WRITE WITH FIRE

Borgo Press Books by Charles Allen Gramlich

THE TALERA CYCLE:

1. *Swords of Talera*
2. *Wings Over Talera*
3. *Witch of Talera*

Write with Fire: Thoughts on the Craft of Writing
Writing in Psychology: A Guidebook (with Elliott Hammer & Du
    Bois Irvin

WRITE WITH FIRE

THOUGHTS ON THE CRAFT OF WRITING

by

Charles Allen Gramlich

THE BORGO PRESS

An Imprint of Wildside Press LLC

MMIX

Borgo Literary Guides
ISSN 0891-9623

Number Eleven

www.wildsidepress.com

FIRST EDITION

CONTENTS

DEDICATION

To the Wordsmiths:

Kathleen Davis, Elora Fink, Steve Harris, Candice Proctor,
Laura Joh Rowland, Emily Toth, and to David Lanoue

ABOUT THE AUTHOR

CHARLES ALLEN GRAMLICH grew up on a farm in Arkansas, near the foothills of the Ozark Mountains, but moved to the New Orleans area to teach psychology at a local university. He's since sold four novels and numerous short stories. His stories, while mostly in the genres of horror, science fiction, and fantasy, have included westerns, children's tales, mainstream, slipstream, and experimental fiction. Charles has also published poetry and nonfiction, the latter ranging from reference works to articles on writing. He is an editor for *The Dark Man: The Journal of Robert E. Howard Studies*, and produces a regular column on writing for an online newsletter called *The Illuminata*. He lives with his wife in Abita Springs, Louisiana, and has a son named Joshua. His blog can be found at:

http://charlesgramlich.blogspot.com/

INTRODUCTION

The following articles and essays on the craft of writing were produced over a fifteen-year span, although most were completed after 2003. Some have been previously published in varied and sometimes difficult-to-find venues such as *Just Write, Writer's Gazette*, and *The Canadian Writer's Journal*. Others were written for my monthly column, "The Writer's Block," which appears in *The Illuminata*, an online newsletter edited by author Bret Funk. Still others appear here as virgins.

Not even the previously published pieces are here exactly as they were first printed, however. I'm an inveterate tinkerer and can never leave anything alone. For such pieces, in honor of their first book publication, I've revised to make them as up to date with current technologies, current references, and my own growth in experience as possible. Most have been expanded significantly because in their original publications there were word limits that restricted what I could say, or what I could get away with.

I've also divided the book into three parts. Part One could probably be subtitled "the tip articles." These are articles about the mechanics of writing. How do you get ideas and shepherd them through the writing and editing process into finished and publishable form? Where do you look for markets? Part Two consists of more general articles about writing and writers. These are my attempt to examine writing, publishing and promoting at a level beyond the mechanics. Part Three, which is shorter, are pieces that are more personal to my own history as a writer, like my essay on what happened to me after Hurricane Katrina struck New Orleans and the Gulf Coast. There is also one original short story, but it's a surprise and I won't say anything more about it until you trip over it.

If you're wondering why you're holding a book on writing by someone who is not famous, well, most writers aren't famous. Most of us work hard at our craft without the benefit of big advances and multi-city tours. Most of us never have autograph parties with lines so long that our hands cramp from signing our names. For many of us, writing is something that we beg, borrow, or steal the time for while our other job keeps the bill collectors at bay.

I'm lucky that as a college teacher in the field of psychology, part of my job is to write and to teach and study writing. I hope that's given me a perspective on the field that can be of use to others, but like most of you reading this I still struggle for every bit of writing success that I get. That struggle has been long, and it's taught me a few things that I've tried to put into the essays that follow. I hope you enjoy.

—Charles A. Gramlich
Abita Springs, Louisiana
October 2007

PART ONE

Writing is hard work. A clear sentence is no accident. Very few sentences come out right the first time, or even the third time. Remember this as a consolation in moments of despair. If you find that writing is hard, it's because it is hard. It's one of the hardest things that people do.

—William Zinsser

SO YOU WANT TO BE A WRITER?

There are writers who are content to put their words on paper and who don't care if anyone else ever sees them. At least, I believe there are such folks, although I've never met one. All the writers that I know, and all the people that I know who tell me they would like to write, are saying—at least in part—that they would like to be published. Being published validates us, and it doesn't matter whether that is a good thing or a bad thing. It just is.

Several years ago, a friend that I'd corresponded with for a long time began to express doubts in her ability to be a writer. She had published a short story a couple of years earlier, and one or two non-fiction essays, but she was very close to quitting writing. Yet, she had talent. It had even been rewarded.

In trying to encouraged my friend, without lying to her about her chances, I had to dredge up and lay out logically my own thoughts about what it takes to get published—and what it would take for me to know that I should move on to another interest. Just below is my response to her. I thought it might be a good place to start this book. As you'll see from the dates, it's over a decade old. Yet, if I wrote this letter today I'd say precisely the same things and the only thing I'd add would be information about the worldwide web.

THE LETTER:

You've asked a question that I can't answer. Do you have what it takes to be a writer, or are you knocking your head against a wall? I don't know. In all honesty, I think you do have some grammar problems that may make selling fiction difficult for you. (Not impossible, difficult.) I had much more academic training than you have before I wrote my first publishable story. But I also honestly think that you have a gift for description, a solid feel for the land and for growing things, and a strong sense of purpose.

There is also something else about your writing that I don't know, and it's not something you've really said anything about. You mentioned in your letter that you "haven't produced any marketable work," or been able "to create material worthy of publication." What I have to ask you very bluntly is: How many pieces of fiction have you completed? And how many pieces have you submitted to a market? If the answer is anything less than twenty-five then I would have to say that you've really made little effort toward publication.

I don't want to sound mean, but no one can judge you as a writer until your stuff has actually been offered on the open market in polished form. That's really the only test. In 1994, I submitted pieces to sixty-nine different markets. I got forty-nine rejections, sold fifteen pieces, and am still waiting to hear on the rest. This was, in fact, a better than average year for me.

Pretty much every day of 1994, whether I felt good or bad, I sat down at my computer and wrote, at least for an hour. The only exceptions were if my son was sick, or if the pressure of school work made it impossible, or if, very rarely, I said to myself that I just couldn't do it that day. I'll bet I didn't miss more than fifteen or twenty days out of the year.

On January 1, 1989 I gave myself five years to get published, and I wrote a promise to myself that I would work on some writing task, no matter how small, each day. That meant I would read a book about writing, or study a grammar guide, or, mostly, that I would just write. I kept very close to that promise, and it didn't take five years to sell my first story.

There is only one way to find out if you have what it takes to be a writer. Write and rewrite and submit—over and over and over again. Don't set a time limit on yourself. That was a mistake for me, I think. It doesn't matter how much time has passed. It only matters how many actual words you've put down on paper and sent out. If I were to lay it out in steps, they might look something like what follows. I'm sure there are other ways of doing it, but this is the way I tried, with some hindsight about what I did wrong:

Step 1. Decide that you'll work on some writing task every single day. Feel guilty if you don't.
Step 2. Pick a manageable task, the completion of one short story.
Step 3. Jot down the story's basic plot in a few sentences. Make sure you have an idea how the story will end, and that the end is in some way surprising. Very importantly, plan for a story that will be no longer than five or six thousand words. To get ideas, use dreams,

real events, folklore and myth, retelling of classic stories, variations on stories you've read or seen on TV, or just make it up.

Step 4. Promise yourself that you will complete at least one good paragraph on your story every day. *One* paragraph! Four to ten lines maybe. And do it no matter how long it takes. But if you finish that paragraph and are really tired then quit for the day. At this rate you will complete a five thousand word story in a couple of months. (Of course, there will be many days when you'll do *more* than one paragraph.)

Step 5. Take some time when you are not writing to look for potential markets for your story. Look for places that pay money first, but don't worry too much about the amount of money or how prestigious the magazine is. Worry about whether they publish pieces like what you're writing. Markets can be found in a lot of ways. See magazines like *Writer's Digest* or *The Writer*. Check out the book called *Novel and Short Story Writer's Market*.

Step 6. When your story is finished, assume that it's not publishable and rewrite it again. Rewrite it at least three times, checking the meaning and spelling of every word that you're not absolutely sure of, checking the placement of every punctuation mark, especially commas. Read it out loud to yourself after every rewrite, and make the changes that jump out at you when you hear them. By this time you may well be sick of the piece. You may think it's absolutely worthless. Ignore that feeling. Put the manuscript in a drawer somewhere for at least a week.

Step 7. Reread the story one last time. Correct anything that seems weak. Make sure the piece is in proper submission format, which means your name and address single spaced at top left of the first page, the word count at top right of the first page, and the story double spaced below. You need page numbers and a short title at the top right of each page after the first one.

Step 8. Write a brief cover letter to the editor of the market you've selected. At its simplest this letter could say something like: "Dear ___. Please find enclosed a story entitled ___ that I would like to submit for your consideration. Any attention that you might give to it would be appreciated."

Step 9. Make sure to include an SASE, an empty, stamped envelope addressed to yourself, when you mail the story.

Step 10. Start another story using the same process.

Step 11. If the first story gets rejected, reread it again, make any corrections that are warranted, and send it out to another market within one week. Repeat as needed, at least twenty times.

Step 12. When you've written and submitted fifty stories this way, and every one has been rejected at least twenty times without a single sale, then this might suggest that writing is not your game. This'll take four to five years. But you have to start somewhere and sometime. Ray Bradbury started out doing one story a week, but I couldn't handle that myself. The steps above were things that I could handle.

Are there strategies that you can use to improve your skills? I think so. Here's some suggestions. Most are ones that I used myself, and/or still use.

1. Get an anthology of stories similar to those you'd like to write. Type one out from first line to last. You might try this exercise several times to get a feel for how published writers do what they do. I know a guy who typed out a whole novel this way.

2. Study books on writing technique. I typically read four or five books a year on writing, as well as various magazines.

3. Get an English textbook. Read it like you were taking a class. Read five pages a day maybe. Do the exercises in the book just like they were homework. Start a note file for yourself and put anything new you learn into that file. I've read through my English text twice this way. And I have a pretty big file of writing notes by now.

4. Try to go to a writing conference. Go to the panels and listen. Ask questions if you can think of any. But mostly listen. I go to at least one conference a year, and I'd go to more if I could get away from work.

5. Do writing exercises. Study an object and then describe it as completely as possible. Listen to conversations at work or over lunch and try to write them down the way you heard them. Free associate, which means just start typing and don't stop to think. Do this for five or ten minutes at a time, then go back and see what you've got. Write out descriptions of past experiences.

6. Make yourself a writer's "list to do" sheet and mark off tasks as you complete them. I also keep a notebook that lists guideline requests and submissions that I make, along with the date and cost in postage.

7. Keep a writing journal and record what you do each day that is related to writing. Be honest. If you're lazy one day, say so. I find this helps motivate me.

8. When you see a magazine that interests you, study their guidelines, which you can often find in the magazine itself or which you can send for through the mail (with an SASE, of course).If you submit a story to them, mention having looked at their guidelines. I

usually say something like: "About a month ago I requested your guidelines for submission, and after looking them over I believe I have a story that meets your requirements."

9. Take a story that you like and analyze it. Count paragraphs, count long sentences versus short sentences, see how many long sentences appear in a row, how many words in a sentence. Look to see how soon the writer introduces action, or the main character, or how soon the first major conflict arises. Study the story's pattern. I do this a lot.

In closing, nobody can answer your question except you. You have strengths and weaknesses like any other writer. You have doubts about your ability, but so does every writer. Ultimately, the fate of your writing is in your own hands. I wish you the best of luck. Write to let me know how you feel and what you're thinking. – *End of Letter.*

I've wondered over the years whether I laid it on my friend too thick? Did I make it seem too hard to be a writer? Should I have mouthed platitudes rather than truths? All I know is, I didn't lie to her about what I think it takes to be a writer. I also know that I never heard from her again.

I hope I hear from those of you reading now.

FIRST WORDS

Personally, I've always enjoyed looking at a blank page and then marking it up with my scribblings. When I was in college I loved getting new notebooks. The snowy white expanse of all those pages was an invitation. Each new sheet held promise. Maybe on this one I'd pen something really cool.

Today, I write on a computer, but when I open a new file and see...nothing, I still get that same little thrill. Perhaps this time I'll write the perfect story, the one that I can see in my head but never quite capture.

A lot of people don't seem to think this way, though. They don't like the blank page. I won't say it makes them afraid, but they don't feel comfortable with it. They need stuff on that page, something to distract the eye or draw the mind. And some people go blank themselves when faced with emptiness. Where do they start? *How* do they start? Below are some suggestions that might help fill that first-page void.

1. *Let yourself write ugly.* You probably wouldn't get up from a night's sleep and go directly out on a date. You'd fix yourself up a bit first. But you don't *blame* yourself for your morning face, morning hair, morning breath. Treat your writing the same way. It doesn't have to be perfect, or even presentable, when it first comes out of your head onto the screen. Get stuff down and then worry about making it look and sound pretty.

No one in the world has to see the first words you produce. You can try out anything you like, use any word that pleases you, make any argument you want to make, and no one can deny or contradict you. No one can tell you: "That sucks!" Who cares if what you put down is ugly? You can always fix it tomorrow.

2. *Don't reread/proofread as you write.* Some folks put down a few sentences or a few paragraphs and then spend the next hour

proofing, checking, and polishing that snippet. This is dangerous because if you try to fix things too early you'll lose track of where you were going with a piece and you'll never get into a flow that allows one idea to build on another. Do you ever get interrupted when you're talking and lose your train of thought? Well, stopping too early to correct errors in your prose can cause the same thing. Your masterpiece could disappear like a morning fog.

How do you avoid rereading when the page is right there in front of you? The word discipline comes to mind (not that I listen), and if you're writing on actual paper discipline is what you're stuck with. But, if you're writing on a computer and the words are too tempting, there are a couple of ways to achieve the same effect mechanically.

If you're on a desktop computer you could just turn the monitor off. If you're using a laptop you might not be able to do that, but you could cover the screen or simply write in white on a white background (which works well for me if I'm taking a typing test). Later, when you're ready to polish, do "select all" and turn the words black. The point is, if you can't see your errors you won't be tempted to fix them until later. And you'll get your scene or story down before it vanishes.

Writer friends of mine often shudder when I suggest they turn their monitor off to break through writer's block. They don't want to give up that much control. But blocks are often about authors striving for too *much* control. What have you got to lose by living dangerously?

3. *Free associate*. In *Zen in the Art of Writing*, Ray Bradbury talked about making lists of nouns or phrases that seemed evocative to him. He didn't think much about them; he just wrote them down, let them come up from wherever they were buried in his subconscious. Later, he began taking nouns from his list and starting prose poems about them, just letting the words flow with little or no conscious direction. Soon a character would appear and Bradbury would be off and running on a story.

Long before I'd read about this habit of Bradbury's, I'd begun doing the same thing with titles. A title like "Shadow Dream" or "Clowns in the Dark" would occur to me, and I'd sit at the computer or over a notepad and riff on that title until something interesting happened. It might be a single scene, or a character that grabbed my attention, or it might be an entire tale written at white heat. Most of my earliest stories were written in this way, including the two whose titles are listed above, as well as my very *first* published tale, "Still Life with Skulls."

If the blank page bothers you, fiddle with this kind of free association for yourself. There shouldn't be any threat or anxiety in that. You're not trying for the perfect opening line, or for a "chilling, masterpiece of suspense." You're "fiddling," just typing whatever pops into your head. But, the human mind tries hard to make sense of things. Even without intentional effort, the mind will begin to connect, attach, associate. Soon you'll have meaning, and the tyranny of the empty page will be broken.

WRITER'S BLOCK NO MORE

Author's Note: One section of this article overlaps a bit with the previous piece but the topic is an important one and worth a revisit. I've grouped the two pieces together as a double whammy.

The title of my monthly column in *The Illuminata* newsletter is "Writer's Block," named after that thorny subject on which reams have been written and for which few successful cures have been proffered. I'm lucky in that I don't suffer from the problem very often. Once I've gotten my butt into the chair, I seldom have trouble getting myself to write. True, I occasionally have problems making myself actually sit *down* in the chair, but that's out of laziness and procrastination, both of which I suffer from in ample amounts. To me, those things are just an attempt to avoid the effort of writing in the first place. They're not the same as "writer's block."

What exactly is writer's block, then? I take it to mean that someone who wants to write or considers themselves a writer sits down at their computer, turns on their fully capable system, and then stares at the screen without finding anything to write about. They never get to the first word, or if they get past the first word they just can't keep the flow going, or if they get further than that they find that what they've written needs to be deleted because it's total "crap."

What causes writer's block? I believe it's fear: 1) fear of embarrassment should others not like what you write, 2) fear of facing unpleasant truths about yourself, or 3) fear that you will have nothing to say. Fear, and the insecurity that it brings, is more powerful than any weapon humans have yet invented. Killing a writing career is nothing compared to what fear can destroy.

As far as I can see, there are only four rules to follow if you really want to be a published writer. These are:

1. You must start writing.
2. You must finish what you start.
3. You must submit what you finish.
4. You must repeat 1 through 3 as long as it takes.

Writer's block violates the very first of these rules and ensures that you'll never get past the initial step. But you don't *need* to suffer from writer's block if you remember one simple fact. The "act" of writing is completely and totally safe.

You write alone. The words are on paper or a computer screen in front of you and no one else in the world knows they are there. Think about how liberating that is. You can say anything you want without the slightest risk of reproach. You *cannot* be laughed at. You *cannot* be embarrassed. Try a hundred ways of putting down your thoughts, and if you don't like them throw them all away. There is *never* any reason not to put words down when you set at your desk. No possible harm can come from it.

So what if you start to uncover a secret about yourself that you feel uncomfortable with? You've got a delete key. If you write on paper, you've got a match. Self-discovery is one of the great benefits of writing, but if you can't handle certain thoughts at certain moments then set them aside for later. If you're like me, you've got plenty of troublesome thoughts to deal with. Start with something less threatening. You'll get to the deeper scars at some point.

But what about the fear that you have nothing to say? Impossible! You're human; you've got plenty to say. I write pretty much every day and I'll tell you what I do when I've stuffed my posterior into the chair and can't figure out what to write. I write anyway, and you can too.

Take a few deep breaths, let your mind wander a bit, and write whatever comes flowing into your awareness. Use free association to put words on the screen and help you combine those words into sentences. Sometimes I just start typing and let my fingers do the thinking for me, but if I need a bit more structure I'll start with my childhood, with phrases like "my mother was," or "my father was," or "I grew up in," or "I hate," or "I loved…."

At worst, you are getting your writing juices flowing. Better, you're getting practice at excavating your past for the detail that makes a writer's work come alive. Best, as you type, those old ideas and experiences may begin to percolate and combine until you find yourself racing far along a road you never expected to travel.

That's where the fun begins, and writer's block ends.

TIPPING THE ODDS IN YOUR FAVOR

Author's Note: The article that follows is one of the earliest pieces on writing that I ever sold, way back in 1994. As much as anything, it was written to myself as part of the process of discovering what I truly thought about writing and publishing. I was somewhat surprised to find in rereading that I still stand by these same principles today. Although I've updated the section on marketing information, I've left the rest of it pretty much as it was. There used to be a bibliography with this piece as well, but I expanded that and moved it to the end of the book. I've made the occasional modern day editorial comment in parentheses and italics.

I'll start this piece by suggesting to you that I am more qualified than Dean Koontz or Clive Barker to write an article on getting published in the small press. Do you believe me? Even if you do not—and I don't always believe everything I say myself—I hope you will give me a few minutes to try and convince you that I'm right on this point.

I mention Koontz and Barker because they are among my favorite writers, and I'll admit, reluctantly, that they are better at it than I am. But, neither of the two has to think very much about getting published at the small press level anymore, and thinking about what you are doing is the key to breaking in at the smaller magazines.

Clearly, the Koontzes and Barkers know how to get published, but how many of them have to agonize over a cover letter they are sending to the editor of *Small Press Horror*? And how many of them have to worry about getting their stuff to stand out from the slush pile of manuscripts sent in by hopeful new writers? I'm not saying that their name guarantees a sale—it certainly does not—but it probably does guarantee that their stories will be read carefully.

Struggling new writers on the other hand, like myself and like many of you reading this article, have to agonize and worry. We have to write good stories, and then we have to get an editor to notice what we've written. Even after twenty-five short story sales, as well as various articles, essays, and poems, I still have to spend my non-writing time thinking about how to get published. I have to be consciously aware of the things I try, and of whether or not those things work. So far, there's been no six figure book deal to distract me from the small press. *(Strangely enough, that's still true today, over ten years later!)*

Given the time I've spent thinking about publication in the small press, it would be surprising if I hadn't come up with some ideas about what works and what doesn't. Those ideas are in this article. Give them a once over, compare them with your own thoughts, and then decide for yourself whether I'm really more qualified than Dean Koontz to write about small press publication. By the way, I'm better looking than he is too.

I. The Writing Itself: Tips on Making Your Stories Stand Out

1. *Write Short*: Small press magazines have limited space and most would rather buy two 2,500 word stories than one 5,000 word one. The reasons are psychological. First, people who buy short stories want them short, something they can finish without investing much time. They read one on the subway, or in the twenty minutes before bed, and they can still feel the pleasant sense of having accomplished something. (Psychologists call this closure.) Second, everything else being equal, folks tend to buy the magazine or anthology with the most stories in it, even if they're getting the same number of words for their money. Having more stories often makes the reader feel as if they are getting a bonus. Editors who sell magazines and books know these kinds of things, and they want to cram as many stories as possible into their pages.

In my opinion, the best way to break into selling fiction is to write short-shorts, stories of less than 1,500 words. Four out of my first seven sales were around that magic 1,500 mark. Another was just over 2,000. In addition to the benefits of brevity indicated before, I believe that short-shorts enjoy two other advantages over longer stories. Editors can better afford to take a chance on an unknown writer's four page story than on her twelve page one, and short-shorts can be fitted to a magazine's space requirements more easily than longer stories. Oddly, though, you may actually have to work harder on a short-short than a short-long, but the extra effort should pay off in the greater likelihood of a sale.

2. *Write Genre*: I've sold to both, but I believe it is easier to sell to genre magazines than to literary ones, particularly in the genres of

fantasy, horror, and SF. It's not that the writing itself is easier, it's just that it is easier for a new genre writer to attract an editor's attention with unique ideas or a distinctive style.

Take a basic plot idea such as boy meets girl. In literary writing you are limited to realistic or at least semi-realistic interpretations of that one sentence. In genre writing, you can add such variations as boy meets monster, boy meets alien, boy meets machine, boy meets himself, boy desperately wants to meet girl, any girl. With a wider range of available twists, it's going to be easier to do something surprising. The "new" sells, and the genres give you more freedom to explore that "new." The following paragraphs illustrate what I mean in terms of ideas and style.

Unique ideas. Unique ideas are difficult to find and most published stories are "variations on a theme," a slightly unusual way of looking at vampires, for example, or a different approach to dragons. One current trend, in genre and in mainstream fiction, is toward increasingly graphic descriptions of sex and violence. Sex and violence are not new to fiction, of course. What is new, at least to popular fiction, is the "graphic" nature of the descriptions. This marks a "variation on a theme" that has given many recent stories a feeling of newness. I'm not indicating my approval of the trend here, just stating an observation that I've made. *(This article was written when "Splatterpunk" horror was new on the scene. Although horror fiction and film have continued to push the limits of violence, most other genres have not "gored" it up. Sex, on the other hand, has become more graphically depicted almost across the board.)*

Now, how can new writers identify the variations on a theme that will give their work the shine of originality? The best way that I know is through reading, reading fiction so that I can find out what other people are doing and avoid it, and reading a wide range of nonfiction so that recent historical and scientific discoveries will inform my writing. The writing mind can only use what it has available to construct a story. That means you better feed it everything you can, and nonfiction will generally feed you better than fiction.

As examples of what I mean, in the last few years we've had the unearthing of epanterias—a carnivorous dinosaur larger and meaner than Tyrannosaurus Rex—the discovery of a Roman house complete with dinner settings beneath the leaning tower of Pisa, and the melding of firefly genes with tobacco plants. *(All new discoveries in 1994.)* If you absorb enough such material, it will soon begin to percolate through your writing and add a new taste to your work, or, considering my reading habits, a new stink.

Distinctive style. Besides good ideas, another thing that can gain you favorable notice is a distinctive style. This lies not in what you say but how you say it. Compare Harlan Ellison's "I Have No Mouth, And I Must Scream" to Ray Bradbury's "Rocket Summer" if you want to see differences between unique styles. The problem is that your style must come naturally if it is to be any good. Although I believe it is possible to deliberately "craft" a style for yourself, I also think such craftings seem stilted and strained. And they often degenerate into mannerisms. You can, however, fertilize your prose in a way that will promote the growth of your own style. One way to do this is through a process called "layering."

My first step in "layering" is to write the entire story in short, declarative sentences using nouns and verbs only. Second, I go back and combine some short sentences in order to break up the staccato quality of the prose. This also involves recasting some sentences into the passive voice, and the process takes a long time because the story has to "sound" good to me when it's read out loud. Third, I put in a layer of adjectives and adverbs to modify the bare framework of my sentences, and I don't care if they're a little thick at first. Fourth, I read the story out loud to myself again, paying closest attention to the music, the cadence. To me, written style is as much sound as it is word choice and syntax. Finally, I prune the whole thing to get rid of any excess modifiers or clichés, and to clear away any dead phrasings that obscure my meaning. This also takes a long time.

Now, I certainly don't use "layering" every time I write, but I do it occasionally because it demonstrates the way in which a writer's voice is put together—from the inside out. No two people carrying out such an exercise would put their prose together in exactly the same way. That's unique style.

Finally, though, don't despair if it looks like your voice will never be a standout. You'll just have to write better stories, which is what Isaac Asimov did, and what Stephen King does. Both writers have had their prose described as undistinguished.

3. *Rewriting and Editing*: Writing well also means rewriting a piece as many times as it takes to make it good. I rewrite my stuff until I'm sick of it and have to put it away. Then I take it out later and rewrite some more. If a piece gets rejected, I rewrite (or at least re-edit) again before it goes out a second time, and I look it over every time it comes back. For me, and I suspect for all writers, rewriting has been the key to publication. I've learned to enjoy it.

Although sometimes overlooked, a major part of rewriting should involve an effort to get the grammar and punctuation of a piece just right. Some people don't worry much about grammar. After all, isn't that what editors are for? The answer is "no" for anyone who wants to get their work published. I have over twenty books on grammar, punctuation, and usage, and I try to read a bit on the subject whenever I can. To make things easier, I extract the most important information and keep it in a computer file for quick access. *(See the Bibliography at the end of this book for a number of works that can help with English usage.)*

4. *Resources*: Good resources are essential to helping you write well. You probably already have a dictionary—unabridged I hope—and a thesaurus, and in the previous section we talked about a writer's need for guides on grammar and usage. You may not know, or think, however, about some of the other books that can help you. In my own writing, I use my encyclopedias almost every day, and they often take the place of the specialized references that I would like to buy but can't afford.

When I do need more detail than encyclopedias can provide, I pull out my library card and head for the nearest branch. Most city libraries will have books on the topics you're interested in, whether that be warfare, weapons, or witchcraft. University libraries are even better if you can get access. Those of you who live in rural areas or small towns, like the place where I grew up in Arkansas, may have to prepare yourself to spend more money on references than your big city colleagues. Book clubs and catalogs kept me in reading, for prices that weren't too steep, and there are always magazines, on just about any topic that you might need.

Most libraries will also carry books on the writing process itself, which can be helpful and encouraging when you're feeling isolated. Some, like this article, are collections of "tips." They give you hints and ideas to think about. Others examine more theoretical issues such as plot, voice, and character. Still others are cheerleaders. Each type can be helpful, and I've included a few of my favorites in the Bibliography.

(If written today, the above section on "resources" would have much in it about the internet, and I've included other articles on the net later in this book. Still, having access to hard copy physical resources has much to recommend it, and there is still a lot of information in books that is not yet available on the web. Even though I use the net frequently today, I still buy and use many reference books as well.)

II. The Magazines: Tips on Getting an Editor's Attention

5. *Contact*: If possible, make contact with editors prior to sending them stuff. This means by letter, not by phone. I'd never call an editor who I didn't know pretty well. What I do is send for "Writer's Guidelines." Most magazines have them, and they often provide information that you can't get anywhere else. I think it also makes a good impression on editors, especially when your *submission* cover letter can say something like: "Several months ago I requested your guidelines for submission, and I have now completed a story that I believe meets those guidelines." There are also "market reports" that collate guidelines, or at least the appropriate addresses, and I've included a few in the "Marketing Information" section.

Another good idea is to send for sample copies of magazines you want to submit to. I say it's a good idea, and it is, but it's not something I routinely do. The reason is money. I just can't afford it. I do buy sample copies of magazines where I hope to submit a lot of stuff, and I buy samples from magazines that offer them to writers at reduced cost. Libraries will also subscribe to some of the bigger genre magazines, but, in general, I find that the guidelines provide most of what I need. At the risk of sounding preachy, though, I do feel that writers need to support the small press as best they can. If we sell to them, then we ought to buy from them too. Small press writers and editors have to work together if either is going to survive.

(Here again, the internet has made it much easier to find writer's guidelines, and often to check out sample copies of magazines. Email is also an easy way to make contact, but most of today's editors are swamped with emails and yours isn't likely to stand out. Commenting on sample issues or on websites is one way for you to make an impression.)

Of course, the best way to make contact with editors is to meet them in person, and that usually means going to writing conferences, which can be tough if you don't live near a large city. I never attended a science fiction conference until after moving to New Orleans. There weren't any within 150 miles of my hometown. I'm hooked now, though. In just a few years, for a very small outlay of money, I've met a lot of writers and a good number of editors, including some who bought pieces from me later. I've also found out about markets that I wouldn't have heard of anywhere else. Conferences have proven to be a definite plus for me as far as making contact goes. I'd suggest you give one a try, even if it takes driving a few hours to get there.

6. *Professionalism*: Professionalism means doing the things that make an editor's job easier, and it means doing them even when you aren't paid like a professional. The first step is to read the guidelines and follow them with care. Although each magazine is different, there are a few common courtesies that most editors will appreciate. These include a brief cover letter, which should *not* summarize the story unless you are specifically asked to do so. And don't downgrade yourself or your talent in your letter. Mention some past sales if you have any. Otherwise, just say something like: "Any consideration that you might give to the enclosed story would be appreciated.... Thanks very much for your time."

In addition to the cover letter, send a copy of your story that is easily readable, with the print as dark and clear as possible. Try reading it under fluorescent lights. If you have to squint, so will the editor, and she won't thank you for it. Also remember to put your name and address and an approximate word count on the first page of your story (Name and address at top left, word count at top right), and put a page #, a partial title, and your last name on every page. Allow ample margins (inch and a half at left, inch everywhere else) and use plain white bond paper. *(Two extra points for today's writer: 1) use Times New Roman or Courier New, in 12 point, as your font, and 2) even when emailing stories still show the same concerns for cover letters and story formatting.)*

Don't forget to enclose an SASE (Self-addressed stamped envelope).Unless you send one, you probably won't hear back from a magazine, and you probably *will* irritate the editor. Editors use SASEs to send contracts to writers, or, at worst, to return their manuscripts. The writer has to make sure there is enough postage on the SASE to get a story back that's not being used. It's often cheaper to have an editor discard the story and reply on a self-addressed and stamped postcard that the writer has included. This is cheaper but I almost never do it. I like to get my stories back. *(I email most of my submissions these days, but I still occasionally find a market that wants paper submissions. That means they still want an SASE as well.)*

7. *Marketing Information*: After you finish a story, then you have to find somewhere to send it. Some people say there aren't many markets for fiction right now. They're wrong. There are markets; there just aren't many that pay well. Fortunately, the markets are often strong in the genres I've been talking about. Unfortunately, many of those markets are not going to be in your geographical area, and the only way to discover them is to use a "market guide." Such guides usually come in two forms, books that compile large lists of

markets, and newsletters and magazines that report on fewer markets but are more frequently updated. Both types of guides often double as writing tutors, with articles on plot, setting, characterization, *etc.*

For my own writing, I started off with book guides. I now prefer to go with newsletters /magazines because I like to get information on new markets and on changes in editors and addresses as quickly as possible. Both kinds of guides have their uses, though, and you might want to try a couple of different ones and see how you like them. Below are names and/or addresses for some of the more popular guides in each category.

Book Guides: Note: Most of these can be found in the big chain bookstores and libraries will often carry copies. *(Today, of course, most can be ordered from Amazon or Barnes & Noble, and there are online sites for them as well. The websites below are newly updated for this book.)*

Literary Market Place (LMP). (literarymarketplace.com). The most comprehensive annual guide available on publishers, including US and foreign publishers, as well as small press publishers. It also contains contact information for many agents, but it is expensive.

The Writer's Handbook. An annual work that lists core markets and publishers and also contains many articles and essays on writing by established professionals.

Writer's Market. An annual release that covers a huge selection of paying markets for both fiction and nonfiction. This is from *Writer's Digest Books. (Available at writersdigest.com, Amazon, or toll free at 1 800 448-0915.)*

Novel and Short Story Writer's Market. Annual, also from *Writer's Digest Books.* Covers fiction markets only, both paying and non-paying. Includes articles on fiction writing.

Newsletters/Magazines: *(Again, addresses and websites are updated for this book.)*

Byline Magazine.(bylinemag.com). Articles, markets, and frequent writing contests.

The Gila Queen's Guide to Markets. (gilaqueen.us). One of the most comprehensive and frequently updated market newsletters available. The editor is Kathryn Ptacek, who has many contacts among editors and publishers.

The Writer. (scriptmag.com). Magazine. Contains markets and articles on writing.

Writer's Digest. Magazine. Market information as well as articles and tips on writing.

III. Afterward: Tips On Surviving The Writing Roller-Coaster

8. *Perseverance*: You will get rejection letters and I know they'll get you down. They do me. So wallow in self-pity a while. Gripe and growl around the house, or go to the video arcade and blow some quarters on cathartic violence. But then go back to writing. I won't give you any platitudes about "getting back on the horse." Hell, you probably don't even have a horse. What you do have is a writing tool of some sort. And you have a need to write that is big enough to have kept you reading this article. That's all I know about you. You know the rest.

9. *Money*: Forget about the cash flow for now. It's very nice to get paid for writing, and it makes you feel professional, but you aren't going to make a living at it at first. You aren't even going to make enough to pay the rent. There just isn't that much money in the small press, or in the big press for that matter, unless you write a bestseller.

What's the answer? Don't do it for the money. I've got a good job and I write weekends and nights. Any money I make, and I do make some, goes into fun things, like motorcycling or books. If you can last, and can keep getting better, the money will come. Until then, the best of luck.

WRITING WITH PURPOSE

Why does anyone want—or feel like they need—to learn how to write? And for this question it doesn't matter whether we're talking about fiction, nonfiction, or both. What do people hope to accomplish by the solitary and, frankly, somewhat odd behavior of writing?

Do they want to amuse their friends with their quick wit, or perhaps amaze them with their erudition? Or do people think that good writing will help them get better grades in school or earn more money in their jobs? Could it be that some would-be writers want to get famous, maybe go on a national book tour where they sign autographs for fanatical legions of admirers and have talk show hosts like Oprah clamoring for their attention? Maybe some folks just want to get rich and conclude that if Stephen King can do it then so can they.

Although some of these possibilities are more likely to occur than others, all of them are perfectly legitimate reasons for writing. In fact, there are no illegitimate reasons to write. Each writer has his or her own inner purpose, and his or her own unique way of putting information down on the page. Ernest Hemingway often wrote standing up. Truman Capote and Mark Twain preferred lying down to write, while Edgar Allan Poe liked to have his cat on his shoulder while he created. I prefer the more standard "sit at my desk and stare at the computer screen until words begin to appear," but anyone who writes will find their own path.

Given the many legitimate reasons for writing, and the many ways of going about it, is there any point in trying to identify a primary or *best* reason to write? I believe there is. I believe that we can, in fact, start by eliminating all but one reason for writing, and that is writing to communicate. This doesn't mean that other reasons are wrong or bad. It means that they are secondary to the need to transmit information, which is really basic to *all* writing. No one gets rich or famous from writing unless they can convey something interesting to a large number of people.

Some people just like the act of writing, the simple behavior of putting words down on a page and then changing them around. They care more about the process than they do about seeing the finished product in print or earning money from it. And even though I don't completely follow that model with my own writing, I honestly believe that it's the best attitude to have. It certainly helps insulate a writer against the inevitable criticisms and rejections.

But for those who need a publishable written product and cannot just enjoy the writing process, the first thing they need to learn is how to clearly communicate ideas, facts, emotions, and experiences. Of course, whole books have been written about that subject. I'm not going to cover all that territory in this short essay.

What I will say is this: to communicate effectively, whether in fiction or nonfiction, the writer has to think like both a writer and...*a reader*. The writer's primary purpose is to make the reader's work as easy as possible. At every point, with every sentence and every paragraph, writers must ask themselves: "What is my reader hearing from me?" "Am I saying exactly what I think I'm saying, exactly what I intend to say?" And unless the writer achieves this (or at least a close approximation) then no other purpose for writing will *ever* be achieved.

So how do you think like a reader? You've *been* a reader, probably for most of your life. Go back to that reading for your answer. But learn to read "critically." You've read passages in books before that confused you, scenes that you couldn't visualize, dialogue that you couldn't follow. Chances are you skipped over those passages to something clearer, or tossed the work aside. Reading critically means not skipping those passages, not tossing anything aside until it's been dissected. Ask why a scene doesn't work. Is it you? Or did the writer do something wrong? Did they leave out some critical piece of description? Did they fail to make it clear who was doing what to whom? Did they scrimp on necessary background information?

Even the passages that work must be studied critically if you want to understand writing from the viewpoint of the reader. What is it about a great scene that grabs you? Is it the characters, the concrete details, the prose itself? Most likely it's some combination of these elements, but only by careful study can you determine how much of each element is the critical amount. In this way, writing is much like chemistry. Or, maybe alchemy would be a better analogy, for writing is nothing if not taking common everyday elements like words, grammar, and punctuation and transmuting them into gold.

But you must go beyond critical reading to truly achieve clarity. Critical *writing* is also important. This doesn't mean that you must always strive for conscious awareness of everything you're doing in your prose; it means that, sometimes, you need to cut under the flesh of a story to the bones. How important is word choice, sentence length, paragraph length to producing a specific effect, such as creating suspense? What makes some dialogue sound stilted, other dialogue sound natural? How does punctuation change the flow of words? To analyze such qualities I think it's best to begin by studying the work of other writers, work that you are not so close to as your own. I'd suggest you choose writers for study who are better than you at the craft.

One effective strategy is to *retype* passages or stories from writers that you are interested in studying, not as a mere exercise but as an honest attempt to understand the process the other writer followed. Don't even allow yourself to edit the other writer's work at first—which you'll probably want to do—but faithfully reproduce it before going back and trying to make it your own. Retyping a story this way puts you in the writer's shoes, with your feet on the stones of the trail that he or she followed. Just reading a story, even if you're trying to study it, is more like driving that same trail in a Jeep. You might see the obstacles, but they won't bruise your heel. You need those heels bruised.

Once you've retyped another writer's passage and studied how he or she put it together, *then* revise the piece as if it were your own. Think about the changes you've made. Why did you recast a passive sentence as an active one? What made you add or remove an adjective? Why did you change the punctuation? Answering these questions will show you how your decisions are different from the other person's. It will make the reasons behind your writing decisions clear to you.

Good writers *do* make better grades in school and make more money in their jobs. Good writers also sell articles, stories and novels, and they hear from people who have connected with their work and enjoyed it. Good writing pays off. But that payoff only comes to those whose ultimate purpose is clarity. The readers demand it.

DON'T TALK, WRITE!

Writing and talking are two ways of communicating ideas. Talking is more familiar to most of us and, unfortunately, it's often common for new writers to write much like they talk. Although this is fine for a personal letter to a friend, or even for the first draft of a short story, it's not good enough for a query letter to a prospective agent or publisher, or for a story that is to be submitted to an editor. Formal writing is not the same as talking, and this causes us writers some enormous difficulties but also gives us some enormous benefits.

To get a feel for the way people talk, try listening to a casual conversation among your friends. Don't eavesdrop. Just listen for a while instead of talking. Notice the insertions of "uh" and "you know" into the conversation, the short pauses while someone tries to think of something to say, the interruptions as one person cuts off another.

Spoken language gets its message across, but there are always false starts, considerable backtracking, and the use of "reactive" speech, which means that each person's response builds upon information just provided by the other person. Written language cannot proceed this way, both because it looks confusing on the printed page ("I...uh...well...we wanted), and because there is only one person present at a time, first the writer and then the reader.

Another thing that is true of talking—but not of writing—is that there is a substantial amount of non-verbal communication involved in a spoken exchange. You can emphasize your words with hand gestures, punching the air with a fist or pointing a finger, and you can show indecisiveness with a shrug. You can judge how clearly your point is being made by watching the other person's facial expressions, rushing on at smiles and nods, backtracking at frowns and head shakes. A spoken conversation uses body movements for punctuation and is filled with immediate feedback on the speaker's success, or lack of it, in conveying a message or telling a story. This just doesn't happen in writing—though question marks and other punctuation symbols are a feeble attempt to add some of the same qualities.

The audience that you are trying to reach with your writing might be in the next city, or the next state, or the next country. They can't shake their heads at you if they fail to understand something you tell them. This is the major weakness of writing, and because of it you have to think about what you are saying much more carefully when you write than when you talk.

If you say something confusing while chatting with someone, then it takes very little energy for them to ask you a question. But if you confuse someone who is reading your words, the easiest thing for them to do is either tune out your message and just scan the piece, or to throw it aside and turn to something else. These are not good outcomes, particularly if the individual reading your work is the same person you'd like to have purchase it. To communicate effectively on paper you have to anticipate questions the reader might ask, and then provide him or her with everything needed to answer those questions.

What kind of questions do readers ask? There are two good ways to find out. First, develop your own reading habit, and especially cultivate the ability to read critically, which we talked extensively about in the last essay. Second, let some friends (or a writing group, which we'll talk much more about later) read your story or article and tell you where it confused them. Choose those friends carefully, though. Don't pick people who will only brag on your writing. Good as that might be for your ego, it won't help you sell to an editor who doesn't know you.

Pick people who will be honest and listen to them with an open mind. I also suggest that you pick people who generally *like* the sort of thing you're writing. If you're writing a romance then don't select your readers from among people who hate romance and have never read them. Such folks will point out the wrong things; they'll be criticizing the *genre* rather than your particular contribution. Always pay special attention to those things that several people point out as a problem.

Keep in mind, too, that general comments such as, "I liked that character," or "this scene didn't work for me," aren't of much use to you. You need to know the "whys" and "what fors." What did a character *do* that made a reader like him? What specific elements of a scene didn't work? You may have to ask questions to get the details you want. Just don't sound angry or defensive, as if they've criticized your baby; you asked them for feedback after all. And don't try to explain what you *meant* for a passage to say. The writing has to explain itself. You're not going to be there for every reader after a piece is published. That would be "talking."

Taking criticism is not easy, but it is absolutely necessary if you are going to get better. This doesn't mean you have to agree with everything your friends say, or make every change they suggest, but it does mean that you should give their comments careful consideration.

And remember, don't talk. Write!

WRITING WITH CONFIDENCE

Having confidence in your own abilities is crucial to writing for publication, and there is absolutely no way to gain confidence without trying and succeeding. You may have to modify your idea of success, though, at least at first. Don't expect agents to trip over each other to sign you up on the basis of a few short stories, and don't expect publishers to call and beg for the rights to your first novel. Don't expect national book tours and stays at five-star hotels. Don't even expect to sit down and write a great novel or short story the first time you try, or the second or third times either. It almost certainly won't work out that way. With practice, you may start getting closer to a good *draft* on the first try, but it will take a while to get to that point, as it has for everyone who writes.

It's also highly unlikely that your first polished efforts will be sold for big money (unless you're already famous or infamous for some other reason). If you sell your first story for *any* money, I'll be surprised. Even if you earned "A's" on your college papers there probably won't be many magazines willing to pay for the privilege of publishing you until you've honed your skills to a professional level.

Instead, start your writing career with modest goals that can be more easily met, like finishing your story, proofreading it, and improving your grammar and punctuation. (You'd be surprised at how many people who say they want to write never actually finish any of the stories or novels they start.) Once you know that you can meet *these* goals, then select tougher goals and either apply them to the same story or to a new one. Don't try to take huge leaps forward and don't try to improve everything at once. Newly hatched confidence can easily be hunted down and killed by bad luck or by predatory critics. Mine was, and it took me years to coax it back to life.

In addition, though, remember that we often get a skewed impression about how competent other people are. We see a great performance by Jodie Foster and think, "Wow, this lady can act." We pick up a novel by James Lee Burke and admire how superbly written it is. We see LeBron James slam-dunk a basketball and we just stare. In each case we think how lucky some people are to be born with those kinds of skills. And in each case we are wrong.

Sure, LeBron probably would be better at basketball than most of us even if he had never practiced it. But each of us could be better than we are if we worked hard enough at it. People are not born experts. They may have innate talents, like size, speed, or coordination, but most people have to work hard to make their jobs look easy. Writing is the same. Being a good writer is probably both a gift and a learned skill. Some people *may* just be better than others. But almost everyone can learn to write publishable stories and books that will earn them both money and respect.

One key to gaining confidence is knowing, without a shadow of a doubt, that you understand what you are writing about. Try penning a short essay about something you know how to do very well. It might be how to play solitaire, or how to make a cake, or how to work your iPod. This kind of exercise can be difficult because you have to put into words things you normally do automatically. However, it should also illustrate one effect of knowing your subject. You don't have to worry about getting the details wrong. This is what that old adage of "write what you know" means. It doesn't mean that you can only write of things you have personally experienced; it means that you should write about things you have learned enough about, things that you've made an effort to study and understand.

Remember, also, that not even best selling novelists know everything about the art and craft of writing. Published and unpublished writers are both involved in the process of *learning* to write. The writer with fifteen novels under her belt might be a little further along the curve than you are, but she's also been working at it longer. You can master the basics of writing and then tell your own stories in ways readers will want to hear. It may require a considerable amount of hard work, but it is not beyond your talents.

Finally, though, there is one last point to consider. Confidence and obsession are two different things, so avoid the trap of trying to make sure your story or novel is perfect. This doesn't mean you should let laziness keep you from correcting errors that you know exist, but it does mean that there comes a time when a story or novel is as good as it is going to get with your current level of skill. At some point you have to let that puppy out into the world. You have to send it off to editors and publishers. And you have to write something new, something that will take you a bit further along the road toward confidence, and toward writing success.

RQW3R

Author's Note: This is another of my early articles, and, again, was at least in part an attempt to describe for myself the exact strategies I was following as I wrote and submitted. I believe it has something interesting to say about generating ideas.

"Where do you get your crazy ideas?" I often get asked.

Well. All right. I'll admit that I've never actually been asked that question—except by my wife and she wasn't talking about writing—but I've imagined myself as the kind of famous author who *gets* asked that question. I even have an answer ready just in case it happens. It's called RQW3R, and I hope you'll let me tell you about it.

RQW3R is a variation on SQ3R. You see, I'm a teacher by profession, and SQ3R, which stands for study, question, read, recite, review, is something that I frequently hammer into my students. It's a study strategy that I used in school, and it worked so well that it was natural for me to adapt the concept to my fiction. Here is what my version (RQW3R) means.

The first "R" stands for READ. Reading is, after all, the well-spring of most ideas in fiction. Direct experience is also necessary, but most of us who write fantasy, horror, or science fiction will be writing about things that we have not, and probably *cannot*, directly experience. Reference books, novels, magazines, and newspapers can vicariously provide us with the experiences that we lack, and, indirectly, with the ideas that flow from those experiences. Many of my ideas come from reading nonfiction, and I'll give you some examples in the following paragraphs.

A few years ago I sold a long piece called "Haunting Place" to *Nether World*. It's about a man who kills his girlfriend while high on PCP, but who has no memory of the act when the drug wears off. Later, the man suffers a head injury and develops epilepsy. Every time the seizures occur, he relives the murder. This story did not come out of nowhere. It was based on a case study described by Dr. Oliver Sacks in his book *The Man Who Mistook His Wife for a Hat*.

Another story of mine, "Machine Wash Warm; Tumble Dry," which sold to *Crossroads,* came from a newspaper piece about an odd murder, and "Roses and Thorns," which appeared in *Tales On The Twisted Side*, was stimulated by a magazine article on flower gardens. Now, I'm not a medical doctor or a murderer, and I've only planted rose bushes when forced into it by the women in my life, but that didn't matter because my reading provided the ideas and background information needed to tell the stories. Your reading will do the same for you.

If step 1 of the RQW3R method is reading, then step 2 is using that reading to generate further ideas, the kind that don't strike immediately after you put down a book or an article. This is where the "Q" comes in. The "Q" stands for QUESTION, and this is how it works for me. First, I select a scenario for myself. Second, I ask myself questions about that scenario. I might, for example, imagine myself walking down the street late one evening. I ask myself a question. What do I see? Well, I see houses, lights, cars, and—

But wait a minute. What do I see that no one else sees? What do I see that is different or odd? The questions force me to generate answers, which in turn lead to more questions. The resulting sequence might be something like the following:

QUESTION:ANSWER:

What do I see? I see two dark shapes in the street.
What kind of shapes? Well, they're not human.
What are they then? They're werewolves.
What are they doing? One is chasing the other.
Why?

Suddenly I have a mystery, one that I generated myself and which I'm just a little curious about. Now I sit down to write that mystery out on paper, asking and answering more questions along the way. Pretty soon I have a story, one that I sold to *Nightscript* magazine under the title "Lovers."

This is also the technique that I used to create the story "Messiah," which appeared in *Dead of Night* magazine. I imagined myself at Jesus Christ's crucifixion and asked myself what I saw. I saw a vampire, which led to a lot of questions, which led to "Messiah" and to a several other projects as well. Those "other" projects all sold to the anthology series *Prisoners of the Night*.

So, one of my main strategies for coming up with ideas is to ask myself questions, bizarre questions, silly questions, all kinds of questions. Some of my answers—perhaps even most of them—go nowhere. But some of them take me to stories that curiosity demands that I tell. And there are a million questions. What if it began to rain just inside my house? What if my son is really an alien being? (The latter has been answered in the affirmative.) What if I had been born rich instead of so good looking?

The last two components of RQW3R are "W" and "3R." The "W" stands for WRITE, and it always helps me if I start writing before I know the answers to all the questions. At least for me, part of the real fun of writing a story is finding out how it ends. The "3R" stands for REWRITE, REWRITE, REWRITE. Whoever said that "Writing is really rewriting" knew a lot about the craft. In fact, three drafts is a bare minimum for me. I usually have to do many more.

Well, it's time for me to close now. I just thought of a question that desperately needs answering and I hope you'll excuse me while I go work on it.

QUERY: What would happen if a struggling young writer were to kidnap a rich New York publisher and demand a book contract instead of a ransom? Now there's an idea.

FIVE HABITS OF PUBLISH*ING* WRITERS

What separates published writers from the unpublished? I used to think (back before I was published) that it was a lot. I know now that it's not very much, and with the explosion of the world wide web it's getting less all the time. But of all the people who get published on the net these days, and of all the people who have their novels produced by print-on-demand presses, how many are making a career for themselves in writing? How many are making money? And are they likely to see their readership grow? That's why this article is not about getting published but about publish*ING*, about the habits that will help if you want to build a career in writing. Check them out. See if you agree or disagree. And write on.

Habit 1: Making time for writing. Publishing writers make time for writing, and they do so consistently, day in, day out. No one can write without time to sit and think and plot at the keyboard. But if you wait for time to find you, it never will. You make time for going to the movies, time for watching TV, time for spending with your loved ones. You also have to make time for writing, and one of the easiest ways to start is to first identify your *free* time.

Pay attention to your schedule for a full week. You don't have to jot down what you do every single minute, but notice where you spend your hours. (Feel free to use the "Activity Schedule" form at the end of this article if you'd like.) How much time do you spend getting ready for your work day? How much time do you spend actually on the job? What kind of lunch and dinner schedule do you have? How much TV do you watch? How much do you talk on the phone?

Then, depending on both the free time you have and on how long you think you can sit at the computer, map out an hour or so a day—or more—for writing. Maybe if you're a student you have an extra hour between afternoon classes. Or, many of us could probably use the hour before we go to bed, when we're usually watching TV.

Many writers who are well known now, like John Grisham, wrote parts of their first novels on their lunch breaks or as they rode the subway. But whatever time you find for yourself, it's critical that you actually use it consistently for writing. Do not play Minesweeper during that time. Do not check your email. Write.

For people who are starting out, I'd suggest that you try to write at least four days a week—I usually write six—but I'd also suggest that you don't try to write for five or six hours at a time. Start out with forty-five minutes to an hour, and build up from there as you get familiar with the process and the work. Writing is an intensive act and, at least for me, a few hours can be pretty draining, especially if I'm spinning fiction.

Habit 2: Look up things about which you are unsure. Learn to keep a dictionary and a grammar guide close at hand while you're writing. If you're not sure of a word's meaning, look it up. If you can't recall how a semicolon is used, look it up. Almost everything you need to know about writing is written down somewhere. Make it a habit to check yourself against such sources. This will take effort at first—the easiest thing is to be lazy—but it'll soon become routine. You'll *soon* find that you need to look things up less and less. The information will be there in your mind, ready and waiting to be used.

In addition to a dictionary and a grammar guide, I keep a thesaurus on my desk and a little book called *The Elements of Style* (3ʳᵈ edition) by William Strunk, Jr., and E. B. White. *The Elements of Style* is under a hundred pages but is one of the best books you can buy on how to express yourself well. Encyclopedias are also good to have around, and I like to have the internet handy to check facts and spellings. (Be careful not to let yourself get caught up in surfing, though.) I even started my own computer file of writing notes, to help me with pesky problems ranging from the use of adverbs to the meaning of zeugma.

Habit 3: Do multiple drafts of everything. The habit that might improve your writing the most is to rewrite everything you do. Just assume that your first draft is not good enough. Do it over again. This seems like work, and that's exactly what it is. But, after all, you would never expect to build a perfect chair the first time you tried carpentry, would you? Even if you did, you would still have to sand it, and polish it, and paint it. Writing is the same way. You don't build a perfect, or even a publishable, story or novel without effort.

When people ask me how many drafts to do I suggest they try at least three. But it really depends upon the writer and the piece, and even on the section of the piece that's being worked on. Most writers rewrite the openings and the endings more than the middles because they know how critical it is to hook the reader at the start and leave them satisfied at the finale.

Habit 4: Use writing as a way of challenging yourself. Any job that you do over and over in exactly the same way is going to get boring after a while. Never let this happen to your writing. Vary not only the words, but the tone and style from one story to another. If you usually write in third person, try first person for a change. Play games with your writing if that helps keep your interest. For example, try cutting a word from each paragraph of your final draft, or try to remove all the adverbs. Some such experiments will fail, but each time you try something new you'll be using writing muscles that you didn't know you had, and *that* will make you a better writer.

Habit 5: Read. This is something that I don't think can be stressed enough, and I've stressed it several times already in this book. Quite simply, good writers are also good readers. This doesn't mean they read only classics. More likely, it means that they read a little bit of everything, novels, textbooks, magazines, newspapers, the backs of cereal boxes. Reading provides you with ideas, including the facts that you need in your stories, but it also gives you a sense of language, of how words are used. The more you read, the better you'll write.

Getting published is not the same as publish*ing*. Using a comparison from sports, most amateur athletes have a "great" game at least once in their life. Maybe the balls all bounce their way and the breaks fall on their side, or maybe they just play better than they've ever played before, or ever will again. That game doesn't make a career.

A career in sports, or in writing, requires consistency. You don't have to be great all the time, but you do need to be good almost every time. Practicing the habits listed above will help with the "every time." If you've consistently made time for writing you'll be ready when deadlines loom, as they will in a writing career. If you've made it a practice to look things up you'll be prepared for the research that you'll *have* to do. If you can take rewriting for granted you'll be able to keep massaging your first drafts until they are publishable. If you can challenge yourself you'll avoid boredom and will steadily improve your skills. And if you read, all the other steps will come just a little easier.

ACTIVITY SCHEDULE

	TIME	M	T	W	TH	F	S	SU
AM	8:00							
	9:00							
	10:00							
	11:00							
PM	12:00							
	1:00							
	2:00							
	3:00							
	4:00							

	5:00							
	6:00							
	7:00							
	8:00							
	9:00							
	10:00							
	11:00							
AM	12:00							
	1:00							
	2:00							

	3:00							
	4:00							
	5:00							
	6:00							
	7:00							

QUICK VERSUS SLOW SUSPENSE

Suspense is an element in all fiction. Suspense is what keeps readers reading, keeps them turning the pages, no matter what the genre. Suspense is wanting to know what happens next, whether to see if the world will be saved, or just if the hero and heroine will get together. When the suspense is generated by the threat of vampires, monsters, serial killers and other "creatures of the night" it is usually called "Dark Suspense," and that's the kind I'm personally most interested in. This kind of suspense is based on *fear*, either of the unknown, or perhaps of something that is all too familiar.

Because we are all constantly bombarded with over-the-top suspense in entertainment, as in movies from the current crop all the way to old favorites such as *Alien, Predator*, and *Die Hard*, modern folks have become somewhat blasé about "entertainment" suspense. That has made it increasingly hard to induce this critical emotion, not only in movies but in writing as well.

A writer who is about twenty years older than I told me once that when he saw the original version of "The Thing," an old Science Fiction horror movie from the fifties, he literally wet his pants when the monster appeared on the screen. He was young when he saw it, but some twenty years later, when I was about the same age, I saw the same movie myself for the first time. All I could think of when the monster appeared is that it looked like a giant walking carrot. It wasn't scary to me, but not because I'm a braver person than the older writer. By then I'd seen much worse on screens large and small.

The ante has been raised for modern writers and filmmakers. The need for suspense is greater than ever, and it's harder than ever to do it effectively. That means we have to think carefully before we commit anything to paper. We have to analyze how suspense works and how to create it. The next few essays in this book are on that very topic. In this first, somewhat introductory, essay I'd like to argue that there are two kinds of suspense, *Quick* and *Slow*, and that writers need to keep the differences between the two in mind as they spin their tales.

Every novel needs *Slow* suspense. Thriller and horror works need a lot of the *Quick* kind as well. Depending on their length, short stories can have very little to a fair amount of *Slow* suspense, but they definitely must have some of the *Quick* kind. Any written work can probably benefit from a mixture of the two, but *Slow* suspense is clearly superior and much harder to create. It has to develop as the storyline develops. Let's talk about the easier kind first, the *Quick* kind.

Here's an opening piece from Joe Lansdale's story "The Steel Valentine":

> *A man did not club you unconscious, bring you to his estate and tie you to a chair in an empty storage shed out back of the place if he merely intended to give you a valentine.*

Here's the opening from Lansdale's book *The Nightrunners*:

> *Midnight. Black as the heart of Satan. They came rolling out of the darkness in a black '66 Chevy; eating up Highway 59 North....*

Here's the beginning to Peter Straub's *Ghost Story*, a masterpiece of suspense.

> *Because he thought that he would have problems taking the child over the border into Canada, he drove south, skirting the cities whenever they came and taking the anonymous freeways....*

In these examples there is little or no characterization. There's been no time for it. Instead, there is scene setting and action, and threat. But it's enough to create both a mood and an initial curiosity in the reader, which is the primary function of *Quick* suspense. In a short story these two things might keep the reader hooked all the way through, as long as the scenes remain interesting and the action rockets along. In a *very* short story you'll have time for little else. I've written quite a few tales under 3,000 words and developing *Slow* suspense at such a length is virtually impossible. Suspense has to be there at the moment the story ignites.

Although *Quick* suspense is important to novels as well as short stories, especially at the beginning, it simply cannot carry an entire book. You need *Slow* suspense, too, and *Slow* suspense develops primarily from characters. Most readers will agree that the *Lord of the Rings* trilogy starts off pretty slowly. It begins with a birthday party, for goodness sake. Not much *Quick* suspense there. But by the time Frodo and Sam sneak into Mordor to destroy the one ring, readers are frantic with worry because over time they've come to respect and love the two hobbits. It is this concern for characters that creates *Slow* suspense.

It has probably always been hard to create characters that readers care about, and I don't think that TV and movies have hurt that process as much as they've hurt a writer's ability to develop *Quick* suspense. When people fall in love with a character, any threat to that character will generate suspense, the good, *Slow* kind that engages the readers' deepest emotions rather than just making their pulse race a little faster.

Because I talk about developing good characters in two other essays in this book, I'm going to refer you to those essays and move on from here to two more pieces on suspense. First we'll have "Six Steps to Creating Suspense," followed by "The Mechanics of Suspense." After that will be the two essays on character development, "Creating Sympathetic Characters" and "Characters: The Best and The Rest." Together, these five essays should clarify the process involved in developing *Slow* suspense.

SIX STEPS TO CREATING SUSPENSE

When I wrote *Cold in the Light*, I knew that because it was a horror/thriller I needed some *Quick* suspense. I needed some bad things, or mysterious things, to happen to people right off the bat. But I also knew that I then had to convince readers to care about the characters enough so that they'd keep reading past the initial "trauma." I needed *Slow* suspense. Let me tell you what I tried, much of which was unconscious at the time I tried it. But I think these are the kinds of things that are important in developing suspense, especially of the *Slow* variety.

1. *Write with Emotion*: When I started shopping *Cold in the Light* around it was rejected a few times for being "over-the-top." I didn't really consider this a valid criticism of a thriller novel in this age of *Independence Day* and *Spider Man*, but I think that the reason the charge was leveled against me was because the action/horror scenes for that book were written while I was in an intensely emotional state. I worked myself into that state deliberately, worked to get my adrenaline pumping and to psych myself up the way athletes do when they take the field.

When I first started writing, long before I worked on *Cold in the Light*, I used what I would almost call "props" to help me get in the mood. Before writing battle scenes I would listen to loud, heavy music, the kind called heavy metal, which always pumps me up. I often did exercises just before writing action scenes, any kind of callisthenic to speed up my breathing and my heart rate. When working on horror I sometimes wrote in the near dark, or with a few lorn candles scattered about.

As I got more familiar with writing I found that I didn't need the music, or exercise, or candles. I could put myself into an intense state simply by sitting down at the computer, or, if I needed a little something extra I'd read action passages or scary passages from previous stories I'd done, or from stories by writers I admired. I believe that it was such "emotional" writing that came through in *Cold in the Light* and earned me the label of "over-the-top" in some folk's minds.

I'm not going to tell you that I write every word and scene in that intensely connected state. It's physically exhausting, for one thing. But I think that when you want to create a strong emotion like suspense in a reader then it helps to give your own emotions some room to run. If *you're* feeling flat, there's a danger that you're prose, too, will be flat.

2. *Challenge Characters with Harsh Conditions:* We could call this the "It was a dark and stormy night" effect. Despite the cliché of that line, the environment in which your characters move is, in many cases, as important as the characters and the action itself. In my short story, "Chimes," a woman and her son are alone in a house waiting for a hurricane to come. As storm-wrought chaos descends on the world outside, a psychological chaos enters the home itself. The parallels strengthen the tension for the main character.

In "Chimes," however, the harsh environment of the hurricane was not something the main character had to *directly* struggle with. In *Cold in the Light*, in contrast, much of the action takes place at night and in the forest. The villains are at home in the dark and the woods. The heroes are mostly city folk, and like all humans they are at least a little bit scared of the dark. Pitting the heroes against both the villains *and* their environment is an effective way to create reader tension.

3. *Cliffhangers and Goals:* Since the days of the matinee serials, and before, writers have known the value of a cliffhanger for creating tension and suspense. Page turners are page turners because the page the reader just finished generates a "need to know" feeling for what happens next—on the following page. But cliffhangers work best if they come out of goal directed behavior for the characters.

For the heroes, cliffhangers occur when they meet an obstacle on their way to a goal. It seems like they're going to make it and, "boom," something gets tossed in their way. That's when you drop the scene or end the chapter. Let the reader wonder, "Oh my God, what are they going to do about *this* barrier?"

In contrast, cliffhangers happen with villains when obstacles are *removed* from their path, when it suddenly becomes easier for them to reach *their* goal. Since the reader's hopes lie with the heroes, when the villain suddenly acquires new weaponry, or new knowledge, or any advantage, then this ratchets up the suspense level for the reader. If you're using cliffhangers, then this is where you introduce it when the villain is on the scene. Let the reader wonder: "What is he/she/it going to do with the new information or new weapon?"

4. *The Telling Detail:* When seen from the point of view of characters, the details that they focus on can do much to increase suspense. I remember once when we had a fire in an office at Xavier University, where I teach. We couldn't get the fire extinguisher to work so I was running into the bathroom to fill up a trash can with water. While all the drama was happening, while all the shouting was going on, I noticed for the very first time a dark stain on the porcelain sink that looked like a man in a cloak. I don't know what that says about me, but it told me a lot about the "telling detail," that piece of…whatever…that captures a character's attention in moments of peak stress.

For example, in *Cold in the Light*, at various times, I have my villain focus on the details of smells. At one point he *sees* a certain odor trail as being a weave of yellow butterflies. Then, laughing, he begins to run wildly along that trail, letting the butterflies smash and die against him with broken wings. I did this to try and show the mindset of the character, to create a sense of madness in him, which, I hoped, would increase the readers' tension as they rooted for the heroes to stay ahead of their pursuer.

In "Chimes," the female hero awakens to hear the wind chimes under the eaves of her house ringing. She thinks to herself that she should have brought them in before the hurricane hit. Then she remembers. She *had* brought them in. They were downstairs in her living room where no wind could move them. That single detail, the ringing of chimes where no chimes should ring, set the entire story in motion, and I hope it curled the hair on the back of my readers' necks.

5. *Exploit Your Characters' Weaknesses:* For *Slow* suspense the characters who the readers care about need to be vulnerable. They need to be afraid and in danger. They need to have weaknesses. In addition to her normal fear of the dark, one of the main heroic characters in *Cold in the Light* shows an intensely fearful response to the sounds of night frogs croaking near water. The reader doesn't find out why until the end of the book, but you can bet I kept pushing that character closer and closer to watery places.

Characters who fear heights should face heights. Characters who hate the outdoors should be locked out of the house. Remember the scene from *Raiders of the Lost Ark* when Indiana Jones says: "Snakes! Why did it have to be snakes?" Of course it had to be snakes. He wasn't afraid of rats.

Now, I'm sure that everyone reading this book is a very nice person. But it's part of our job as writers to be mean to our characters. Make the readers love them, then give them the shaft.

6. *Kill Your Characters:* Here, I'm *not* talking about the kind of characters that populate many books and movies and whose sole job is to get killed. I had some of those characters in *Cold in the Light*, too; their main purpose was to provide a means by which the villain could show how *bad* he was. No, by killing your characters I mean some of your *main* characters, some of the ones you worked hard to develop and which the readers have come to like.

About a third of the way through *Cold in the Light*, a character who I had lavished lots of time and attention on, a character that I hoped the readers would identify with, was killed. I hated doing it, but it came naturally to the story and I let it happen. I was trying to put myself in the reader's shoes, maybe thinking as the reader that: "if he could kill that guy then *no one* in the story is safe. Anyone could die. At anytime."

Quite a few readers told me they hated me for killing that character. But they got over it. They kept reading. To create *Slow* suspense the ante has to be high and the risks have to be genuine—for the *characters* that the reader loves. You know that character who you really like, the one who's so similar to you? She could be the next to buy the farm.

Gotcha!

THE MECHANICS OF SUSPENSE

The strongest kind of suspense arises out of a story's characters, but there are some mechanical ways to increase suspense as well. The following are strategies that many writers have found effective in their stories and novels. Take them for a spin and see if they can work for you.

1. *Condense the Time of the Action:* There is a reason why so many movies have ticking clocks in them. When the bomb is about to go off, when the hero is racing against time, the reader's pulse starts to jump and his level of tension rises. In my novel, *Cold in the Light*, I had the action take place over a period of two days and three nights, yet one reader wrote to tell me that he would have preferred it to happen in one day. I told him I'd keep that in mind for my next thriller.

Time pressure on the hero can lead to suspense, but remember that it will only work if the reader cares about the hero and about the people the hero is rushing to save. No one is going to read a story about an empty building that is about to blow up in five minutes. They *are* going to read a story about a man who is going into a building before it blows up to try and save his three-year-old son.

2. *Use Short sentences and Sentence Fragments:* When people are rushed, or feel rushed, their tension level rises. Nobody wants to feel rushed through an entire novel, but when it comes to the suspense and action scenes a reader *needs* to feel the pace of the story pick up. Short sentences and sentence fragments lead to physically rapid scanning on the part of readers. Their eyes leap to cover the page and this has a tendency to crank up their emotional level as well. This won't work if the reader doesn't care about the characters. Given concern for the characters, however, this can be an effective technique, as long as it isn't employed too often. Sentence fragments, in particular, can be irritating when overused.

3. *Use Short Paragraphs:* Short paragraphs work much the same way that short sentences do. And by short I mean paragraphs of only two to four sentences each. Sometimes of only one. This will create a large amount of white space on the page over which the reader's eye will skip rapidly. (Having a lot of dialogue works similarly.) Both the reading pace and the emotional pace will ratchet up, as long as the reader gives a hoot about the characters, of course.

Unfortunately, the trend in modern fiction is already toward shorter and shorter paragraphs. But, if you have a contrast of different lengths in your work then shortening the paragraphs during the suspense and action scenes can add drama.

4. *Make Nature an Enemy:* Heat, cold, earthquakes, floods, avalanches, storms, landslides, volcanoes. When characters are in a fight for their lives against a story's villains, it can only add to the suspense to throw in a tornado.

The only caveat here is not to go overboard. One tornado is believable, and it might come with rain that causes a flood or a landslide. Two tornadoes is stretching it, and a tornado, earthquake and volcano together tells us we're not in Kansas anymore. We're in some kind of "B" movie like the ones they show only late, late at night on cable.

5. *Throw in Real World Surprises:* In real life, people get flat tires. They run out of gas. They get sick. They bump into people they know. They have a thousand other experiences. If used correctly, such everyday "surprises" can significantly increase suspense, *and* can produce excellent cliffhangers.

Consider, an undercover police officer is working a drug buy when he realizes that one of the men approaching him is someone he knows, someone who will recognize him. End the scene now and you've upped the tension. Or, our hero has been secretly tailing a terrorist who knows where a bomb is planted. She started the tail with plenty of gas but they've traveled so far that she's getting worried. She glances at her instrument panel and sees the fuel gage on "E."Drop the scene here and you'll leave the reader wondering how the hero is going to cope.

Anything that tosses an obstacle into the hero's path can ratchet up the suspense. This works especially well if it comes as a surprise in a critical moment. As with any other technique, however, this can be overused. Don't let characters suffer too many slings and arrows of outrageous fortune, and when everyday surprises do happen make sure they keep the focus *on* rather than distract *from* the main conflict.

6. *Cut the Fat and the Metaphors:* Cutting out extraneous wording can significantly increase the pace of a story, and the level of tension in suspenseful scenes. Phrases like "it seemed that" or "she felt like" are often unnecessary anywhere in a tale, and they can be the deadly enemy of suspense. Even metaphors and similes, which are great for scene setting and for creating atmosphere, will slow the pace in action sequences. Tight noun and verb sentences convey the pounding, dynamic rhythm that the reader wants when bad things are about to happen on the page.

CREATING SYMPATHETIC CHARACTERS

Most readers don't like unsympathetic point of view characters. And though they might follow such a character through a vignette or a short story, they won't follow him or her through a long story or a novel. That doesn't mean that characters have to be perfect, and they shouldn't be, but they have to have some qualities that readers will root for.

So how does one create a sympathetic character? There isn't any magic dust that can do so, but there *are* some guidelines that can help. Here are some of the observations that I've made over years of reading and writing, and from studying in my own field of psychology. These are observations, *not* judgments. I'm not saying that people *should* think the way they do. But see if you haven't noticed the same things.

1. Children are automatically seen as sympathetic characters unless they are clearly shown not to be. Most people love kids, or at least think they are cute at a distance. Most readers won't want to see a kid hurt in a story, and I'm not saying that writers should do so. But, kids in danger tend to evoke sympathy from the reader. And, after all, John Saul, Dean Koontz, Stephen King, and Mary Higgins Clark have done it. Or consider *The Exorcist*.

2. To a lesser extent than with children, women are seen as sympathetic characters, especially if they are in danger. Consider *Rosemary's Baby* or *The Stepford Wives* (the book not the lame 2004 movie of that name). This probably comes out of the old stereotype, which has still not been completely dispelled, that women are the weaker sex. For today's readers, though, a woman character will quickly lose her sympathetic "cred" if she merely waits to be rescued. There's a difference between being in danger and being helpless. *Helpless* females irritate modern readers. Also keep in mind that women—much more than children—can easily be

made into villains. All they have to do is be conniving or manipulative. You'll know what I'm talking about if you've ever watched soap operas.

3. The elderly are often seen as sympathetic characters, as long as they are not demanding and are basically healthy. Think of the movie *Cocoon*. People fear old age, though. It doesn't take much to make an old person appear evil. Just let them try to steal someone else's youth. If the elderly character is old to the point of grotesqueness, or if they have some horrid disease that makes them disgusting to be around, then people, even in these so called enlightened times, will recoil. But old characters are going to get the reader in their corner when they are cast aside or mistreated.

4. Characters who have disabilities tend to be seen as sympathetic. Stephen King uses a lot of "good guy" disabled characters in his books, so much so that you can always bet that the disabled or mentally "slow" character will be a hero. Check out *The Stand*, for example, or *The Green Mile*.
But be careful here, too. Disabilities that cause too much uneasiness or even disgust in the reader will not create sympathy without a lot of work by the writer. The world isn't quite ready for the Elephant Man as an action hero. Is this fair? No! And I'm not saying that writers shouldn't push the envelope of what readers will accept; my points are meant as observations, not judgments. Just be aware of the possible consequences to your choice of protagonist.

5. Characters who show sympathy or empathy for others, or who come to the aid of others, become sympathetic characters themselves. Think of firemen, dedicated police officers, doctors and nurses who sacrifice for their patients. Characters become *especially* sympathetic if their aid or empathy is directed toward animals. People have a hard time believing that someone who is kind to others or to animals could be bad. You might notice that Dean Koontz has a lot of good, loving dogs in his books. They're always associated with the heroes.

6. Sympathetic characters show traits or behaviors that are admired. Loyalty. Honesty. Independence. Self-sacrifice. Generosity. Dignity. Flexibility. Integrity. Grace under pressure. These and a hundred other personality aspects that we humans admire are key components to creating characters that readers can root for. Just don't give your character all of them or they'll be *too* perfect. Don't

we hate those kinds of people? Don't we all believe that in the real world "perfect" people are probably hiding a dark secret?

7. Considering #6 above, it may seem odd for me to say next that sympathetic characters need flaws. It's true, though. Impatience. Minor dishonesties such as telling white lies or cheating on one's taxes. Drinking too much once in a while. Getting angry enough to snap at loved ones. These are also common human traits and behaviors. We may not admire them but we understand them. We recognize them in ourselves and when a character shows one we often feel a little closer to that character. We can identify with them because they are similar to us.

Don't give your sympathetic character too many flaws, but a selected few can be a real help in creating a believable person that readers accept and identify with. Remember, though, that your sympathetic character *cannot* possess certain flaws. Pedophilia. Rape. Sadism. These are also behaviors and traits that some humans show. Any character who you hope to make sympathetic should *never* demonstrate these kinds of traits.

8. Outsiders or underdogs can quickly become sympathetic characters as long as they are not *too* far outside the mainstream. Almost everyone roots for David over Goliath. Almost everyone roots for the person who is misused or mistreated in some way. J. K. Rowling's Harry Potter is a great example. He's an underdog *and* a kid. Rambo gains the reader's sympathy in *First Blood* when he, an outsider alone, wanders into a small town and is harassed by the Sheriff. Or look at the movie *Stand and Deliver*, where Hispanic students from tough backgrounds succeed despite the doubts of almost everyone around them. In fact, that last plot line has been seen in many TV shows and movies. I'll bet you can name some.

9. Characters who think and express good thoughts, or who at least get upset with themselves for thinking bad thoughts, tend to become sympathetic. In one episode of Stan Lee's reality show *Who Wants to be a Superhero*, Stan asks his superheroes who *they* think should go home next. Four superheroes say nice things about the others in the group and then name themselves as the one who should go home. A fifth person criticizes another of the superheroes and names *that* superhero as the person who should go. Who do you think ends up getting cut? Indeed! And I'll bet most of the TV audience supported Stan's decision. I know I agreed.

All this ties in to the fact that readers, like most every other human on the planet, want to think of themselves as basically good. Given a chance, readers will root for someone who is a lot like they are—maybe not perfect but at least good hearted. Many of Stephen King's characters are very ordinary in this way. They have doubts. They look for some way to avoid doing what has to be done. But in the end they think, say, and do the right thing.

10. Characters who have experienced loss or who are suffering in some emotional way can easily become sympathetic. Imagine a parent whose child has died, or a little boy whose dog has to be put to sleep (*Old Yeller*, anyone?). We cannot help but feel for such people. In fact, this works so well that the "suffering" hero has become a cliché in action movies where every heroic cop seems to have lost a wife or child, or both, and be on the verge of committing suicide. Think of *Minority Report* with Tom Cruise, or *End of Days* with Arnold Schwarzenegger, or a dozen others. Even the cliché still works, though, and if you can find a new way of presenting "loss" for your hero then you're ahead of the game and should be writing essays like this yourself.

CHARACTERS: THE BEST AND THE REST

Through my blog, which I'll talk about later in this book, I've been having a wonderful online conversation with a bunch of authors about every writing topic under the sun. Recently, we got on the subject of character in fiction, about what makes a "good" character and a "bad" one? And I don't mean in the sense of the hero or the villain. The question was, why do some characters work and others fail? Here's the gist of what we uncovered.

First, one thing we noticed when our group began listing our favorite characters is that most were male. One commentator suggested that sexism played a role in that, but even women writers in our group had more male characters on their lists than female characters.

Does this mean that male characters are good ones and female characters bad? No. Most of the writers I've been communicating with are around my age, and most of us read adventure fiction in our formative years in the 1960s, 70's and 80's. I read primarily Science Fiction, fantasy, and westerns, largely written by men, but the fact is that *most* adventure fiction in those days was written by male authors and had male leads. At that time, even female authors in my favorite genres tended to feature male heroes, as with Andre Norton, or with C. L. Moore and her Northwest Smith tales (although Moore also created a very fine female hero with Jirel of Joiry).

So, if male characters aren't necessarily better than female ones, can the preponderance of male favorites on our writers' lists tell us anything about good and bad characters? I believe it can. I believe we can extract Rule #1 of good characterization from our lists. That is, *good characters act*.

For whatever reason, and much of it was simply a reflection of the times in which our group's reading habits formed, male characters were seen as taking charge, as *doing* things, while females either had to be rescued or simply stayed at home. Of course, there are many powerful female characters in today's fiction, but the key point is that they *still* act. They never stay home, and if they need rescuing they rescue themselves. Good characters can never be passive.

From discussions with my colleagues, it seems to me that another rule of characterization, Rule #2, is that *good characters are multi-dimensional*. This means that heroes can't be perfect. Sherlock Holmes is brilliant, a virtuoso in almost everything he does, but he is also arrogant and impatient, and a cocaine addict. Robert E. Howard's Conan is brave and physically tough, but in his younger days he was a thief and—in the parlance of today—has "anger management" issues.

Even villains today can't be all evil. Hannibal Lecter is a serial killer and cannibal, but we find out in *Hannibal Rising* that he loved his younger sister and that as a kid he often protected weaker children from bullies. Thus, despite his murders the reader begins to develop sympathy for him. Heroes *and* villains need to have both positive and negative traits, especially to attract today's readers.

One point, however! As I mentioned in the last essay but which is well worth repeating, certain flaws will overwhelm any positive qualities that a character might possess. No one has yet featured a blatant child molester as a hero, and I personally hope they never will. Even Hannibal Lecter could not have been written as a child molester and still gain readers', or viewers', sympathy. A combination of positives and *reasonable* flaws make a character more human, more like us. That makes them someone we can root for, or at least understand.

Speaking of "someone like us," I believe that Rule #3 is that *good characters have the same kinds of wants and needs that the rest of us have*. Good (as in effective) characters share in the common nature of humanity. Good characters love their children and want the best for them. Good characters want to be brave but sometimes are afraid. Like all of us, good characters feel strong emotions, whether it be love or hate, sadness or joy. When they work best, even the coldest characters are emotional at the heart, although that emotion may only be the consuming need for vengeance.

I once read that good Science Fiction should take one trend of today's world and project it into the future to see where the trend was going. In a similar way, good characters intensify one element out of the many that we humans hold in common. But without *some* connection to humanity the character fails.

Consider the Star Trek Universe and the supposedly alien character of Spock, or the android character, Data. Spock may have pointed ears, but his loyalty to his friends and his willingness to sacrifice himself for their welfare makes him the kind of "human" that we can all admire. Data wants to become *more* human, but that wish is ironic because the viewers can see just how human he already is as he strives to "fit in" and to "do the right thing." We come to know and love such characters through the very humanity that they show. Their differences may attract us to them in the first place, but it's their similarities to the best parts of us that keep us coming back.

For a final thought on character, if you want to write good ones then an excellent place to start is by reading biographies. I remember being disappointed in Ernest Hemingway when I found out that this "man's man" was not above cheating a little to win a fight, and that he could be as childish as a ten-year-old. I remember my disappointment when I found out that Martin Luther King, Jr., a man who sacrificed much for others, had a weakness for women other than his wife. And I was disappointed to learn that Bobby Fischer, the only American world chess champion, was something of an ass.

But disappointments aside, these three men's faults made them more interesting than any paragon of virtue could ever be. Despite their incredible successes, their faults showed them as human, because they are faults that are shared by the common people I see around me every day. What good fictional characters all three would make.

Biographers know what attracts readers to the characters they write about. Readers want to see personalities who are larger than life in some ways, and yet humanly flawed in others. Shouldn't *your* characters fit that mold?

HARVESTING MEMORIES

I grew up on a farm in Arkansas, and although I've lived in mostly urban environments for the past twenty-eight years, many of the memories of that childhood are still bright. I remember that we lived just under a hill, and how one night we heard a tornado go over the house in the air, and how it really *did* sound like a freight train. The next morning we found fish scattered in the field behind the house and brought them home in a big silver tub.

I remember how I used to keep little green grass snakes for pets, and how one got out of my pocket at supper one night and went scooting across the table directly into my mother's lap. I remember that was the end of my snake keeping. But it wasn't the end of my experiences with snakes. We raised chickens, and snakes would sometimes find their way into our chicken nests to eat the eggs. One day I found a snake that had swallowed two of the wooden eggs that we used to get our hens to lay more. I remember thinking how rough it would be for him when he needed to poop.

So what do these odd tidbits from my life have to do with writing? Well, all of them have been used to provide verisimilitude in stories that I've written. The past is what we all mine for the detail that makes our fictional scenes seem real. Even when I'm writing a story set on an alien world, it is *this* world that provides the sensory details I need to make my readers "feel" the alien sunlight and the alien wind. And it's my memory that provides the relevant experiences.

But a writer's past life can provide more than just detail for stories. It can supply whole plots and complete scenes. Even though I haven't lived a terribly exciting life by Hollywood standards, enough has happened to me—and almost certainly to you, as well—to feed a writing habit for years. From thinking about how a tornado could carry fish came an idea that I used in writing a story called "The Teeth of the Wind." From an old, half-fallen house about which ghost stories were told came the plot for a piece I called

"Your Nightmare or Mine." There are plenty of other examples I could give from my own work.

Although most of you reading this article already know the truth of what I'm saying, I'm afraid that many of you are *making* a mistake that I've *already* made. That mistake is to trust that your childhood memories will always be there for you to explore whenever you need. As we say in Arkansas, it ain't necessarily so.

I turned forty-eight at the end of 2006, and I'm lucky that my memory is still pretty good. But...it's not as good as it used to be. Every time I go home to visit my family, someone brings up something that happened twenty years ago that I've forgotten. Finally, about eight years ago I got smart and started a journal to record as many of my childhood memories as I could. And I update it whenever I talk to old friends or to family who remind me about past events.

I was to discover, however, that even important events that were once vivid memories can fade. For example, in looking over my memory journal for this article I found the entry: "The little yellow Tomcat that I loved." I now have absolutely no memory of that cat, although apparently I "loved" it.

My mistake—at least my first mistake—was not starting my memory journal until I was already forty years old. I wish now I'd begun it at twenty. Or at fifteen. I wish I'd kept a diary from the moment I could write.

Even after I began keeping a journal I made yet another mistake. I just jotted down a line or two about items, such as that yellow Tom, smugly convinced that this was all I'd ever need to trigger my recall. Nope! Had I added more detail about Yellow Tom to my journal I might still be able to dredge up that memory.

So what is the point of this piece? The point is to suggest that you start your own "Memory Journal." Start it now and put into it all the rich details that you possibly can. If you have a chance, take your journal with you on a physical trip back to old homes and old haunts. Look at time-faded photos and write down the remembrances they evoke. And it'll be worth the effort to keep adding to your "memoir" as new memories form or old ones resurface.

I know why I just jotted down a line or two for many of my own early entries. It was because I was lazy, and that was yet another mistake. I always had other writing projects that I wanted to work on, and I knew my journal in and of itself was not going to be published. I shortchanged my journal to write other things. What I didn't realize is that time spent on my journal would pay bigger dividends in the years to come than any other writing related work I might manage.

Hey, why are you still reading this? Get to work on that journal. Don't be lazy. And don't forget.

WRITING YOUR PAST
FOR FUN AND PROFIT

Writers find their inspiration from many sources but none more important than their own childhoods. In the previous essay I talked about keeping a journal to write down one's youthful memories before they fade with time. I've been doing that myself for quite a few years, and it turns out that there are markets for personal essays based upon these kinds of experiences. One early piece like this that I sold ran in *Delasaint's, Southern Writing With An Edge*. Before I talk about writing for, and finding markets for, this type of work, I thought it might be instructive to run the actual essay for you. Here goes:

WHEN ELECTRICITY CAME TO ARKANSAS

My older brother is as tough as a leather biscuit. I know because he proved it to me on a lazy country afternoon back in 1973. My brother—we called him Pabe—and I used to have macho contests to see who was the toughest. He always won—whether it was seeing who could eat the most jalapeno peppers, or who could catch the biggest chicken snake and play whip with it. Then came the summer of the electric fence.

On our farm we raised cattle, and to keep them out of the garden our dad often resorted to stringing a length of electric wire around the vegetable patch. On this one particular day, Pabe dared me to touch that fence. I told him that I would if he would, and that I'd hold on longer than he did. He gave me a sneer that I figured he'd practiced in front of the mirror and wiped his sweaty palms on his jeans. Then he reached out and "took hold" of that fence. I heard him grunt and saw his face get all twisted and crimson, and in about ten seconds he let go. I know because we both counted.

Now, Pabe had just beaten me a little earlier in an extremely important contest by licking twenty-five of mom's fresh chocolate coconut cookies while I'd only been able to lick fifteen. That meant he'd get to eat twenty-five and I'd eat fifteen, because neither of us would eat what the other licked, which was the point of the licking in the first place.

But, because Pabe had beaten me out of some cookies, I was determined not to let him win a second time in the same day. I approached the fence nervously, dried my hands as my brother had done, and latched onto the wire with one swift movement. It felt like a swarm of bumblebees had crawled under the skin at my wrists and were beating their wings wildly trying to escape through my shoulders.

But I'd felt worse. Daddy's spankings were a whole lot worse. I held on and counted, and at twelve, a good two seconds longer than Pabe's record, I let go of the wire and looked up at my brother with my own practiced sneer.

My triumph was short lived, however. Pabe would never accept defeat from his little brother. And after that day I gave up challenging him ever again, something I've held to until the present.

"Tain't nothing," he said. "I dare you to try this."

Then Pabe dropped his trousers and urinated on that thin little electric wire. I don't think he expected to get quite what he got. I think he figured it was a myth that you could get shocked peeing on an electric fence, but a young man's "stream" is often a pretty solid arc of water, and electricity flows through water. I remember the sizzle and Pabe's strangled scream. I remember wondering if he'd ever have kids.

Well, today my brother has both a boy and a girl. Tough as he is, I'm almost certain they're his.

* * * * * * *

Several things seem key to turning a personal reminiscence into a salable essay. First, you need to find a memory that has a beginning, middle, and end. Even nonfiction needs to tell a story if it's going to sell. Second, it really helps if there is humor involved, although there are certainly markets for spiritually profound experiences and for family oriented works. Third, brevity is an important key, and by brevity I'm talking about 750 words or under. Most of the ones I've sold have been around 500.

The need to write short means that you have to be absolutely brutal with your own memories, cutting out every extraneous detail until you have the distilled essence of the experience. In the piece I shared here, notice that there's nothing about the weather, no details about the clothes we were wearing, not even our specific ages. The details are focused on what led up to our "fence" experience, and what we felt or did when we touched the fence. There are also no inside jokes here, nothing that is meant just for those who know my brother and I. You might include such things if you're writing to entertain at a family gathering, but not if you're trying to sell the piece to a national market. No reader wants to feel left out.

Once you've created a personal essay then you'll need to find a potential publisher. You can do an online search on "personal essay markets," or try "personal essay contests." Contests provide great chances for publication and when they're put on by magazines they often pay more than the standard rates for that magazine. I've also listed some links to online guidelines below. All of these markets use personal essays and pay, although not always enough to fill your wallet.

Capper's:
    www.cappers.com/contributors-guidelines
Chicken Soup:
    www.chickensoup.com/
Cup of Comfort:
    www.cupofcomfort.com/share.htm
Good Old Days:
    www.goodolddaysonline.com/pages/magazineinfo.html
Literal Latte:
    www.literal-latte.com/submit_new.html
Midwest Today:
    www.midtod.com/new/writers_guide.html
Reminisce:
    www.reminisce.com/2005/SO05/guidelines.asp

THE FIRST RULE OF ENDINGS

People who write fiction most often revise their openings more than they do any other part of their work. They may even tell a new writer that the beginning is the most important part of a piece. They may particularly stress the opening sentence as the hook upon which all readers turn. I think they're telling it wrong.

I don't mean to downplay the importance of strong openings. They are absolutely essential to selling any individual piece of writing. Unless you can catch the reader's attention quickly, perhaps instantaneously, that reader is going to move on to one of the many other sources of entertainment in their sensation-rich world. Reality shows and X-boxes. DVDs and iPods. They're all waiting and willing to steal your readers.

So why aren't openings the single most important part of a tale? It's because they only help sell the immediate piece that the reader has in hand. More important than the beginning is the "ending," which not only helps sell the immediate piece, but is the *only* thing that sells your next piece. And surely most writers would prefer to have more than a one story career.

I recently read a collection of short SF stories from the 1930s and 1940s that was entitled *Strange Ports of Call*. There were a few excellent pieces in the anthology, including Ray Bradbury's "The Million Year Picnic," but what struck me about many of the tales is that if they were submitted to the big SF magazines of today under my name, or probably yours, they wouldn't sell. They wouldn't sell because they had no real endings, just a sort of..."trailing off." They finished with a whimper rather than a bang, and endings today *need* that bang.

It is the *endings* that people remember about a tale, whether it's in written form or in the movies. Who remembers the *start* of *The Sixth Sense*? But if you saw that movie then you remember the end. Who can tell you the opening lines of *King Kong*, but who can forget "It was beauty killed the beast?" Beginnings may capture our attention, but it is endings that send us clamoring for more.

I'm going to spend a couple of essays talking about endings and how to find the good ones, but I'll finish this immediate piece with the first rule of endings, a rule that many writers don't realize *is* a rule. This is that the opening of any piece of writing *makes a promise* to the reader, and the ending's first and foremost job is to fulfill that promise.

This rule is easy to see in action with nonfiction. Suppose you pick up an article that opens with: "Recent research suggests that Mars was once a wet planet." Don't you want the author of such a piece to tell you about the "research" and why it suggests a wet Mars? Just so.

Now consider a short story that begins: "The three men fled Mars aboard a stolen rocket." This is just as much of a promise as the opening of the nonfiction piece. At the very least the readers must be told who the three men are and why they stole the rocket, and, of course, what happens to them as a result of their theft.

Seems simple, doesn't it? But all of us can probably name some published books and stories that failed at the climax. And I'm told by editors who I know that this is the most common reason why decently written stories are rejected.

The best endings do more than just fulfill the promise of their openings, of course. They create a mood that stays with us even after we close the book or turn the last page. But that's a discussion for another essay. This one's at its end.

THE CURSE OF THE LAZY ENDING

Ending a story or book well is hard, but it's perhaps the most important part of the writer's job. As I mentioned in the last essay, while the opening sells your first work, the ending sells the second. From a marketing standpoint, good endings are what establishes a writer's career.

Even more important, however, is that the ending is where you pay off the readers who have stayed with you through the entire work. They've put their time in. They've trusted you as you've led them along the path you've paved. They expect you to deliver on the promises of your opening.

Two books I've finished recently failed to deliver, at least in my estimation. Both were pretty big sellers, although one was much bigger than the other, and I've very much enjoyed previous works by both writers. This time I was disappointed. And here's why. (Names are left out to protect the guilty.)

Book 1: The hero is cornered by the villain in a dank storm drain at the end. The villain has a gun, and the drop. She's a bit over the top as a character, but we know she's vicious and ready to kill. The hero is a bit more bumbling but has shown amazing resource-fulness throughout. So, how does the author resolve the situation? Surprise! A wild animal attacks the villain from behind and kills her. This saves our hero, who is then pursued by one of the villain's henchmen for another few short chapters before the actual end. It seemed pretty anti-climactic.

To be fair, the reader *had* seen the tracks of the wild animal ear-lier in the book. It didn't come completely out of the blue, and a friend of mine who read the same book said the ending didn't bother her. It disappointed me, however, and I had to read that section over a couple of times to make sure that what I thought had happened did *indeed* happen.

Book 2: The hero and his friends are pursued by a witch who is well developed as a powerful and savage antagonist. She has killed and "eaten" a child for goodness sake. We've seen her transform into an eagle, and a dragon, and have seen her take on a variety of human forms. She has possessed souls left and right who now do her bidding. And so at last the witch faces the hero. He steps toward her, and with a single blow of his sword *cuts off her head*, freeing all the souls she's captured and finishing the final battle before it has properly begun.

Yes, the hero *had* been shown to possess supernatural powers. I assumed that was why the author spent so much time developing the witch into a worthy adversary. Only, she wasn't worthy. She was barely a nuisance to the hero. I've had more trouble swatting mosquitoes.

I have no idea why these normally fine writers ended these two books with such clunkers. Maybe they were just being lazy, or maybe they were distracted or exhausted from the intrusions of real life. Maybe they thought the endings really worked. Whatever the reason, they made *this* reader a little less likely to pick up their next book, and if these had been the *first* books I'd read by them then I certainly wouldn't buy more.

These writers forgot two simple rules for endings. The writer of book 1 forgot that heroes must resolve conflicts themselves and cannot be "rescued" by fate. This type of implausible ending is often referred to as Deus ex machina (God from the machine), and it was criticized as far back as Aristotle. The author of book 2 forgot that defeating the villain must be *difficult* for the hero. Readers expect heroes to win, but they expect them to suffer for their victories. When the hero faced the witch in the climax, I first felt tension. Then I felt cheated.

How am I supposed to feel when I see these two authors' next books on the shelf? Should I give them my money? Should I give them my time? It's not going to be easy to convince me now.

ENDINGS: WHAT'S AT STAKE?

A professionally written story will not necessarily sell. The prose can be good, the characters interesting, the plot possibilities mysterious, and the ending can kill it all if it's cliché, or goofy, or only offers a low stakes payoff for the reader. From TV, consider the infamous *Dallas* fiasco when a whole "season" turned out to be Pamela Ewing's "dream." Consider the miniseries *It* where the monster turns out to be a "giant spider." From print, consider the story where the protagonist realizes at the end that he's been "dead" all along, or the tale where an abusive husband seeking to cheat on his wife meets a woman at a bar who turns out to be—wait for it—a vampire.

There's no decent "payoff" for the reader in these endings. Only an incredibly adroit writer or filmmaker has any chance of pulling off such a climax without losing an audience. (*The Sixth Sense* did it but that was an extremely well done movie.) The "it was all a dream" ending is actually an insult to those who have invested their emotions in a work; you realize you've been toyed with. The guy who "discovers that he's dead," or who cheats on his wife only to meet a "vampire," is a cliché. Such endings are too easy. As for the "giant spider?" Well, that's just lame. Modern readers, especially, want more.

I wrote a tale a couple of years back called "A Curse the Dead Must Bear," and I still haven't sold it. I think it's because the ending doesn't pay off. A man falls down the stairs, breaks his neck, and is declared dead. But his consciousness continues. He is aware of everything around him. He can hear and see (until his son closes his eyes), but he cannot communicate with the "living" and cannot escape the decaying prison of his body. Once he's buried he finds that every other "dead" person in the cemetery is exactly like he is. He can hear them murmuring, cursing, crying, begging, but no one above ground hears a thing. He begins to *hate* the "living" and is comforted by only one thought, that they will soon be in the same boat. The end.

Big deal! I thought the idea that every dead person's consciousness would be trapped within their deteriorating shell was interesting, but that point is revealed midway through the story and other than that what is the reader's payoff? The protagonist cannot *do* anything about his situation. He can only hate, and the target of his hate is perfectly safe. The ending turns on the fact that we're all going to die someday. Now there's a news flash. This is "low stakes," not necessarily for the story's protagonist, but for the *reader*. And it's the reader who matters.

The cheating guy who meets the vampire is low stakes for the reader, as well. We can see that ending, or something like it, coming a long way down the tracks. True, the guy is getting what he deserves, but other than a little "he had it coming" feeling the reader isn't experiencing any emotional kick. The ending doesn't surprise us. It doesn't give us a smile. It doesn't leave us particularly happy, sad, disgusted or afraid. It leaves us flat.

Here's another example, from a well written story that I discovered on a website a year or so ago. A guy plans to commit suicide because he can't stand his life. He struggles to find the courage. But when he finally gets up the guts to shoot himself he finds that his consciousness continues and he's in Hell. End of story. Low stakes. Disappointing. Especially when the prose had been promising up until the very end.

For any story, but especially for such twist-ending tales, the first ending which occurs to you as an author may well be one you've read or seen before. And if *you've* read or seen it, then others have too and they won't find the ending or the twist convincing or satisfying.

How do you avoid endings that don't provide the reader with a payoff? One way is to consider the low stakes ending as the tale's *beginning* instead. Cheating guy meets vampire at the *start* of the story, and gets turned. He goes home to torment his wife, thinking how much fun he's going to have now that he's a supernatural abuser. But he finds that his wife has been having an affair, too, with the female vampire who turned him. They planned to make him a vampire all along, but only a weak vampire, because now they just want him to watch them and suffer. Forever.

It doesn't matter how big a story's stakes are for the characters, only how big they are for the reader. Plenty of great stories have been written where what's at stake for the characters is only the success or failure of a relationship, not stopping a terrorist threat or saving the world. But if the reader is emotionally involved, if he or she is surprised by an ending, or if she laughs or cries, or if he just says, "cool," then you've done your job as a writer. You've made your ending worth the effort the reader put in getting to it.

THE PHYSICAL SIDE OF WRITING

Writing is generally considered mental work, but there's much more to the physical side of it than people think. In the summer of 2007 I took off from teaching and for the first few weeks I poured most of my time into writing, spending anywhere from eight to ten hours a day at the keyboard. I made great progress, but I also had to pay a physical price for it with back aches, neck cramps, numbness and tingling in the legs, a stiff shoulder, wrist, and hand on my mouse side, and eye strain. In fact, while my mind reveled in the work, my body made periodic threats at a strike. Fortunately, I began to find some ways to appease my body without losing a lot of time from writing. If you're going to write long hours then you need to think about some of these things for yourself.

1. Stay hydrated. Everything works better when it's lubricated. Instead of soda, I keep a bottle of water at hand and refill it as necessary. If I want a change of pace I drink something like Powerade or Gatorade. You don't want a lot of sugars and caffeine, but you do need fluids. And despite the fact that five of the Americans awarded the Nobel prize in literature have been recognized as alcoholics, beer, wine and whiskey aren't suitable "fluids," at least not until you're done with the day's writing.(The five, by the way, were William Faulkner, Ernest Hemingway, John Steinbeck, Eugene O'Neill, and Sinclair Lewis.)

2. Take frequent mini-breaks and stretch your body. Just a minute of bending and moving helps me, and I never have to get more than a few feet from the computer. My mind never leaves the problem at hand. Even while sitting at my desk I'll take a moment to roll my neck and stretch an arm or a leg.

3. Switch positions in your chair frequently. I have a habit of sitting with my left leg curled up on the chair and my right leg over

it. I'm trying to alter that pattern on a more regular basis, although it's hard because the position has become a habit. Stiffness and pain often arises from maintaining the same posture too long.

If you start to have aches and pains, don't forget to check your chair to see if part of the fault lies there. Because of how I sit, my chair sometimes presses steadily against the back of my legs and impedes the blood flow, leading to tingling in my lower legs and feet. Most desk chairs can be adjusted in height, though, or maybe it's time to get a new one. Make sure, new or old, that your chair has plenty of padding. After this summer's long hours I've taken to laying down an extra pillow when I position my posterior for work.

4. Have your eyes checked. I've given in and admitted that my eyesight isn't what it used to be and have used my word processor's zoom capabilities to significantly increase the apparent size of the font, often to 150 percent of actual size. I've also gotten a new prescription for my glasses, including a specific prescription for working on the computer. I was surprised at how big a difference this made in my ability to write from a more relaxed pose. I also keep the lights on bright, and since this can generate a fair amount of warmth I have a fan handy in case of overheating.

5. Watch what you do in your off hours. Try to avoid requiring the same things of your body when you're off as when you're writing. For example, I've cut way back during my free periods on playing any computer game that requires a lot of repetitive mouse work. I also don't read in an upright chair anymore, which is what I write in. I sit or lie where I can take the pressure off my legs and my slowly flattening rump.

Like any job, writing takes a physical toll. But if you keep yourself hydrated and move frequently you can minimize the aches and pains that come along with the words. It's hard to concentrate if you're uncomfortable or hurting, so stay loose, and stay productive.

ONE WAY TO PUT A STYLE TOGETHER

Style lies in *how* something is said rather than *what* is said. It is an author's way of "working on words." Some writers—Ray Bradbury, Ernest Hemingway—are known as much for their style as for their excellent stories. Other writers—Stephen King, David Morrell—focus much more on the plot and action and are known for styles that try not to call attention to the writer at work. Neither approach is particularly better than the other, although I confess a weakness in myself for prose that is both beautiful and functional.

Occasionally, newer writers get overly focused on style. They worry *when* or *if* their own personal style will develop. They worry if their style is any good. Sometimes they set out to "craft" a style for themselves. That's usually a mistake. Although a distinctive writing style will certainly get you noticed, it may *not* increase your sales. The problem is that a style must come naturally if it is to bring readers *to* your work instead of driving them away.

Deliberately crafted styles often seem stilted and strained. And they easily degenerate into mannerisms that let the reader see too much of the writer pulling strings behind the scenes. Writing must serve the reader's needs rather than the writer's ego, and prose that is consciously "artsy" is more likely to irritate readers and editors than to impress them.

Nor should a writer's style be set in concrete once it *has* been established. Style changes as a writer's personality changes—compare Ray Bradbury's earlier and later work—and a good style is flexible enough to be used for different types of writing. You won't want to write a nonfiction essay in the same style as you would use for a horror story, or for a chatty letter to a friend. The only rules as far as I can see is that "good" style avoids clichés and wordiness, that it puts the right words in the right places, and that it is not a copy of anyone else's style.

When I first started writing, way back in my teens, my prose generally sounded like a poor pastiche of whatever writer I was reading at the time. I did poor Bradbury, poor Louis L'Amour, poor Frank Herbert. Only when I stopped parroting others and let my own personal feelings and expressions come through on the page did I begin to sound like something different, like something unique. That didn't happen overnight. Nor did my style remain static once it developed. It has continued to change as my experiences and views on the world have changed.

To see how *your* style is put together, and to take a step toward gaining control of your own unique voice, try the process of "layering." The first step in "layering" is to write a story—or a piece of a story—in short, declarative sentences, using mainly nouns and verbs with as few other parts of speech (adjectives, adverbs) as possible. Here's an opening paragraph from such a story:

> *Jack heard a scream. It came from the house. He ran toward the sound. He drew his pistol. He hoped he wasn't too late.*

The bare bones of the story are here, but the "sound" is terrible, like a never changing drumbeat. To break up this staccato quality, step two of "layering" involves combining some short sentences into longer ones. Recasting a few active sentences as passive ones may also help; this dramatically alters the sound of a tale:

> *Jack heard a scream from the house and ran toward the sound. His pistol was drawn. He hoped he wasn't too late.*

Step three is where you put in a layer of adjectives and adverbs to modify the bare framework of your sentences. Don't worry if the modifiers are a little thick at first. Pruning comes later. No editor will see purple prose like: *Jack heard a savage scream from the decrepit old house and ran furiously toward the harrowing sound. His heavy pistol was drawn tight into one massive fist. He hoped he wasn't too late to save an innocent life.*

Step four is where a story really becomes your own. This involves putting in details that make the story specific rather than general. Do you want your character to be named "Jack?" Maybe something else would work better. What kind of scream does the character hear, and does it come from a house or from some other structure? What kind of pistol is he holding? Whose life is he trying to save? Notice the changes made to our sample paragraph this time. They're capitalized:

> *DRAKE heard a SHRILL scream from the ABANDONED RAILWAY CAR and RACED toward the harrowing sound. His heavy L-FRAME RE-VOLVER was drawn tight into one WHITE-KNUCKLED fist, AND he PRAYED TO GOD that he wasn't too late to save HIS ONLY SON'S life.*

Finally, step five is "pruning." This is where you get rid of any excess modifiers and select only those few details that you want to highlight. It is best here to read sentences out loud while working on them. Strangely, written style is often as much about sound as it is about word choice and syntax. The cadence of the work is impor-tant.

> *Drake heard a shrill scream from the abandoned railway car and raced toward the sound. The L-Frame revolver was heavy and tight in his fist, and he prayed that he wasn't too late to save his only son's life.*

"Layering" is not something to use every time you write, but it does demonstrate the way in which a writer's voice is put together— from the inside out. No two people carrying out this exercise would fit their prose together in exactly the same way. That's unique style. Make it your own.

WRITING FOR EXCESS
WITH "BARBARIAN'S BANE"

Excess and exaggeration are often funny. Think of the over the top facial expressions of such comedic actors as Jim Carrey, Steve Martin, or Bill Cosby (or for those really old folks among you, and you know who you are, the Three Stooges). Think of jokes you've heard about how dumb blondes are (two blondes walk into a building...you'd think one of them would have seen it), or how awful lawyers are (The example I have is too obscene to share with this group; I hardly know you.) A lot of humor turns on the spit of excess and exaggeration, and below are three possible ways to do this in your writing by using "lists."

1. Consider this, you're writing a fantasy story where you have a character refer to barbarians as dirty and smelly. This isn't funny. It's not supposed to be. But what if you "wanted" it to be funny? Why not have those barbarians be: "noxious, noisome, flea-bitten, scraggly, stinky, smelly, wretched, filth-encrusted, lice-ridden, scab-picking, snot-eating barbarians." Humor is such a delicate emotion and is so difficult to write that it's hard to judge something as funny without the context around it, but at least with an exaggerated list such as this the "possibility" of humor exists.

2. A second way to use lists to create humor is through exaggerating "within" the list rather than by extending the list. For example, consider our hypothetical story about barbarians again. Say we are naming barbarian *types* in the story. We refer to them as "nomads, savages, and Vikings." This is just a list, not a terribly accurate one, and certainly not funny.

But what if we add one more thing to that list, something that contrasts or undercuts what we've said before. Such as: "he hated barbarians and all their ilk, from nomads, to Vikings, to anyone who would drink red wine with fish." Adding the red wine and fish is an exaggeration that presents the possibility of humor. Few would intentionally consider the ancient Vikings and the modern "class-challenged" restaurant diner to have the same level of barbarity. In this case, you've led the reader down the garden path and then tripped them into the thorns. Now that's funny.

3. A third way to achieve humor in lists is through alliteration. Alliteration is when several words in a sentence begin with the same letter (often "s" or "t") so that the sentence has a pleasant music to it. For example, consider the law firm of Smith, Smythe, and Schmidt. That's alliteration. Contrast that with the law firm of Carbuncle, Megussuah and Bored. Alliteration is a wonderful technique, when used sparingly, to accentuate or jazz up one's writing. But, in the hands of a humorist, alliteration is a weed growing rank in the garden of prose. Consider again our fantasy story. In it we have a rather effeminate sorcerer who "stamps his sandal on his balcony." "Stamps" and "sandal" represent the alliteration. But exaggerate it to get humor: "The Sorcerer stamped his silken-soled sandal on the smoke-stained stone of his sadly-soiled balcony."

The examples given in this essay actually come from a story I wrote entitled "Barbarian's Bane," which was published in a now defunct magazine called *Dragonlaugh*. Since I hadn't written much humor before, I gave the subject quite a bit of thought before constructing the story. Seeing as how the story is fairly short, I think I'm going to run it here to provide a context for the examples I've used. Maybe you can even extract other ways to uses lists for humorous effect from its paragraphs. At worst, I hope you get a few chuckles.

WORMS IN THE EARTH:
BARBARIAN'S BANE

In those days there were Worms in the Earth.
Big worms. Gigantic! Worms so mighty that
the earth shook with their writhings. And
one day those worms came forth and attacked
the shining cities of man. The destruction
was really bad.
  —The Book of "Hopefully" Lost Tales

The barbarians were gone now, but that did little to cool the fevered hate that Farthane the necromancer felt for them. That hate was a black and coiling thing, with smidgens of rust and verdigris in the gruelish mix. He was sick...to death, of barbarians and all their ilk—of nomads, Neanderthals, and Nazis, of savage tribes, troglodytes, and yuppies, of anyone who would drink red wine with fish.

"Why me?" Farthane remonstrated to the foul and brooding sky that roiled like an ulcerated stomach over his nighted castle.

(It was a good question, and one that any being, corporeal or otherwise, who happened to gaze upon Farthane at that moment might well have echoed. 'Tis fortunate then, for those of us who are gazing upon the necromancer at this moment, that Farthane did not leave the question merely rhetorical. Let's listen in.)

"Why did they have to pick my haunted forest to traipse through? And why did they have to kill my Ogres and Trolls, my Will-o'-the-Wisps and Drachen, my Poltersprites and Skogsnufvas, my Shopiltees and Callicantzarois, my mantichore for Crom's sake? What need was there to eat my cannibal trees and pluck the wings from my pegasi? And why," he gestured at the cloud-bruised sky, which declined to answer but instead spat a dollop of drizzle down his neck, "why did they have to trample my ghoulish gray garden of grim geraniums?"

Farthane sighed as he gazed down then in tormented sadness at his ruined flower beds, and upon the scorch marks that had taken the clear-coat right off the obsidian walls of his keep. Why, the "animals" had besieged him—besieged HIM!—and had nearly burned him out before he'd manage to raise a bevy of Babylonian bimbos from the dead and send them out through his secret underground exit (formerly called his sewer) as a distraction to the besiegers. (He was aware that the only thing barbarians like more than looting and pillaging is sex. Just look at how many of them there are.)

Now, after the lust-addled barbs had been enticed off to the south by the alluring mummies, where they would almost certainly lose track of their former purpose of battering down Farthane's walls and doing harm to his actual person, the necromancer was free to ask the gods his "whys," though he did not truly expect a response from the putrid heavens. Besides, he knew the answer to all his questions anyway.

"Because they are barbarians," he muttered to himself. "That is the only reason they need for destroying the livelihood of an honest sorcerer-in-good-standing such as myself."

The spade-shaped beard on Farthane's chin, replete with newly silvered hairs, quivered with agitation. His pale and usually languid fingers curled around his arcane staff with a grip that threatened to crush the delicately filigreed jade-work with which the stave was adorned.

He pondered...and pondered some more...with narrow eyes narrowed in a narrow face. He must have his revenge. It must be a big revenge—one that every future barbarian child would learn at the knee of every future barbarian unwed mother (which he imagined them all to be). They must be taught, forever, that they could not with impunity impugn his power and leave their muddy boot prints and discarded cockatrice bones on his flying carpets. They MUST suffer! He stamped his silken-soled sandal on the smoke-stained stone of his sadly-soiled balcony.

"Must, must, must!" he ejaculated. And, turning with an intent resolve, he made his way through the piles of spent arrows, death's-head daggers, throwing axes, and razor-embedded Frisbees that littered his battlements to enter his castle of stark renown.

Deep into his palace Farthane stalked, making his way to what he called his "black" room (though a visiting imp had once been heard to remark, "why doesn't he call it his 'blacker' room since his whole castle is most wholesomely black?"). Drawing from his fastidiously immaculate shelves his most ancient and potent grimoire—the Necronudicon (older than the Necronomicon and with better pictures besides)—he turned the laminated bat-wing pages until he found the one spell he sought, the one cantrip that he had never used in his rather short long life.

"The Worms in the Earth," he breathed, as he scanned the words scrawled on the vellum sheets with the blood of hundred-year-old virgins. And he cackled most appropriately.

The spell was short (how many hundred-year-old virgins do you think there are anyway?), but the words were filled with a puissance that drummed in the walls as he spoke them. At the first word his vengeance began. So, of course, he spoke the second as well. And the third he scrawled in the air with a fingernail that blazed with lavender and mauve light.

A fourth and fifth word followed, and the world of his castle trembled, dust puffing up from the closely set Acme bricks of the floor. At the sixth word a spider sitting irritated in a corner of the ceiling changed her web-board from "felicitations" to "shut the Hell up."

But now Farthane spoke the seventh and final word. And he watched in the room's enchanted mirror as the earth of his desecrated garden zippered open, and the nightcrawlers of his calling crawled forth, dripping with mucous, moist with glabrous slime.

"The Worms!" he shrieked. "The Worms in the Earth!"

With segmented heads questing like pseudopods, the creatures reared up from the soil that had birthed them, as if to seek the sorcerer who had called them from their nocturnal domain.

Farthane frowned as he noted that those rearing heads lifted only a scant inch or two above the ground, and that in length the longest of the worms would barely outstretch the penile bone of a male highland gorilla (about two inches). Somehow, he had thought the "Worms in the Earth" would be...bigger.

Quickly checking his spell, the necromancer could find nothing wrong with his casting. Every word had been spoken correctly, with just the right sibilant hiss, with all the required umlauts and glottal stops. Every motion of his hands had been choreographed with precisely the right air of languid languor. Shrugging, a bit nonplussed yet determined to carry through with the program, Farthane replaced the book in its niche and, leaning close to his enchanted mirror, shouted through it to the beings he had raised to do his bidding.

"Go forth!" he ordered. "Go and lay waste to those who would dare abuse, profane and/or desecrate my palace and myself. Destroy themmmmmm! Utterly!"

Again our necromancer cackled (a necessary skill for such as he, and one at which Farthane was quite proficient). And the worms obeyed, jerking, sliding, writhing away to the south in pursuit of the barbarian horde. And as they jerked, slid and writhed, a most wickedly wondrous thing happened (from Farthane's point of view). In their thousands, the worms began to flow together, began to...melt into each other, slimy flesh melding to slimy flesh like plastic soldiers tossed together into a fire. These new worms began to fuse together in turn, growing larger and larger and larger and larger and larger and larger and larger—until they formed one Worm, a truly gigantic Worm, a gargantuan, monstrous, humongous, Brobdingnagian Worm.

Farthane stood frozen in awe as he watched that incredible "joining," and soon his feet started to tap, started to dance, started to soft-shoe—until he was capering about in his black room, holding up his black robes with their stitches of silver and the phrases of power sewn upon the front ("Loud chants save lives") and back ("If you can read this the witch fell off"). He was suddenly in rare good humor.

As he gazed into his occult mirror and begin to imagine the delicious revenge that should be his once the Worm fell upon the barbarians like an avenging angel (a rather appearance-challenged and "mucousy" angel, it is to be admitted), Farthane shivered in almost orgasmic pleasure and his good humor grew more good.

"I shall see their wagons and belongings crushed like flour tortillas," he intoned. "I shall see the barbarians and their infernal dogs rolled like enchiladas in the felt of their own yurts. And though a thousand plus a thousand warriors attack my Worm with axes and swords and lances and horned helmets, they shall only be...squished. Each and every one of them. Like mud between the toes of a barefoot boy.

"Ah, too soon it will be over. And across that crimson sward of carnage, only the lonely wind will murmur, and the only living thing will be MY titanic Wurmmmmmmm! I shall be called Mighty Slayer, Foe Destroyer, Barbarian's Bane."

Farthane giggled within his castle of bleak resolve. He chuckled, chortled, and chirruped. But then the necromancer's laughter went chill and hollow, and faintly nasal, and his capering slowed to a mere shuffling of sandaled feet.

Through the miracle of his wizard's glass, Farthane observed a single, bored-looking shamaness of the barbarians stalking out from her roisterous encampment to face the Worm. She appeared to be drinking the kind of beer that is not served with a slice of lime, and was wearing a T-shirt that read: "Yes, I'm magic. No, you can't touch my dark cauldron."

But it was neither the drink nor the shirt that had seized Farthane's horrified attention. It was the small, rust-flecked amulet the woman held pinched between her thumb and forefinger.

When the Worm saw that amulet it paused, quivering along the entire length of its jello-like bulk. Its head lifted, thinning at the neck, whipping back and forth in agitation as if some ancestral memory was striving to break through into its dim awareness.

In that instant, Farthane's sorcerously enhanced senses connected with the microcephalic brain of his monster, who had once, if you recall, been billions of much tinier worms. And in that instant of oneness with his creation, Farthane remembered: the squelch of boots in fresh mud, the biting grate of a spade stabbing into earth, and the terror of being jerked into the air from his bed of rich soil to writhe in the hands of men who were going...fishing.

The shamaness tossed her amulet down in front of the Worm, then turned to reenter her camp. Farthane was hurled from the mind of his creature to stand shivering, gasping, moaning within his castle of lorn longing. He shut his eyes, knowing what was coming, knowing that the results for his palace, gardens, and menagerie would be far worse than anything done by a few noxious, noisome, flea-bitten, scraggly, stinky, smelly, wretched, filth-encrusted, lice-ridden, scab-picking, snot-eating barbarians.

No, Farthane didn't want to see, but after a bit he could not help but open his eyes again. It was as he had thought: The amulet, a steel fishhook, lay on the ground where the barbarian witch had thrown it.

And the Worm? Well, the Worm had turned.

WRITING WITH ATTITUDE

There are as many ways to write as there are writers. Some writers are morning people. Others work in the evening. Some writers have computers with all the latest gadgets to help them. Others work with a pen on paper. The important point is that they all *do* write. There is no easy button for writing. You've got to hit the keys and keep on hitting until you beat the piece that you're working on into shape.

Writing takes both skill and discipline, and, of the two, discipline is probably more important. In fact, almost everyone has the basic verbal skills needed to write; most humans grow up with language and use it every day. Why, then, do some people find it easier to write than others? At least part of the answer has to do with discipline. Disciplining yourself to write requires a few basic attitudes, which are discussed in the paragraphs that follow. See if you agree. See if you have other attitudes to add.

Attitude 1: Make "writing" important in your life. I'm going to say something a little harsh here, but I think it needs saying. We might assume that anyone who is reading this book has made writing important in their life. But is that assumption correct? I know people who talk and read incessantly about writing but *never* write. I don't really think they want to *write*. I think they want to *have written*. If you're serious about this writing thing then you have to set aside time to actually put words on paper. Talking about writing is fine; reading books and articles on writing is good. But neither can be allowed to substitute for the writing *act*.

Attitude 2: Know that writing is hard. Writing well requires effort. Sometimes the words *flow*, but more often you have to drag them kicking and screaming into the phosphor light of the computer screen. To write well you have to forego the easy choices. The dialogue that "pops" into your head is probably from a movie. The first metaphor that strikes you is generally a cliché. The easy literary gold has already been found by writers before you. Now it's time to dig and drill and sweat. Now it's time for the dictionary and thesaurus, and it's time to learn those grammar rules that you wish you hadn't ignored in high school.

Writing is also hard because it requires personal sacrifice, and this is especially true if you have a day job that pays the bills. You may watch fewer movies, play fewer video games than your non-writing friends. (Personally, I've given up on series TV; I never have time to catch two episodes in a row.) Most writers that I know spend a lot of time alone. They miss ball games, social events, phone conversations. They give these up for writing.

Attitude 3: Know that jealousy of other writers is usually misplaced and always *unproductive.* It's very tempting, and I've done it myself, to compare one's writing production and successes to another writer's. Resist this impulse. If you're like me you'll usually end up feeling negative about your own work. Why haven't you written more? Why haven't you sold more? Well, tempting or not, the comparison is useless.

Every writer is on the same road, and if someone is further along that road than you are it probably only means that they started earlier, or that they walked faster because they had fewer obstacles. I know a lot of writers younger than I who have sold more and to bigger markets. Some were writing professionally as journalists while I spent five years in a research laboratory earning my doctorate. Others had life situations that let them focus big hunks of time on their writing while my time was split in more ways.

And, of course, luck always has a role to play in what any writer accomplishes. If someone has more writing success than you even under similar circumstances, maybe they were lucky in making the right connections, or having the right material to offer at the right time. But, even if they have done more with the same level of luck, it still doesn't matter. What matters is what you do from this day on. There are no age restrictions in writing, no such thing as mandatory retirement. The page is forever young.

Attitude 4: Know that "time" is your biggest advantage. The best thing about writing, the most powerful tool that you have, is that you have *time* to work your words over until they are just where you want them. In a spoken conversation people are impatient, sometimes rude. Any pause that you take to think is met with facial expressions and eye movements that demand a response from you *now*. Quite often, people won't even let you finish speaking before they interrupt to add their own thoughts, or just to interfere with your argument.

Writing happens in private, between you and the computer or you and the page, and no one knows what words you've used until you let them. No one can jump in and interrupt your argument or story before you even decide what it is. No one can force you to consider their opinions before you've had time to consider your own. You can take the time to ponder and tinker. If you've ever said something in speech and then wished you could take it back, you should appreciate writing. Up until your piece is submitted to a market, you *can* take it back.

Attitude 5: Remember that, especially for fiction, writing and editing are two separate steps. Some writers edit as they write, finding themselves unable to move forward with a new paragraph until the previous one is polished. If that works for them then there's nothing wrong with it, but such a practice may obscure the fact that writing and editing are separate processes in your mind.

Writing fiction is primarily an emotional act. Logic and rationality have little to do with enjoying a good scary novel or a space adventure with starships and bizarre aliens. Even literary fiction is more about what characters *feel* than what they think. If authors don't write with emotion then readers aren't going to read their work with emotion either.

In contrast, editing is a rational, thinking act. You have to have your emotions under control; you have to be ruthless. Does every word serve a purpose? Is that beautifully constructed sentence necessary? Do you really need that character you loved creating? Emotions *enhance* a story, but *obscure* the meaning of individual words and sentences. Editing must focus on exactly those elements that emotion obscures.

In the end, both processes are required to work a piece into publishable form. You write it, you edit it. You feel it, you think it.

SELLING AND RESELLING
WITH "TO THE POINT"

As long as a piece you've sold wasn't "work for hire" you still own some or all of the rights to it and should definitely keep the reprint market in mind. Work for hire usually means that a publisher or corporation hires a writer for a specific task and then owns all rights to the product. Encyclopedias commonly work this way. They pay writers to create particular entries but then take full ownership of the resulting material. More rarely, fiction may be sold on a work for hire basis. This occurs sometimes with ghost written material, or in a few other cases.

In contrast, print magazines that publish in the United States tend to purchase first North American serial rights, which gives them the right to publish a piece one time in print, and the full ownership and use then reverts back to the author. Online magazines will usually purchase first "world wide" rights, which gives them the right to publish a piece on the net and to leave it up for a given period of time. Sometimes other rights are acquired by a publisher, such as the right to archive a piece or the right to publish a piece in a "best of" collection at a later date. These rights will be specified in your contract, to which you should definitely pay attention.

Say a magazine buys the rights to publish your story in their online magazine and to keep it up for a period of two months. After that two months is up they should take the story down and the rights will revert back to you. At that point, you are completely free to sell this piece to any other market who might want it. You should, of course, inform any market that you submit the piece to that it is a reprint and has been previously published.

Some magazines won't accept previously published material and they'll usually say so in their guidelines, but many magazines *do* use reprints, especially if it's been a while since the piece was published or if it was published in a small venue, such as a local newspaper or a small press magazine with limited circulation. Selling reprints is a way to significantly increase your writing income. It also keeps your name out there and increases the chances that your masterpiece will be seen by big publishers, agents, and even film-makers. I've sold some of my stories three or more times, in some cases for more money than I was paid by the original publisher, and often to far wider exposure.

For nonfiction the situation is even better. Not only can you re-sell a published piece (non work for hire, that is), but the ideas and information inherit in the piece are always yours and you are free to recast and rework those ideas and facts however you want for other potential markets. Say you like to travel and have sold travel pieces on trips that you've taken to Boston, Orlando and New Orleans. Maybe a writing magazine or local interest magazine would be in-terested in such pieces as well if you restructured them to focus on famous literary icons who lived in those places. That would be Ed-gar Allan Poe, Jack Kerouac, and Tennessee Williams respectively.

Recasting ideas and facts in this way can save you a tremendous amount of time on research and thus increases your productivity. Just keep your reference notes in some kind of organized fashion so you can shuffle through them to find particular information with relative ease. I tend to use folders with pockets in them, and staple materials together within the folders on specific topics. These I keep alphabetically under article title in a file cabinet. I never throw re-search materials away.

There are yet other ways, though, in which you can resell mate-rial that you've already sold once. I thought I might end this piece with an example from my own work. Earlier in this book I included an article entitled "Tipping the Odds in Your Favor." A couple of years after "Tipping the Odds" was published I saw a market that wanted tip articles under 400 words and was willing to pay well for them. I had nothing new, so I stripped "Odds" down to what I saw as the absolutely bare essentials. By then the internet was growing quickly so I also added some comments about the net. The results follow, and I hope this will illustrate one way to reuse and repackage information for resale. It might also serve as a reminder of some of the important points about writing that I've made in the previous hundred pages.

To The Point

I. Stand Out Stories

1. *Write Short*: Most markets will buy two 2,500 word stories over one of 5,000 words. Short story readers want quick reads and lots of them. Editors cram their pages with as many stories as possible.

2. *Write Genre*: It's easier to sell genre stories than literary ones. Surprising editors is easier. Take, "boy meets girl." Genre writers can add boy meets monster, boy meets alien, boy meets machine, boy desperately wants to meet girl, any girl. "Surprise" sells.

3. *Rewrite* (most important rule): Rewrite until you hate it; rewrite rejected pieces again.

4. *Resources*: You need a dictionary, thesaurus and grammar guides. The internet is great but don't blindly accept facts you find there. Remember library cards and encyclopedias.

II. Getting Attention

5. *Contact*: Contact editors (letter or email, not phone) and request "Guidelines," the best help—outside the publication itself—on cracking a market. Researching a publication impresses editors. Search for internet samples and guidelines. Sign guest books to show you visited.

6. *Professionalism*: Follow guidelines. Send brief cover letters but *don't* summarize plots. Mention previous sales if you have any; don't apologize if you don't. Use dark print, white paper. Put your contact information (name, address, phone number, and email address) at top left of page one, and word counts at top right. Put page #s, partial titles (headers), and last name on each page. Enclose a self-addressed stamped envelope (SASE) for editors to use.

For online submissions you won't need the SASE, but you still need the contact information, cover letter, and professionalism. Don't let the casual nature of online communication lull you into thinking casualness is always acceptable. Be safe rather than sorry.

7. *Use Market Guides*: Book guides compile large lists of potential markets (*Writer's Market, Novel and Short Story Writer's Market*; at *Writer's Digest*, www.writersdigest.com). Newsletters report fewer markets but update frequently (*The Gila Queen's Guide to Markets*; at www.gilaqueen.us). Don't forget the internet as a source for market information.

III. Survive

8. *Persevere*: Rejections hurt. So wallow in self-pity, but then write. Don't quit.

9. *Money*: Forget it. It's nice to get paid but you won't make a living at first. Few writers get rich. Keep getting better. The money will come. Good luck.

THE WORKING MAN'S CURSE

For those of us who don't write full time, which probably means most of you reading this book as well as the fellow writing it, our real jobs can be a curse on our writing lives. A few weeks back I was really starting to roll on some projects, and ideas for more were foaming around me like crawfish in a boil. Then I came to work one morning to find a seventy page research proposal waiting impatiently on my desk for consideration.

I make my living teaching at Xavier University in New Orleans, and at Xavier I'm also chairperson of the committee that reviews such research projects. I had two days to read this one's densely scribed pages, to understand and evaluate them when they were written in scientific jargon and "proposalese," and then construct a letter requesting more information or approving the project as written.

In those same two days, however, I had to grade essays from nearly forty students in one of my classes, had to administer a test for a colleague, administer two tests for myself in two other classes, grade those two tests and one that I'd given the week before, develop a test for a class the following week, and serve as acting departmental chairperson while our regular chair was at a conference. This was in addition to the usual run of letters, studies, student questions, and the regular doses of academic bullshit; I'm not even counting around-the-home chores.

How could I possibly keep writing in the face of these hurdles? Well, the answer is that I couldn't do very much, at all. Sometimes, no matter how we resist it, the work from our regular jobs fills our cups to overflowing and every instinct to survive tells us to push our writing to the side. But even though I couldn't do what I wanted to do in writing, I could take *some* actions.

I keep a folder on my computer(s) called "ThingsToDo," and in it I have files labeled "ideas" and "markets." At least one of my computers is seldom far from my side, and when a plot or a situation occurs to me I open the "idea" file and jot down in a few quick sentences the basics of my thoughts. If I'm away from the computer I'll often carry a notebook with me to jot down ideas, and on the road I haul along a miniature tape recorder for the same purpose. Transferring my notes or sound bites to the word processor can come later. Even if I'm busy with "work" work, I can record ideas in a few quick moments, and later when I have more leisure I can mine that file for its good ore.

In the same way, if I find a market listing that looks promising I can take down the online address of it or can indicate in my "market" file enough information to find it again when the time is right. For example, WD, June 06, p52 indicates *Writer's Digest* and the month and page number for a market listed in it. And, I keep these "to do" files on my desktop so that every time I start my computer they show up in my face where they won't be forgotten.

A bigger problem for *me* where "work" work is concerned, however, is that it can ruin the momentum I have going on a particular writing piece. If I'm blazing along on a story and I suddenly have to leave it, even for two or three days, I tend to struggle when I finally get back to my desk. It's harder to recapture the mood or style of the piece. Or worse, I've lost some of the emotional interest that I had in the project. Often, I have to read and reread the piece before I can get going again. This is bad enough with a short story, but how could anyone ever finish a novel under those circumstances?

When I'm working on a writing project it is this dangerous loss of momentum that *makes* me go home after work and finish at least one decent paragraph—no matter how much toiling I did for the university that day or how tired I am. I've found that even finishing one paragraph a day can help me keep up the momentum that I've developed on an article or story. And, completed paragraphs inevitably lead to completed pages, and completed pages to completed stories /essays /books. Sometimes, all you can hope for is just to make progress. Sometimes that's enough.

Addendum: Is there ever a time when you just pack it in, when you don't even try to get a paragraph done? Let me introduce you to what I call my "Week of Love," an actual sequence of events that happened to me in 1999.

1. <u>Monday</u>: Car radiator bursts on way to work.

2. Mechanic has to make house call. Actually, a parking lot call, where we leave the car while wife drives me to work in her van.

Mechanic tows the car, charging me appropriately. Finds while working on car that the left rear tire has a nail in it and can't be fixed. Replaces tire for a slight additional charge.

3. Tuesday: Car is in shop so I drive the van. Van battery dead when I get ready to leave work. Attempt to jumpstart battery fails because the cable post falls *out* of the battery. Turns out relatively new battery is rotted away.

4. We have van towed. Both vehicles are in the shop. But, hey, I have a motorcycle.

5. Wednesday: It rains really, really hard. I get, shall we say, wet. Both going to work *and* coming home.

6. Wednesday afternoon: We get car back. Yeah!

7. Wednesday evening: Van is ready and I take wife to get it in my car. On way back a rock is thrown up on the highway and cracks the car's windshield directly over the driver's side. Hard to miss a big glass star in the middle of your viewing field.

8. Thursday: I drive car with cracked window to work. I find it booted when I go out to the parking lot to leave. Problem is that I forgot to take the parking sticker back out of the Van from earlier in the week. Fact that I got two hours of sleep the night before does not help me deal well with the booting of my car.

9. Thursday, in addition: After waiting nearly an hour for the campus police to unboot my car, I get home from work to find that UPS has delivered the new monitor for my computer. Finally, something good has happened. The old monitor (less than three months old) had developed a warped line through it that couldn't be corrected. But now I can replace it, and maybe see what I'm writing again without it looking like it's written on a funhouse mirror. I take out new monitor and find that:

a. the instruction manual is for a different monitor than the one in the box. It has extra parts. But, that doesn't really matter because monitors are easy to hook up. Except that:

b. the three prong plug on the new monitor has one of the prongs hidden behind the plastic casing of the monitor. It was installed incorrectly at the factory and *cannot* be plugged in.

c. I call technical support to get them to issue me another new monitor. Spend half an hour on hold. Spend 15 minutes explaining to the guy who keeps telling me to unplug the monitor that I've never been able to plug it *in*. Finally get my point across. He says I need to return the monitor because it is apparently defective.
Oh *really*?

9. Friday: Pack up defective monitor and take to post office. On way van has blow out on right rear tire.

10. Saturday and Sunday: Remain home for entire weekend. Touch nothing.

Needless to say, I didn't get many paragraphs done that week. I cut myself some slack. I think you could to. Just this once.

PUNCTUATE IT AND FORGET IT!

I thought I would revisit one of the simplest things writers need to do to make their work readable, but one that troubles some of us more than it should. I'm talking about punctuation, and I know it troubles *me*. The genesis for this piece comes from grading term papers in my psychology classes. Too often I find papers that are virtually unreadable because of poor grammar or because the punctuation looks as if it's been tossed in like croutons in a salad. I've grown tired of writing "Lost me" or "I have no idea what you mean" next to student sentences, so last year I decided to create some quick primers for use in future classes. I thought the one on punctuation would be easy to write, but I found that I had to look up many things myself and had to pick some colleagues' brains to get the answers I needed. Perhaps many of us could use a refresher, so, without further ado, I present: "Punctuate It and Forget It!"

Periods and Commas:

The clearest, and often the best, writing consists of short declarative sentences that end with periods. Declarative sentences present one thought. The period ends the thought. The last two sentences were examples, but this one isn't because it has an added phrase.

Sometimes a writer wants to link a few thoughts together in a single sentence, and that's fine, as long as the sentence doesn't just keep going and going. However, when tying thoughts together on paper you need to consider the reader's need to "breathe." To give them a little pause, a chance to catch their breath before the next thought, you insert a comma. The comma goes *between* two thoughts, not in the middle of one. The last sentence illustrates this. Consider how confusing it would be if it had read: "The comma goes between, two thoughts not in the middle of one."

Question Marks and Exclamation Points:

Question marks are one of the simplest forms of punctuation to use. *All* they do is indicate a question in print. (What time is it? What was that sound? Who goes there?) Exclamation points indicate emphatic emotions. (It's Miller time! That sound was my heart breaking! I don't know but he's got an axe!) Question marks appear in fiction and nonfiction both, although they are most common in fictional dialogue. Exclamation points appear much more in fiction than nonfiction, again mostly in dialogue. Exclamation points should be used sparingly anywhere. They call attention to themselves and quickly lose their power.

Semicolons:

Semicolons are used to connect two *complete* sentences at times when you don't want to use "and" or "but" for that task. For example: "Johnny rode to town; he took his gun." Replace the semicolon with a period and you have two separate declarative sentences, each of which serves as an "independent clause" in the longer phrase.

Semicolons *only* connect two complete sentences so they are never absolutely necessary. You could just write: "Johnny rode to town and took his gun," or "Johnny rode to town. He took his gun." Why use semicolons then? Because they call special attention to the connection between two thoughts, much more so than using an "and" or separating the thoughts with a period. "Johnny rode to town; he took his gun" is dramatic. It focuses attention clearly on what the writer wants you to notice most, the link between "town" and "gun."

Colons:

Colons are very different from semicolons, despite the similar sounding names. Colons are much more versatile for one thing. They appear in formal letters (Dear Ms. Manners:), in time measurements (it's 4:20), and in memos (TO: & FROM:). They are frequently used to separate titles from subtitles, usually in nonfiction. This book's title is an example.

Colons are also used to introduce lists (They bought: hats, coats, gloves, boots, scarves, and snowshoes), and to call attention to a phrase (There are two kinds of people in the world: my kind and your kind). They may also appear before quotes (The Martian said only one thing: "Take me to your Wal-Mart"). However, in the last case a colon is only used when the introductory phrase to a quote is a complete sentence (The Martian said only one thing). If that sentence isn't complete you use a comma (She shouted at him to, "Get a life").

Quotation Marks:

Quotation marks appear frequently in both fiction and nonfiction. In fiction they're used mostly to indicate dialogue ("It's a hard way to make a living," the gunslinger said, or, "Who's ready for their poison?" the nurse asked). In nonfiction, quotation marks are generally used to indicate words that are taken directly from another person's writing or speech. Here's a quote from William Zinsser's book, *On Writing Well*. "If your job is to write every day, you learn to do it like any other job." Here's a quote from one of my doctor's recent speeches to me. "Pushups are fine but you'd be better off doing push-aways from the table." When one quote appears inside another quote you put single (') quotation marks around the inside one (The boy said, "I hate it when my Dad tells me to, 'Grow up!'")
Another place quotation marks are used is to indicate a word that is meant ironically or is being given a special meaning that is uncommon or off center in some way. This is often done with innuendos (When asked about her divorce the woman just said she was tired of trying to raise the "dead" every night). Here's another example: (The scientist called on "Chaos" theory to explain a recent increase in severe tornadoes.) There are quotation marks around "Chaos" because here it is used in its special meaning as the name for a particular scientific theory.
Quotation marks most often cause problems for writers when they occur with other forms of punctuation. When used in free text, for example, periods, commas, exclamation marks and question marks generally appear *inside* quotation marks while colons and semicolons appear outside of them. (Examples: "That's a mistake." "I can't see forever," she said. "You liar!" "Who's asking?" He quit politics after the "debacle of Watergate"; he no longer felt fit to serve.) Unfortunately, there are exceptions to some of these generalities so you may occasionally need to consult a source with more detail than this short essay can provide. The Bibliography in this book lists two good resources, *The Elements of Grammar* by Margaret Shertzer, and *The Elements of Style* by Strunk and White.

Dashes and Hyphens:

The dash is an excellent punctuation tool even though it's not used all that often. It typically shows up more in nonfiction than fiction. In manuscript form, it's written as two contiguous hyphens (—), but most modern word processors will convert these to a single long dash (—). Dashes often come in pairs and in the United States they are usually connected to the words on either side (Faulkner's sentences are generally longer—by far—than Hemingway's).

The main function of the dash is to call attention to a specific bit of information (My brother—who is twenty years older than I am—doesn't understand me very well). It can also be used to indicate an "aside," where in nonfiction an author adds a personal observation to material that is otherwise meant to be objective (The President overestimated his support among female voters—a mistake that illustrates his hubris).

In fiction, the dash is most helpful in dialogue where it indicates words or thoughts that are broken off suddenly or which are interrupted by another speaker. Say you have a character who starts to curse and then realizes his grandmother is present. You might indicate this by, "What the He—" Or maybe there are two characters arguing. Character 1 says, "You never let me finish a—" Character 2 interrupts with, "Because you never say anything worthwhile." The dash after the "a" indicates that character 1 never got to finish his or her sentence.

The hyphen is used equally in fiction and nonfiction. It simply connects two words into one word so as to emphasis their relationship (sky-blue, bite-size, well-fed, butt-ugly).

The Ellipsis:

An ellipsis is used when words are omitted from a quote, or in dialogue when you want to show a character's words "trailing off." It's indicated with either three or four periods (....), depending on whether it comes in the middle or at the end of a sentence.

In nonfiction, when you only want to quote sections of a longer passage, the ellipsis is used to indicate where words are left out. In *Zen in the Art of Writing*, Ray Bradbury describes one of his stories thusly: "And then, one night, the dog comes back from a journey to the graveyard, and brings 'company' with him." Using ellipses you could render this, "...one night, the dog comes back...and brings 'company'...." The ellipses show where words have been removed from the larger quote.

In fiction, the ellipsis is used primarily in dialogue. Suppose you have a character who is unsure of what they are about to say. You might write something like, "Well, I thought that..." This indicates that the speaker is censoring his or her own speech rather than being interrupted by someone else. The ellipsis can also be used in the middle of dialogue to indicate a pause, for whatever reason, in the person's speech ("Tell Ryan that I...hate him.") I suggest that you use the ellipsis sparingly in dialogue, but sometimes it is just the right tool for bringing nuance and character to life on the page.

Italicizing for Emphasis:

Most people know that italicizing is used for book and movie titles, but they may not know that it's also a good way to give emphasis to a word and to inform the reader where the inflection should be in a sentence, especially in dialogue. Consider a character who says, "The traitors in our midst *will* be rooted out" versus the unitalicized "The traitors in our midst will be rooted out." To me there is a subtle difference; the character who speaks the first line has a stronger personality and is a little angrier than the one who speaks the second line.

Real life speakers add such tonal qualities to their words all the time, but it's more noticeable on the printed page and can lose its effectiveness if overused. Personally, I always fear that *I'm* overusing it, and it's because I want the reader to sound out a sentence just the way I intend them to hear it. Most of the time there are ways to construct a sentence to convey the same tone without the italics, but don't toss this one out of your tool box. Sometimes it's the *perfect* choice.

PROBLEM WORDS

Words are the writers' medium, and sometimes their curse. If you're like me, you often struggle to use them precisely. And sometimes you fail. I keep a personal "writing dictionary" to help me with my problem words, and I recommend that everyone who writes do the same. I also give out guidelines on troublesome words to students because I see from their papers that they're fighting the same battles. Arranged alphabetically below are some of the words from my lists. These are ones that, because of their difficult spellings and meanings, particularly plague writers. Examples of correct usage are given in parentheses. I hope this helps with the good fight.

Affect / Effect: The affect/effect issue used to bring me nearly to despair about my ability to write. Only after carefully recording it in my writing dictionary did I finally get a handle on it. These words are homonyms, meaning that their pronunciations and spellings are very similar while their meanings are different. Affect is almost always a verb, except for a special use in psychology where it serves as a noun. Effect can be either noun or verb with equal ease.

As a verb, affect most commonly means "to influence." (How did the development of cell phones *affect* you personally.) Affect can also mean something similar to the word "poseur." (He *affected* the attitudes of a world famous author.) Here, it means "to pretend to something." In psychology, affect is a noun that refers to behaviors such as facial expression, tone of voice, and body posture that reflect a person's feelings. (Her *affect* did not change when told she'd just sold her first book for a six figure advance.) Yeah, right!

Effect, when used as a noun, almost always means "result." (The *effect* of alcohol depends on how much you drink.) The word "effects" (note the plural) can also mean "goods that you own." (He left all his worldly *effects* to his dog.) When effect is used as a verb it means "to cause." (The invention of antigravity will *effect* sweeping changes in people's daily lives. Or. Robert E. Howard *effectively* invented the genre called Sword & Sorcery).

Allude / Elude: Allude means to "hint at." (The Senator *alluded* to an affair between her husband and the President.) Elude means "to get away from." (The famous author was able to *elude* the paparazzi by using a doppelganger.)

Already / All Ready: Already relates to "time" and means that something is occurring sooner than expected. (The guests are *already* here.) All ready is useful only if you are talking about multiple people getting ready for something. (We are *all* ready to leave for the ball game.)

Alright / All Right: Remember the old saying, "ain't ain't a word?" Neither is "alright." *All right* means that "things are basically OK." (I'm feeling *all right*.)

Among / Between: When you want to discuss a relationship that involves more than two people or things you usually use *among*. For just *two* people or things you use *between*, and it might help to remember that "tween" means "two." (Examples: The six members of the writing group do not get along *among* themselves. Or. Just *between* you and me I think most members of the writing group are psychotic.)

Assure / Insure: I *assure* you that I want to help you write better. Here, assure means "to promise or guarantee." *Insure* means "to offer protection." (Will you *insure* my house against flood damage? I live in New Orleans.) The word "ensure" is simply a variant spelling of *insure*.

Breath / Breathe: I still fight with this one. *Breath* is the substance (air) that you take in and exhale during the process of breathing. *Breathe* is the action itself. Thus, "take a breath" means to draw in some air while "breathe" means to make your chest rise and fall so that oxygen can be brought into the lungs. The results may be the same but the way it's phrased is different and the pronunciation is different. The "e" in *breath* is pronounced like the "e" in "left" or "next" while the "e's" in breathe are like in "teeth."

Capital / Capitol: *Capitol* means specifically a "building," and only a building. *Capital* is *never* an individual building, although it might mean "the whole city" in which the *capitol* is located. (We went to Austin, the capital of Texas, to see the beautiful architecture of the Capitol Building.)

Compare / Contrast: Were you ever told as a student to "compare and contrast" various scientific theories? *Compare* means to focus on the similarities between two things. *Contrast* means to focus on the differences. Critics of the United States sometimes like to *compare* us to Hitler's Germany. Patriots would much prefer to *contrast* the two nations.

Councilor / Counselor: A *council* is a group of people who are chosen for a specific task, like a student council, and a *councilor* is no more than a member of such a council. A *counselor* is someone who "gives advice." Lawyers are often referred to as counselors.

Covert / Overt: These words should be easy to remember because they are opposites, but their similarity in appearance can cause confusion. *Overt* means out in the *open*. It's something that everyone can see. (Sex on television is certainly more *overt* these days than it was in the fifties.) *Covert* means "under cover." (The Watergate break in was intended as a *covert* operation but went badly wrong.)Notice the "o's" in overt and open, and the "c's" in covert and cover.

Desert / Dessert: I once wrote: "The raiders came storming across the dessert on horses as black as sin." Imagine my chagrin when an editor asked me whether the "dessert" was chocolate or some other type of confection. *Desert* is the arid region I should have been referring to. *Dessert* is something tasty like ice cream or cake that most people crave after they finish a meal. *Desert* has another meaning, too, however. If a husband abandons his family he is said to have *deserted* them.

Discreet / Discrete: These two words are also homonyms and are often confused. *Discrete* means "separate" or "distinct." (Science fiction, fantasy, and horror are discrete literary genres.) To be *discreet* means to be "careful" about what you say or how you act. It means the opposite of being controversial or flamboyant. People are saying the same thing when they tell you to "walk on eggshells" around someone. (Be *discreet* when you talk about politics with grandpa. He gets upset easily and he always packs a pistol.)

Disinterested / Uninterested: If you were accused of a murder that you didn't commit would you want a judge who was *disinterested* in your case, or *uninterested* in it? You'd better hope that judge is *disinterested*, which means "impartial" and "unbiased." *Uninterested* means that he or she just doesn't "give a sh**."

Exhausted / Exhaustive: When you're *exhausted* you're really, really tired. When you're *exhaustive* you're very, very thorough. (After my *exhaustive* examination of everything ever written about *Star Trek* I was *exhausted*.)

Explicit / Implicit: *Explicit* things are "clear" and "specific." (He left *explicit* instructions for how to run his business while he was gone.) *Implicit* things are supposed to be "understood" but are not written down or clearly stated. Most of us understand that there are certain ways we are expected to dress at work even if the employee handbook doesn't provide a dress code. The dress code is *implicit*.

Farther / Further: I've confused these more times than I can count, and part of the reason is that few people make clear distinctions between the two these days. When you use *farther* think of "far." *Farther* means a physical distance. (It's *farther* to Mars than it is to the moon.) *Further* means "to a greater extent" but doesn't refer to physical distance. (Humans are further removed from gorillas than we are from chimpanzees.) This means, according to the theory of evolution, that the human line separated from the gorilla line at an earlier time than it did from the chimpanzee line. It doesn't say anything about how close we are in physical distance.

Flaunt / Flout: These are misused by writers all the time. When you *flaunt* you "show off." (The writer *flaunted* her bestsellers in front of her colleagues, until one colleague murdered her out of jealousy.) *Flout* means to "deny the power of" or to "scorn" something. You *flout* authority or convention. (The writer flouted the literary establishment when he refused to accept the Nobel Prize in Literature.)

Former / Latter: Use these terms only when you're talking about two items, never three or more. *Former* is the first of two; *latter* is the second of two. If you're talking about "books" and "movies" then books is the former and movies is the latter.

Good / Well: If you *smell good* it means that you've probably recently bathed or have put on some deodorant. If you *smell well* it means that your nose is keen at detecting different odors. Good is an adjective that modifies nouns. It can't be used as an adverb. Thus: "He did well in the writing contest" is perfectly correct, but "He did good in the writing contest" makes me shudder and consider slitting my wrists.

Hoard / Horde: I once sent a "hoard" of "raiders across the dessert," but at least I caught the error before submitting it, unlike with "dessert." A *hoard* is a collection of items, such as a dragon's "hoard of gold." A *horde* is a great group of people. Raiders can be a *horde* but not a *hoard*, even though they may *hoard* the wealth that they steal from their victims.

Imply / Infer: Even on *The Simpsons* they get this one right. At least Lisa Simpson does. In one episode she says, "I imply, you infer." Imply means to "hint" but not to say clearly. Infer means to "draw conclusions." The person who is doing the *talking* implies; the person *listening* infers.

Its / It's: It's is an abbreviation of "it is" and is never used for anything else. Its is a possessive for it. (The monster lost *its* appetite after eating the bestselling horror novelist).

Lay / Lie: Here's another one that troubles me to this day, especially when you add in the *lay, laid, laid, laying* and the *lie, lay, lain, lying*. The main thing that helps me is that *lay* always requires reference to some object. Consider, "He went to *lay the book* on the desk," or "He *laid the body* in its shallow grave." "Book" and "body" are objects that are placed somewhere. *Lie* does not need an object. Some examples are, "I'm going to *lie* down," and "She was *lying* on a bed of thorns."

Lightening / Lightning: Although I know the meaning of these two words I've been known to misspell them and no spellchecker will catch it. Lightening means to "remove weight" from something. *Lightening the load* is a common expression in all kinds of books and movies. *Lightning*, of course, is the electrical discharge in the sky that is followed by thunder.

Marital / Martial: Sometimes marriage is a war, but these two words still have very different meanings. *Marital* refers to marriage.

When someone asks for your *marital* status they want to know if you are married. *Martial* pertains to war. *Martial your forces* means to gather your army for battle.

Naval / Navel: *Naval* pertains to ships and navies. A *navel* is your belly button. A *navel* orange is so called because it has something that resembles a belly button, but which is actually an undeveloped twin of the primary orange.

Principal / Principle: Here are some more words that sound alike but have very different meanings. A principal is usually, but not always, a human. A principle can *never* be human. Your high school had a *principal*, which means "chief or "manager." The amount of money you have invested in something is also called the *principal*. In both these cases "principal" is a noun. However, it can also be used as an adjective meaning "primary." (His *principal* goal in attending the dance was to meet the woman he wanted to marry.) *Principle* is always a noun, and it means a "rule" or "law." Most of us have ethical *principles* that we follow, such as the "golden rule," and there are many *principles* of science, such as the principle of natural selection.

Rout / Route: A *rout* usually means a terrible defeat. A *route* is generally a "pathway" or "direction." (Once the New Orleans Saints scored their third touchdown the *rout* was on. Or. What *route* would you suggest I follow to get to your place.)

Simile / Metaphor: A simile suggests a resemblance between two things by using the words, "as," "as if," or "like." (After the dark horrors of the night the sunrise was *like a salve* for my soul.) A metaphor makes the resemblance between two things more direct, without using words such as "like."It says that one thing *is* another. (Defeat was a razor across his ego.)

Than / Then: *Than* is a conjunction, *then* an adverb. *Then* always has something to do with "time." (We ate first, *then* went to the movies. He was at home for an hour and *then* drove to the office.) *Than* is seen in such phrases as, "Better you *than* me," and "Things are worse *than* they used to be."

Who / Whom: Here's another word pair that terrifies me. *Whom* always sounds pretentious to me in speech so I generally use *who*. Fortunately, *who* is the more common term; if you have to guess, pick *who*. The way I *try* to remember the two is that *who acts* while *whom is acted upon*. *Who struck whom* gives the flavor of this. *Who* precedes action while *whom* follows it or has action directed *at it*. (Examples: Who shot Liberty Valence? Liberty Valence was shot by whom? Who is laughing in there? The ones laughing in there are whom? Who is accusing them? They are accusing whom?)

Conclusions: The problem words I've covered in this essay are only a smattering of those that cause writers difficulties. Fortunately, there are more detailed guides available and I've already mentioned two particularly good ones earlier in this book. These were *The Elements of Style* by Strunk and White, and *Dictionary of Problem Words and Expressions* by Harry Shaw. Words are your tools and you need to choose them carefully and use them precisely. If you're like me, that sometimes takes study and struggle.

A GRAMMAR PRIMER

There's no way this small essay will explain every grammar concern that might confront you as a writer. You'll need a book meant for that task, some examples of which are listed in the Bibliography. But there are a few problems and issues that are so common they need desperately to be addressed. The examples are italicized.

Subject/Verb Agreement:

Subjects and verbs have to agree in number and tense. Consider, *Short stories is easy to write.* This is too simple of an example, but it clearly illustrates a problem with agreement in "number." "Short stories" is a plural subject; "is" is a singular verb. Plural subjects have to have plural verbs. *Short stories are easy to write.*

Sometimes the situation is not so simple, however. Consider, *Each member of the writing group are capable of brilliant prose.* This doesn't sound too bad but it still isn't correct. "Each" is singular but "are" is the verb here and it is plural. The sentence should read: *Each member of the writing group is capable of brilliant prose.* Some other words that require singular verbs are "either, neither, everyone, someone, nobody."

"Collective" nouns create a particular problem for subject/verb agreement. These are nouns like "jury, committee, faculty, assembly, team, army." Generally, these words are treated as a *unit*, making them singular. They need a singular verb, as in: *The jury is returning to the court*, or *The army is getting prepared for battle*. Perhaps unfortunately, you can construct a sentence that refers to the *individuals* within a collective noun. In this case the words become plural and require a verb that is plural too. *The faculty were confused over the proposed pay cut.*

An even greater problem with subject/verb agreement comes when you introduce clauses into sentences. *A high blood pressure medicine, when used with a good cholesterol busting drug, exemplify the best medical strategy for preventing heart attacks in many patients.* Adding the clause, "when used with…," suggests that there are two subjects here and that you should use "exemplify" for the verb. The subject is still "a high blood pressure medicine," however, and it needs a singular verb like "exemplifies."If you take out the clause you can more easily see the problem. *A high blood pressure medicine exemplify the best medical strategy….* That doesn't sound right, does it?

Tense:

"Tense" means the time at which a particular action takes place. The three basic tenses are: past tense, present tense, and future tense, illustrated by "I wrote yesterday," "I'm writing now," and "I'll write tomorrow."

Nonfiction seems to present more potential "tense" problems than fiction, but there are some simple rules to help you keep the three tenses separate in articles and essays. One, use past tense to talk about something that has happened before the time in which you're writing. *The Battle of the Bulge was… Gandhi spoke of… Hemingway wrote…* Two, present tense should be used to define terms. *Metaphors are… Haiku is a style of poetry.* Three, future tense is best for writing of things that haven't happened yet. *Global warming could sink half our coastlines.*

For fiction, the problem seldom arises because most stories are told entirely in the past tense. *The evening arrived on a chilling wind. And there was sleet that sent the people of Locknaar scurrying from the streets as the sun failed. Shutters were locked, fireplaces lit. Families huddled together as ice thickened on the buildings. Only in the Temple of Silver had men and women gathered for a reason other than warmth.*

Here, words like "arrived," "was," "were," "huddled," "thickened," and "gathered" indicate the past tense. But it is a recent past tense and the story still has immediacy. We feel ourselves caught up in the events in a way that we wouldn't if they seemed like ancient history.

Alternatively, the same scene could be written fully in the present tense. *The evening arrives on a chilling wind. And there is sleet that sends the people of Lochnaar scurrying from the streets as the sun fails. Shutters are locked, fireplaces lit. Families huddle together as ice thickens on the buildings. Only in the Temple of Silver do men and women gather for a reason other than warmth.*

Words like "arrives," "is," "are," "huddle," and "thickens" show that the action is occurring in real time here, unfolding even as we read it. More and more stories and novels are being written these days in the present tense, and some readers and writers like the unparalleled immediacy and intensity of this style. There are risks, however. First, the present tense is still uncommon and many readers feel uncomfortable with it because they aren't used to it. Second, most writers have been trained in the past tense and may not be able to switch gears easily, and mistakes in tense seem more noticeable when the prose is in present tense. Third, I've found that while action scenes really sing in the present tense, it's harder to do character development. Present tense creates such a sense of momentum that any slowdown in story to address character calls an uneasy attention to itself.

Past tense is the standard; it's probably what all your favorite books were written in. And it's hard to criticize the tense used by Ray Bradbury, Edgar Allan Poe, John Steinbeck, Ernest Hemingway and Jack London. If you should decide to use present tense, I suggest you try it in a short story first. Get used to how it handles before you tackle your own present tense version of *The Lord of the Rings* trilogy.

Prepositions:

Prepositions are words such as "in," "to," "with," "at," "for," "from," "upon," "among," "between," "behind," and "about." They indicate the relationship between a noun or pronoun and some other word in the sentence. *He undressed behind the hedge* is an example of this usage. "He undressed" is connected to "hedge" by "behind."

It is a common belief, but a wrong one, that a writer should never end a sentence with a preposition. The most likely reason for the belief is that in casual speech people often add an *unnecessary* preposition to the end of a sentence. *Where should we go to*, or, *Where have you been at* are examples of this. The prepositions, "to" and "at" are not needed here. But, *what movie are you going to* is perfectly fine. The "to" is necessary and putting it at the end saves you from such obfuscating constructions as *what movie is it to which you are going.*

Conjunctions:

"And" and "but" are examples of *conjunctions*, and conjunctions are meant to join other words or phrases together. Other conjunctions are "unless," "either," "or," "neither," and "nor." Because conjunctions are meant to *join* two verbal elements together, many people believe that it is unacceptable to *begin* a sentence with one. If the *history* of English is to be considered, that belief is nonsense. The *Bible* uses "and" and "but" to start many sentences. Shakespeare also knew how powerful these words could be at the beginning of a sentence. As long as they are not overused as openers they can work wonders to increase the drama and poetry of sentences.

Adjectives & Adverbs:

Adjectives modify nouns and pronouns, nothing else, and there are a myriad of them in the English language. Some common examples, with the adjective always appearing first, are: red brick, tall man, ugly dog, rich dessert, blue sky, fast car. Some writers will tell you to avoid adjectives as much as possible, but there's nothing wrong with adjectives by themselves. The problem comes when adjectives are used poorly.

Adjectives, for example, can become cliché to the point where they add nothing to a noun they are supposed to modify. Don't all desserts seem to be "rich?" "Aren't most of the cars in fiction "fast?" We hardly even notice such descriptors anymore. And is "blue" really a necessary modifier when we're talking about the sky? Unless you're on an alien world or need to call attention to the sky for something *out of the ordinary*, why even write "blue."

Adjectives are also misused when they are piled one on top of the other until they obscure rather than enhance the nouns they are attached to. *The elegant and expensive bright red sports car started with a low, throaty growl that reminded him of some sleek and savage jungle beast.* There are just too *many* adjectives here. The sentence is bloated with them, although all of them are perfectly fine modifiers by themselves.

Adverbs are typically used to modify verbs, but they can also be used to modify adjectives as well, and even to modify other adverbs. All adverbs are supposed to answer one of four questions: How, When, Where, and To What Degree. Examples, with the adverbs underlined, are: *Bob laughed <u>insanely</u>. Janice lost her job <u>recently</u>. The lion crouches <u>there</u> in the jungle. The team's chances of winning the game have been <u>utterly</u> destroyed.*

Most adverbs end in "ly," which is generally a reliable way of recognizing them, especially when they don't follow a verb. *The <u>brutally</u> expensive sports car...*, or *the <u>frantically</u> screaming mother...* Adverbs are not useless, but they are less useful than adjectives and are often used to prop up weak verbs when the best thing for a sentence would be to alter the verb. For example, *he cried brokenly* might be written better as *he sobbed. He ran quickly* would be better as *he sprinted.*

Conclusions:

English is a beautiful, complex, and sometimes confusing language. Just consider plurals. Most words add an "s" to make a plural, like ghosts, fossils, vampires, monsters, sinners. But look at goose and geese, deer and deer, wolf and wolves? Look at words like data, criteria, curricula, colloquia and phenomena, which are all *plurals.* The singular forms are datum, criterion, curriculum, colloquium, and phenomenon.

The confusion comes, in part, because English has borrowed so many words from other languages, and because the language itself has evolved dramatically over the past few hundred years. Most of us learned the exceptions to English rules as kids, and we often write correctly because it *sounds* right to us. What sounds right is not inevitably right, however, and only by practicing and continuing to learn can we make sure that our work is as good as we can get it.

Books on grammar and word usage are a necessity for a writer, not a luxury. But even a good dictionary can answer many of your questions. And maybe you should start keeping a *personal* file of writing problems. Anything that troubles you about words and their use should go into that file. I have such a file; I refer to it constantly. It grows, and grows.

REWRITE, REWRITE, REWRITE

Better writers than I have said it before, but the truth can always stand repeating. Good writing is rewriting. When I finish a story or article I just assume that it's not good enough for publication and I start revising, and revising.

Something that happened to me in graduate school taught me a little bit about why multiple drafts are a good idea in writing. It occurred when I said to a female friend that she must hate getting up in the morning and having to worry about putting on makeup. It seemed a bit unfair to me, since most men just comb their hair and maybe put on some deodorant before seizing the day.

My friend's response was enlightening, however, not about the fairness or unfairness of putting on makeup, but about the reasons why a writer should always do more than one draft of a piece of work. She said that she "liked" to put on makeup. She'd get up in the morning, look in the mirror, and go, "Yuck." Then she'd fix her hair, put on a little of this and a dab of that, follow it all with a touch of lipstick, and by the time she was done she could look in the same mirror and say, "OK, not so bad."

This is actually a pretty good analogy for writing. First drafts are our early morning face. They have at least a little bit of that "yuck" quality. But then the polishing starts. We get rid of a few excess words, what writers call "fat." We break that long sentence into two shorter ones that are more clear and to the point. We try to figure out what in the world we were thinking when we wrote that opening paragraph. By the time the polishing is finished we have a product that is more likely to evoke "OK, not so bad" than it is to call up "yuck."

How many drafts should a writer do? The only answer is to keep rewriting until the work is finished. When asked point-blank, I usually say something like "three." But any number is inaccurate if accepted as a *rule*. Every writer and every piece is different. Some people polish as they write and do fewer total drafts while others produce extremely rough first drafts and rewrite extensively. Most writers rework beginnings and endings more than middles because they know how imperative it is to catch readers' attention quickly, and to give them something at the end to engage their emotions.

One key to rewriting is to get a little emotional distance from the work before you start. Putting the completed draft aside for a week or two is probably the best way to do this. There's always a danger that you'll forget important "threads" of the work if you put it away, and if you're worried about that take careful notes on those threads. However, emotional distance is needed because rewriting requires rationality and ruthlessness. Every scene and every phrase has to be weighed on its importance to the whole, not on whether you think it's pretty prose or not. The scene that made you cry during a cathartic moment while writing it may not work when you return to the manuscript in a different mood. If it doesn't, it needs to go. You don't always have to "kill your darlings," but you should certainly make them struggle for their survival.

A second key to rewriting is making sure that all the diverse pieces fit where they are supposed to fit. Here, you're like a conductor guiding an orchestra; you have to make sure the violins come in at the right time. Writers who work from an extensive outline have an advantage here because they can just update the outline with any changes or additions/deletions they made, then check to make sure there aren't any continuity flaws, or that characters don't enter and leave scenes at the wrong moment. If you didn't develop a detailed outline *before* you wrote, then making one after is a good strategy. It can work like a set of instructions for assembling a bicycle. Which part (scene) goes where. Which step follows which.

A third element to focus on in rewriting is fact checking. I'm not talking just about the *actual* facts of your story. If your tale is set on Mars then of course you better know the planet's topography and rotation. But you also better know the "internal" facts of your story. This includes such things as the hero's eye and hair color, but it also includes the personality traits and quirks of all your characters. It's during rewriting that you make sure your tale is consistent, and many writers do this by keeping a story "bible."

Every character is recorded in your "bible" with relevant information like height, interests, fears, and personal history. Any other important points are also kept here, such as the plants and animals that your characters may have noticed, or salient details of the environment where the action takes place. These bibles can get quite elaborate in science fiction and fantasy and some have been published as books of their own, especially for series like Tolkien's "Lord of the Rings trilogy," or the "Dune series" by Frank Herbert.

Finally, the rewriting phase is also where you check your grammar, punctuation, and word usage. It may be the last thing you do with a manuscript, but it isn't the *least* thing. Neither editors nor readers want to wade through poorly structured sentences filled with grammatical errors. The fewer errors you have the more likely you are to sell your work.

The world is rich with written material for readers to choose. They don't want to read clumsy first draft work, or struggle to extract meaning from convoluted sentences. They want an immediate sense of what the writer is trying to convey, and they want to be both entertained and informed by what they're reading. Rewriting until each word, phrase and paragraph is clear and accomplishes its task is the surest way to catch and hold any reader's attention.

BY EXAMPLE

While I've already talked at length in this book about issues such as punctuation, style, and grammar, I haven't really discussed an important element in actually submitting something for publication. That element is the "cover letter." It's generally the first thing an editor sees, and while it won't sell your piece on its own, it creates an impression that can either help or hinder you. If it's bad enough it might even get you rejected before the editor ever looks at your actual submission.

My best advice for the cover letter is to be clear, honest, at least semi-formal, and short. Even in this day of quick email contact, not everyone is your best friend and you shouldn't treat an editor as if he or she is a buddy. Remember that you are actually making a "business" contact with the editor. You want to sell them something. Do you like it when people who are trying to sell *you* something are long winded? Or cutesy? Don't you want them to get to the point? Don't you hate it when they resort to tricks?

One way to get an idea for how to write a cover letter is to look at examples of ones that worked for another writer. Below are some that worked for me. I can't guarantee the same result for you, but at least it'll give you a place to start. Many of these are from fairly early in my career, before I'd sold much stuff.

Note: Any additional comments that I have concerning the letters are underlined. I've taken out spaces here and there to save room in this book, but you should double space your letters, of course. The editors and addresses of the magazines listed in this essay were correct at the times these letters were sent but I'm sure most have changed now. And remember that SASE is a "self addressed stamped envelope."

email – gramlich@hotmail.com
phone – (555) 555-5555

Charles A. Gramlich
666 White Horse Lane
New Orleans, LA 77777

March 24, 2000

Nick DiChario, Editor
HazMat Review
Box 507
Rochester, NY 14603

Dear Mr. DiChario:

I recently found the guidelines for *HazMat Review* in *Writer's Digest*, and I have some poems that I thought I would submit for your consideration. Any attention that you might give to them would be appreciated.

Some of my poetry has been published in magazines such as *Star*Line, Midnight Zoo, Rouge et Noir*, and in the anthology *Once Upon a Midnight*. A poem from the anthology received honorable mention in the 1996 *Year's Best Fantasy and Horror*.

An SASE is enclosed and I ask that you please drop the pieces back in the mail to me if you find that you can't use them. I can also submit by email, if that would be convenient. Thanks very much for your consideration and time.

Sincerely yours,

Charles A. Gramlich

Encl.

email-
phone -

Charles A. Gramlich

———-

———-

April 3, 2000

Norm Davis, Poetry Editor
HazMat Review
Box 507
Rochester, NY 14603

Dear Mr. Davis,

   I'm glad you liked "Border." No problem from my end for you to hold onto it for a while. I appreciate your interest. I'll also be happy to see a sample issue of *HazMat Review*. I'm always looking for good magazines for myself, and to recommend to folks who read the kind of stuff I do.
   Thanks again for accepting "Border," and for sending me a sample copy. I look forward to it. Good luck with everything.

Best wishes,

Charles

Sample Letter 3: For submitting a story.
Again, if you haven't had anything published,
leave out the second paragraph.

phone -
email -

Charles A. Gramlich
———-

———-

January 20, 1998

Joe Monks, Editor
Agony in Black
360-A W. Merrick Rd. #350
Valley Stream, NY 11580

Dear Mr. Monks:

I recently found the guidelines for *Agony in Black* in the *Gila Queen's Guide to Markets,* and enclosed is a story that I believe may fit those guidelines. It's called "Wall of Love," and any attention that you might give to it would be appreciated.

Some of my stories have been published in magazines like *After Hours, Strange Days,* and *Dead of Night,* and in anthologies like *Dark Terrors, Dark Voices* and *Prisoners of the Night.*

An SASE is enclosed and I ask that you please drop the story back in the mail to me if you find that you can't use it. I can also submit on disk or by email, if either of those would be convenient. Thanks very much for your consideration and time.

Sincerely yours,

Charles A. Gramlich

Encl.

Sample Letter 4: Another poetry submission letter to an editor I'd already sold something to.

email -
phone -

Charles A. Gramlich

———-
———-

September 26, 2000

Michael Pendragon, Editor-in-Chief
Songs of Innocence
PO Box 719
Radio City Station
NY, NY 10101-0719

Dear Mr. Pendragon (Michael),

I've been checking out your website(s) over the past few weeks and came upon the description and guidelines for *Songs of Innocence*. I thought I might submit the two enclosed poems for your consideration. They are free verse but I think they fall within the general "romantic" guidelines for the publication. Any attention you might give to them would be appreciated.

An SASE is enclosed, and I thank you very much for your time.

Best wishes,

Charles A. Gramlich

Encl.

Sample Letter 5: A letter requesting guidelines for a magazine or contest. One thing this does is let you make contact with the editor. Then, when you submit something you can mention that it's "after examining their guidelines." It never hurts to let the editor know that you are serious about considering their needs.

Guideline Request

email -
phone -

Charles A. Gramlich

———
———

November 27, 2000

Lori Fraind
11027 Becontree Lake Drive
Apt. 303wd
Reston, VA 20190

Dear Ms. Fraind:

I wonder if you might send me your submission guidelines. An SASE is enclosed and I thank you for your time.

Sincerely yours,

Charles A. Gramlich

Encl.

Sample Letter 6: Here's a letter for a story submission I sent by email.

phone -
email-
website = http://www

Charles A. Gramlich

———-
———-

January 10, 2001

Jack Fisher, Editor/Publisher
Flesh and Blood

Dear Mr. Fisher:

    I recently found the guidelines for *Flesh and Blood* in *Inklings*, and attached to this letter is a story that I believe may fit your guidelines. It's called "Haunting Place," and any attention that you might give to it would be appreciated.
    Some of my stories have been published in magazines like *After Hours*, *Strange Days*, and *Dead of Night*, and in anthologies like *Dark Terrors*, *Dark Voices* and *Prisoners of the Night*.

    Thanks very much for your time and consideration.

                         Sincerely,

                         Charles A. Gramlich

Then the story is either attached to your email or copied into the body of the email itself. Make sure to check the guidelines to see which one the magazine wants. Give them the wrong one and you're giving them a simple reason to reject your piece.

    Now, just to help ease your worries, the first story I ever sold was to a magazine called *Twisted*, and I did everything wrong in the cover letter. Good material has a good chance of selling. Just don't prejudice the editor against you if you can help it. As long as you are clear, respectful, and *brief*, you'll move the editor's gaze past your letter and onto your story or poem. That's where you want to focus the editor's attention.

BEFORE YOU SUBMIT, DON'T FORGET

Before mailing, or emailing, a story off, there are some things to check one last time. If errors are present and you don't find them, then the editor certainly will. And he or she may hold them against you when it comes time to send you either a check or a rejection slip.

This article consists primarily of a list of those things that need to be checked one last time before the envelope is sealed or the "send" button pressed. Try to compare each of your manuscripts against it. The results should be fewer errors, and more sales.

Checklist: Put a check beside each step as you complete it.

___ 1. Give the story a final proofreading *just* for mechanical errors, which includes word by word, sentence by sentence checking of grammar, spelling, and punctuation. You're not reading for story here, but for mechanics. Some people like to read *backward* at this point so they won't get caught up in the story line. It would be great if, after finishing a piece, you could let it sit for a few days or more before giving it the final proofing. This makes it much easier to catch mistakes.

___ 2. Check your fonts. Most magazines like to see submissions in 12 point type in either Courier New or Times New Roman. Unless the publication specifies, go with one of these two rather than some fancier font.

___ 3. Check your format. Include your name, contact information and a word count at the top of your submission, and make your margins about 1 inch all around. Make your text flush with the left margin but let it be ragged on the right. Pay special attention to page numbers and headers. I've *forgotten* page numbers in email submissions but I wouldn't advise it. Typically, you start numbering on page 2. Also, there should be a "header"—your name and a short phrase from your title—at the top of every page from page 2 on.

_____ 4. Double-check the magazine's submission requirements. Different magazines require different things so make sure that what you submit is *exactly* what the guidelines ask for. If they say "no email submissions," they mean it. If they accept email submissions but want "attached" files, give them that. If they want stories copied into the body of an email then give them that. *Note:* if you copy a story into an email you better make sure to go over it *after* it's copied to check formatting and paragraph breaks. You may also have to make sure that italics are indicated properly in the piece.

_____ 5. Although not one of the most important tasks, do check to see that you've spaced properly after periods, commas, and other forms of punctuation.

_____ 6. When you're physically mailing a story, you should read the final printed copy out loud to yourself one last time. This will help in proofreading, of which you can never get enough, and will also ensure that you haven't lost a paragraph somewhere or transposed a couple of pages. My students turn in papers with mistakes like that all the time, and they're expecting a good grade.

_____ 7. Make a personal hard copy of the finished story and put it where you can find it again, or make multiple backup copies, either on disk or on a *different* computer from the one where your original is stored. Someday, somehow, your computer is going to crash, or worse. Don't lose everything you've written. I have a friend who had most of a novel completed when her computer was stolen. Over 300 manuscript pages gone. And she had no backup. She quit writing.

_____ 8. Address your story, via a cover letter, personally to the editor. They like to see their names, too. Guidelines will usually give you the editor's name, and these can often be found online or from looking at the front matter in a copy of the magazine. Don't be overly familiar. If the editor's name is listed as James Reasoner don't address him as "Dear Jim.""Dear Mr. Reasoner" is the appropriate way to approach. If you can't tell whether the person is male or female, use their entire name, such as "Dear Terry Holland."

_____ 9. Don't forget the SASE. If you're physically mailing a manuscript then include a self addressed, stamped envelope with your submission. If you want the story back, say so in your cover letter and include enough postage on the SASE for the story's return. I usually ask editors to discard my manuscript if they can't use it, and I enclose a self addressed envelope with one stamp on it so I can get their note of acceptance or rejection. It's just cheaper that way. Without an SASE you are unlikely to ever get your story back, or even hear from the magazine again. You may also be biasing editors against your future submissions.

_____ 10. Start something new. Don't wait to get an acceptance or rejection on one story before starting a new project. Patience is not always a virtue.

_____ 11. If a story gets rejected, get it back in the mail, or out by email, as soon as possible. Keep your stories in circulation. They can't earn you money or publishing credits hanging around at home like a lazy post-adolescent.

PART TWO

Vigorous writing is concise. A sentence should contain no unnecessary words, a paragraph no unnecessary sentences, for the same reason that a drawing should have no unnecessary lines, and a machine no unnecessary parts.

—William Strunk Jr.

WRITING GROUPS

Are you a member of a writing group? Should you be? In an earlier essay in this book I talked about finding people who would give honest feedback on your work to help you improve. Well, a good writing group could provide exactly that. A "bad" writing group might do more harm than good, and, believe me, there are bad groups crouched out there ready to pounce.

I wrote for a couple of years on my own before I joined a group, and I sold a few stories. The idea of a writing group never even crossed my mind until my first one formed almost by accident. Xavier University, where I work, is a small, four-year, liberal arts university in New Orleans that fosters a close relationship between members of its faculty. In late 1989 Xavier sponsored a faculty retreat where one exercise involved forming small groups to talk about our academic writing. By chance, two members of my group also wanted to write fiction, myself and Michelle Levy from the English Department. A short time later, another English Prof—David Lanoue—joined us, and we three constituted the core of a group that met pretty much every week for the next decade.

I wrote two novels and rewrote a third while in that group, and all of them were published. David also wrote a couple of books around that time, *Haiku Guy* and *Laughing Buddha*. Both were published; both are beautiful works. In fact, though the group eventually dissolved David and I still meet on occasion to discuss writing. We've become good friends and allies.

My first group was a critique group. Each week we shared and criticized each other's stories, and I believe this helped me tremendously early in my career. The criticism *itself* helped, of course, because other members of the group often caught mistakes that I was too close to the work to see. But the group also helped by giving me deadlines to meet. The others didn't *make* me write, but I always wanted to have something to share when it was my turn at the meetings. After all, the others were writing. And how could I appear lazy in their eyes? So I wrote and wrote, until writing became a habit. I've long thought that *this* was actually the most important role of that group. And I believe from conversations I've had with David that he would agree.

I enjoyed my first group so much that I sought another one as soon as it broke up. This one didn't work as well, although both the other writers in it were good folk. It was also a critique group, but by that time I needed less critique and more general discussion of writing and writers. Part of the problem, too, was that it was physically inconvenient for me to meet with the second group, and as a result I probably didn't put as much into it as I should have.

I'm in a very different kind of group today. There aren't any critiques, but I get support when I'm struggling or when I'm emotionally drained, and I have a sounding board for ideas. We have wide ranging discussions on writing and writers that both inspire and inform me. The group members come to my signings and they've turned me on to speaking engagements and other opportunities. I started a blog as a result of conversations that begin in that group, and it's been a lot of fun as well as a source of inspiration.

How do you find a group if you're interested in one? Let me count the ways. First, call the English Department of your local college or university. Ask to speak to the chairperson, or to any faculty member who is a writer. Most university English Departments also publish a student magazine. Talk to the faculty advisor for that magazine. One of these folks will probably be aware of a writing group and if that group is interested in new members. At worst, ask if you can post an announcement about starting a writing group on the Department's bulletin boards. Colleges have writers at all levels of the craft.

Second, check local bookstores and read their flyers and the notices sections of the free newspapers they provide. Third, check libraries. Many groups meet at bookstores and libraries and might be interested in having new members. Groups that are actually looking for members often include announcements about their meetings in local newsletters and newspapers, or on bulletin boards. You can do the same thing if *you* decide to start a group. You might need to be a little assertive, but there are lots of people out there who are interested in writing groups and are just looking for an excuse to get involved.

Fourth, join a writing group online. These are many and varied, and there are advantages to internet based groups. You never have to leave the house, for one thing, and you don't have the hassle of deciding where to meet and trying to make sure the time is suitable for all members. Groups that meet physically either have to worry about finding a quite public place, which is not always easy to do, or they meet at one member's house and someone is probably responsible for providing drinks and snacks. Such issues don't trouble online groups.

An online group can also typically be much larger than a group that meets physically. For critique groups, instead of having three or four members share their stories for feedback in a given hour or so, stories can be posted so that dozens of members have the chance to comment at their convenience. No one is rushed, and shyer members may feel much more free to share and comment than if they had to do so face to face. If it's a closed group then such postings of stories do *not* count as publication, so that's not a danger.

Another advantage to online groups is that they may actually save you a little money in comparison to physical groups. You have to pay for an internet connection, of course, but you'd probably have that anyway. You won't have the costs of gas and no wear and tear on your automobile, and you won't have to pay to make copies of your manuscripts to hand out to the group when you're sharing. Copies can become expensive.

Finally, and *potentially*, since online groups pull members from the whole internet there is probably a better chance of finding folks who share similar interests to you in writing. (It may be your *only* chance if you live where there are no other writers.) For most of the physical groups I've been in, I've also been the *only* member interested in writing science fiction, fantasy and horror. This can cause problems, especially for critique groups, when one member doesn't appreciate the work of another. This is the main reason I finally left my first group.

Physical groups also have some advantages, however. In my experience, physical groups often foster closer bonds between members than online groups. This doesn't mean that closeness *can't* develop in online groups, only that it doesn't occur as easily. Since writing is largely a solitary pursuit, meeting physically with other writers provides some needed social interaction, and gets you out of the house where you can observe first-hand the world that provides the grist for your stories.

When you have signings or give talks, the members of a physical group can be there in the audience, giving support with their bodies instead of just their words. I've also found that people are somewhat less likely to offer aggressively negative feedback that hurts rather than helps writers when you meet face to face. And, physical groups tend to have less turnover, which means you spend less time acclimating new members to the group. I've been frustrated in some online groups at how often the same issue or question comes up again and again as new people enter the fold.

I don't believe a writer has to join a group to write. But I do believe that my groups have enriched *my* writing life and have aided my career. They might do the same for you. So, if you plan to join a group, or start one, here are some things you need to consider, gleaned from my experiences. See what you think and let me know if you agree, *or* if you find out differently.

First, I don't think a physical group works well with less than four members, but eight is too many. If you have only three, what do you do when someone misses, as someone will? You have to cancel, and maybe this was a time when you *needed* feedback. On the other hand, if you have more than six or seven in the group there's not enough time for everyone to share, and, inevitably, someone ends up listening all the time while others talk. They'll grow disgruntled and bad things will result. Trust me.

Second, make sure when the group forms—physically *or* online—that all members are in agreement about whether there are going to be critiques or not, and about what genres people feel comfortable working with. A good discussion on what people are expecting from the group is a necessity. People can have very different ideas on what a writing group should be.

Third, the relative skill and experience levels of the group members must be considered. It would be great to be in a group where one or two members are better than you are, but if there is too large of a discrepancy then you are likely to become discouraged. In the opposite way, if you are a lot better than everyone else in the group then you'll spend all your time helping others and won't get as much in return. The key, I think, is to avoid extremes. Most members of the group should be around the same level of skill and experience, without having anyone who is too weak or too strong.

Fourth, writing groups need focus or they'll soon deteriorate into "so and so's problem of the day," or "did you know…something or other about some one or other?" Critique groups have a built in structure, where everyone has to have a chance to share. But the physical group I'm in now doesn't do critiques. Instead, we brainstorm discussion topics at one meeting, then parcel those topics out over a dozen other meetings down the line.

So that each person gets a chance to talk about their own issues, my group always starts with a "round robin" where people discuss what they've been working on and the problems they're having. But, we limit the time for sharing, and then we move on to our selected topic. The resulting discussions are very freewheeling and we get off on tangents all the time, but trying to at least talk "around" a topic insures that our meetings are spent productively in an exploration of writing and are not simply social affairs.

Finally, and most critically, each member of a writing group must be aware of their impact on the other members. Too often, one member sucks up the time talking always about *their* sales, *their* angst, *their* "egos." I've seen groups of wonderful writers break up over this, and it always seems a tragedy to me. But it can be avoided if, 1) time limits are set *and* enforced for physical groups, 2) members speak up for themselves or others speak up for them, and 3) if folks are just cognizant of the needs and feelings of others. Failing that, tell your group about the wonderful writing article you just read and then show them this piece. Make sure to highlight the last paragraph.

PAGE-TURNERS: WHAT
MAKES THEM, WHAT BREAKS THEM

What does it take to suck you into a book so deeply that you lose the real world and *must* keep reading? What kind of book opens in such a way that the first page demands a second, a third, and more? Conversely, what kicks you out of a book early? What lets you toss one book aside and pick up another, or maybe turn instead to TV?

Conversations with various of my writing colleagues have led me to believe that three things are of critical importance in creating a page-turner. These are: 1) Character, 2) Situation, and 3) Quality of Prose. First among them is "Character."

Great characters will cover up a few sins in situation or prose, but an interesting situation or scintillating prose won't make up very long for shoddily constructed characters. For me, even if I'm attracted to a piece because of a fascinating opening, I'll lose interest quickly if the characters don't click. And though I've read works where the prose sings but the characters and situation don't attract me, I read them slowly and would not pretend that I was "sucked" in by them.

Almost as important as character, however, is "situation," which is not—I think—the same as plot. Situation is what we are introduced to in the opening few paragraphs, *before* we have time to figure out what the "plot" is going to be. *I* want a dramatic scene to open a book. I suspect that I put more emphasis on this than some of my writing colleagues, but that most general readers side with me. An author needs to put me immediately into a place where action or emotion, preferably both, abounds.

Unless something is happening on the page when I open a book, I'm not going to spend the time to learn about the "great" characters. And I *cannot* learn much about them from a few lines of opening dialogue. To me, characters are best revealed by what they *do*, not what they say. So please, writers out there, start your characters out *doing* things.

The third component of the page-turner, according to most writer's I've talked to, is high quality prose. I do believe prose quality is important, but I often wonder if it's more appreciated by writers than by the general reading public. For example, *The Da Vinci Code* was *not* beautifully written, and I've never heard anyone compare Dan Brown as a stylist to Ray Bradbury or Ernest Hemingway. Yet, many people have told me they could not put the book down and that they loved the characters and story.

Personally, I love great prose. I seek it out, turning often to writers such as Cormac McCarthy, James Sallis, and James Lee Burke. I believe, however, that most readers want the story and characters first, and that they are happy if the prose just doesn't get in the way. Sometimes, I'm the same. I didn't feel that Stephen King's *Misery* was full of artistically composed prose, but that book still ranks as one of the fastest page-turners in *my* personal history. *Misery* sucked me in and would not let go. A more recent book that I fell in love with was *The Swords of Night and Day* by David Gemmell. The prose was professional but workmanlike; the characters and story made it one of my favorite reads of 2005.

Finally, though, I believe that even the casual reader can appreciate beautiful prose—as long as it doesn't get in the way of the story—and written works that click on all three cylinders create the biggest vacuum effect and become the ones that possess our lives until we exorcise them by turning that last page. From my life, this includes such works as:

1. *Ghost Story*, by Peter Straub. It's a long book but I finished it over a weekend. The first scene, the very first sentence, locked me in. There's a young girl in trouble, or so it seems. And there were more great characters in this book than in any other novel I can name. The prose was both delightful *and* chillingly effective. How do you convey the "silence" of snow in words? Straub does it.

2. *Midnight*, by Dean Koontz. Another dramatic opening, even better than in *Ghost Story* because we know at once that it's life and death. The characters, too, are solid, though not as memorable as Straub's. The prose is crafted, and you can feel the effort that Koontz put into getting it just right.

3. *The Road*, by Cormac McCarthy. What could be more dramatic than two survivors, a man and his young son, struggling across a post-apocalyptic wasteland? Every moment is life and death. And the father is so lovingly etched in the way he cares for

his son. The characters are absolutely real, and yet still serve as archetypes that engage our deepest emotions. The prose reflects the mood and setting so perfectly that it's almost invisible, but each individual sentence is a jewel.

4. *Drive*, by Jim Sallis. It begins with a man in a motel room, dying it seems, with bodies and a gun close to hand. It's the perfect noir opening, and the character, who is known only as "Driver," is developed with loving intensity. Sallis's prose also never fails to satisfy, even here where it is stripped down to its bare essentials in service of the story.

5. *To Tame a Land*, by Louis L'Amour. The opening scene shows a boy and his father standing beside their broken-down wagon in Indian country as the rest of the wagon train rolls past. I'm already hooked, but we see the boy, Rye Tyler, grow to be a man in a harsh land. And L'Amour's prose, while not quite up to that of McCarthy or Sallis, lets us feel the loneliness of the prairie, lets us see the far blue mountains and the midnight stars.

Any of these books is worth study by those who want to see how the elements of Character, Situation, and Prose can be combined into a seamless meld that catches readers like a bear trap. I'm sure there are many other works deserving of consideration. Don't all readers have such lists? Check yours. Reread one or two of them. Let another writer's world take you over. You'll come back better able to take other readers to *your* worlds, better able to make them *turn that page*.

IN PRAISE OF THE NET

I come not to bury the internet, but to praise it—for research purposes at least. I've been working mostly on nonfiction for the last couple of years, not necessarily because I wanted to but because I needed the money. One recent project was an assignment for forty short author biographies, five a month, for Salem Press, which publishes reference works for high schools and colleges. Before the internet it would have been virtually impossible to complete these pieces on time and still do the kind of job I pride myself on doing. Using the web, I averaged seven essays a month and finished with time to spare, and to write other things.

Twenty-eight of my assigned authors were living, and through research on the net I was able to go well beyond just finding their web pages. I was able to make email contact with *all* of them except for one, Peter Straub, who I had enough information on without trying to contact. I was able to directly ask these writers questions about their childhoods and actually get them to read my rough drafts in order to check my accuracy.

For three of the deceased authors, I was able to make email contact with either relatives or agents, and for almost all of my assignments I downloaded—for free—copies of some of their books and stories. This was especially helpful for the foreign authors I had been assigned. I don't read Hebrew or Russian, but I was able to find the translations I needed online. And even if I didn't have to see a complete book or story, I could use the web to locate reference details such as date and place of publication. Amazon proved invaluable for this, as did *The Locus Index to SF* and Fantastic Fiction (www.fantasticfiction.co.uk).

Another project I've been working on recently is a book about Charles Darwin's theory of evolution and natural selection. Fortunately, almost everything Darwin ever wrote can be found free on the net, mostly at Project Gutenberg (www.gutenberg.org). Even when I have hard copies of a particular book I still download a copy from the net because it is so easy to search within a work for a particular phrase such as "natural selection" or "survival of the fittest."

Darwin did not create in a vacuum, of course, but much of the work that influenced him is extremely rare as far as printed copies are concerned. I discovered that I really needed to read Jean Baptiste Lamarck's work on evolution, *Zoological Philosophy*, as well as *Vestiges of the Natural History of Creation* by Robert Chambers. I couldn't find either work in print, which wasn't surprising since they were published in 1809 and 1844 respectively. A few minutes online, however, gave me both books in easily downloadable form, for nothing.

The internet has become much more for me, though, than just a source for hard to find references. When working on nonfiction I often use it in my moment to moment writing. My modem went kaput the other day and I lost a good chunk of momentum because I couldn't fact check important points with a click of my mouse. All I could do was rough draft some sentences with question marks where I needed information.

My topic at the time was the Amish, who most people know as the folks who still use horses and buggies instead of cars and who reject such modern marvels as TVs and video games. I wanted to know when the first Amish came to the States, and how many original settlers there were, and how many Amish are alive today. I also needed information on Ellis-van Creveld syndrome, which afflicts the Amish at a much higher rate than it does the general population, and which often causes polydactyly, the trait of having more than the usual number of fingers or toes. Once I got my new modem connected it took me about half an hour to get all this data and more, including pictures of humans and cats with polydactyly.

To gather the print resources that I needed for my last year's work would have been immensely costly and time consuming. I would never have made my deadlines without cutting corners, and the process of writing the articles would have been much more tedious and much less fun. The internet didn't do my job for me. In fact, I actually did *more* background reading than I would have before the web because of the wealth of easily available material. But, as a result, the finished products were more detailed, richer with examples, and just plain better than they would have been otherwise.

I'll end, however, with two warnings about using the internet for research. First, be careful not to get so caught up in online study that you fail to actually "write." The fact checking and the chances to learn new things are great, but they should be done in service of a goal, that of completing your project. Second, double and triple check every "fact" you find on the net. There's bad as well as good there. For my questions on the Amish, I searched and compared a dozen different websites before coming up with a consensus. Only then did I put anything into my own words. Used with a little caution, however, writers should find the world wide web a true boon.

All hail the net.

BLOGGING PROS AND CONS

In 2006 I started a "blog," and I'm still going strong. It's located at http://charlesgramlich.blogspot.com/. It's my online writer's journal, and I call it "Razored Zen."

For those (very few) of you who don't know what a blog is, it's a personal "log" that is published online where anyone can see it and comment on it. An advantage to having it online is that you can quickly get feedback from others. A disadvantage is that you can quickly get *feedback* from others. What I mean by the latter is that you'd better be careful what you say. Hasty words can bite you good and hard, and keep on biting for years.

Yet, there are blogs everywhere on the internet these days. Some are funny, some serious. A lot of them are put up by young folks, but increasingly I'm seeing men and women in their forties and fifties and beyond who are blogging. Unfortunately, a lot of blogs, whether by young or old, are...boring, at least to anyone beyond that person's immediate friends and family. I don't often care what some perfect stranger had for lunch yesterday, or what lame movie they snored their way through. Most people's day to day lives, including mine, just aren't very fascinating.

So why did I start my own? Well, I thought if I kept the focus primarily on writing then I'd be covering a topic that quite a few people find interesting, and I also thought that it *might* help me with my own writing, both the actual practice of putting words on the page, and the much harder task of promoting my work. I quickly gathered enough evidence to evaluate the first stage, the direct affect on my writing. The second stage, whether it could help me promote my work, took longer, but eventually I was able to evaluate that as well.

I had actually been thinking about starting a blog for months before I did it. One reason I hesitated was out of fear that the blog would cut into my writing time. That fear turned out to be foolishness. Far from slowing me down, the blog kicked me out of a lazy rut I'd fallen into in the wake of Hurricane Katrina, and to be a bit crude it energized my writing like the morning's first shot of hooch energizes a drunk.

I'd forgotten, or was at least neglecting, a cardinal rule of writing, "thou shalt write every day." If I didn't have a project due, I didn't put my butt in the chair. I let myself watch TV, that great killer of minds. But now I start each day with a blog entry, and once my fingers are on the keyboard they pick up a momentum that keeps them moving. And the ideas for projects began coming fast and wild as the need for blog-fodder made me reexamine my writing world. My writing column for *The Illuminata* was one beneficiary. Almost all of my recent column ideas have evolved from my blog, and, in fact, it's been so productive for me that I tend to stay well ahead of the deadlines for my next column.

But what about "promoting my work?" Here, too, blogging has proven to be an outstanding strategy. I began by making sure to keep the focus on writing rather than letting the journal deteriorate into a gossip column about myself. I offered what advice I could, shared the snares and traps that my own writing has fallen into at times, and occasionally posted samples of works in progress to illustrate specific points or just to express an experience. I also visited other writers' blogs and commented on them.

People began visiting my blog in turn, and soon we had formed a little community, almost a small town. It seems strange at times to have made so many good friends with people I have never physically met, or, in many cases, even seen a picture of. At other times it makes perfect sense when you realize that the people in this community share interests and commonalities that one is unlikely to find in an actual small town. I even feel comfortable sharing personal material (gossip if you will) at times now, but I try not to let more than a day or two pass between writing focused posts. I felt like I had arrived after I found a comment on a blog that I had never visited before about what a free "education" my site provided on writing.

After my Taleran novels were published in the summer of 2007, the blog community also pulled together behind me and gave me incredible support, not only in buying the books but in posting reviews and images all over the net. One of my blog colleagues even conducted an online interview with me. In *my* experience, blogging can only help a writer's career, although I believe the blogger needs to work hard to make sure that his or her visitors leave the site with something of value. Give them information, entertainment, or food for thought, and they'll keep coming back.

In the meantime, I'm also having fun and getting a lot of writing practice. And I'm producing polished material. If you'd like to start a blog, it's amazingly easy. Along with several other authors I know, I set mine up at blogspot.com; it took me about ten minutes to get comfortable with it. But there are plenty of blog sites online that will take the effort of formatting out of the process. All you have to do is write. And isn't that what you want to do anyway?

PRO VERSUS AMATEUR

A while back I had a flame war online with a fellow who calls himself a "pro" writer. He doesn't actually make his living solely from writing, although he does make some of his money from literary activities, including writing. He certainly considers himself a pro, however, and typically proclaims that to anyone who will listen. Our war started because I took issue with his arrogance toward those who weren't as widely published as he was, and we proceeded to bash each other mercilessly back and forth until we ran out of insults.

One thing that kept coming up was his references to me as an "amateur." He meant it as an insult, although I didn't take it that way, but his words did start me thinking about the differences between pros and amateurs when it comes to writing. What are those differences? And, in the writing game, is being a pro necessarily better than being an amateur?

The terms professional and amateur each have two different meanings. One definition of professional is of someone who is highly skilled at what they do. Another definition is of someone who is "paid" for what they do, especially if they make their living at it. Peyton Manning is a professional in both senses of the word. So is Peter Straub. On the other hand, the guy who fixed my roof a few years ago was paid for it but he certainly wasn't highly skilled judging from the number of leaks we had afterward.

The two meanings of amateur are exactly the reverse of those for professional. One use is of someone who has little or no skill in what they are attempting. Another use is of someone who is not paid, even though they might be talented. When it comes to singing, I am the rankest of rank amateurs in both senses of the word. My singing takes the term caterwauling to new lows, and no one, *ever*, has offered to pay me to sing. But there are plenty of people who sing beautifully in church choirs all over the world, people who are highly practiced and highly skilled but who do not get paid. They're certainly amateurs, but only in one sense of the word.

I make my living as a college teacher. That's my "profession." But I also write, and most of the time I sell what I write for money, even though it's not enough to pay all my bills. Am I a professional or an amateur? Well, I certainly don't make my living solely from writing so in that sense I'm an amateur. I also write a lot of things for free, either because someone has asked me for it or because it's something I just want to write. In that way, too, I'm an amateur.

However, whether I'm writing for free or for pay, I still require the same level of commitment from myself, the same level of hard work. I refuse to let myself "toss" something off just because I'm not getting paid for it. In fact, for nonfiction, I believe that some of the essays I've written for free have been better than ones I was paid for. The reason is that when I write for paying markets I follow their guidelines and word limits to the letter, even if I think the piece would be better with a different format or at a longer length. In these ways, I always try to offer any market I write for a professional product.

Frankly, the elements of professionalism that are important to me in the field of writing have little to do with "being paid" or with "making my living." (Although I certainly like money as much as the next person.) They have to do with the attitude and approach that I take to a piece of writing.

I know "professional" writers of both fiction and nonfiction who have turned out weak material because they were under a tight deadline or because they *had* to make a sale to pay their rent. I don't condemn them for that; all of us have to feed our families and ourselves. I just don't want to be in that position myself. I'd rather worry about what I create than what I earn.

In my experience in writing, it's not necessarily true that the pro inevitably produces better work than the amateur. In fact, the talented amateur who has worked hard at his or her craft and who takes the time to perfect a story can often create superior prose. Some enduring works have been written by amateurs. J. K. Rowling was an unemployed single mother when she finished the first Harry Potter novel. And, of course, all of today's pro writers were part-timers once. Stephen King was teaching high school English when he wrote *Carrie*. John Grisham considered writing a hobby when he was working on *A Time to Kill*.

To me, being a professional writer means worrying more about the quality of one's work than about the paycheck one receives for it. It means taking pride in what you've given the reader rather than in your own ability to put words on paper. The "pro" writer I mentioned in the first paragraph of this piece seems to pride himself on being able to turn out serviceable work at the last minute to meet his deadlines. I don't think "serviceable" work counts as professionalism when you can do better. Especially when you know it.

EXPAND YOUR MIND

Now that I've gotten your attention with a spurious drug reference, let me make haste to state that your personal habits are no business of mine. I'm not talking about LSD or mushrooms here, or Timothy Leary's suggestion to "turn on, tune in, drop out." I'm talking about expanding your *writing* mind.

Everyone who writes will eventually find themselves getting into a rut. They'll do a new project the same way they did an old project. Because it's easy. And pretty much every human, including me, is lazy.

I recently had an assignment to do forty short biographies of writers for a reference source. The first two or three were hard because I was feeling my way through them. My guidelines from the project were pretty vague so I not only had to decided what to include, but how best to present it. But after the first three pieces, the articles began to flow faster and faster. I had developed a template to follow. The next fifteen articles went like lightning. And then suddenly I started to slow down again. I began to struggle. It took me a while to realize that I was...bored.

Anytime you do something the same way repeatedly it's going to *get* boring. Psychologists know that it's human nature to seek out new sensations, new experiences. Once I figured out what the problem was with the biographies I deliberately altered my approach. I changed the physical location of my computer in the Austin apartment where I was living and working after Hurricane Katrina. I changed the time of day when I sat down to write. Most importantly, I changed the way I actually researched and wrote the articles, altering the format I was using and even the style.

It took me a while to find a new pattern that I was comfortable with; again I struggled through a few articles. But before long I'd discovered a process I liked and the pieces were rolling out of the computer again. When I got bored with *that* process I switched back to the original pattern and was happy to find that I was no longer bored with *it*. Soon the work was done and on its way to the publisher.

I wondered why I'd never had this problem with my short stories and I think I've finally figured out the answer. One, for me, writing fiction more strongly engages my emotions and that insulates me against boredom. Second, I've never tried to write more than a few stories in a row in the same genre. I might do a horror tale or two, then pen a fantasy or a western. And although I like to think there are some stylistic factors common to all my work, my style changes pretty dramatically depending on the genre I'm working in. I never have a chance to get bored with any specific tactic.

Writing novels is different, of course. You may spend half a year or several years living in the *same* world, with the *same* characters and the same style. Since I also work full-time as a teacher I don't get unbroken strings of time to write and don't suffer a lot of boredom in the so called "sagging" middle of a manuscript. Professional novelists that I know *do* suffer from occasional boredom, though, and the secret for them, too, has been to spice their routine with variation.

One novelist I know takes periodic breaks from her computer to write longhand at a house she and her husband own on a lake. Another takes her laptop to various coffee houses around the city, changing her venue as routine starts to creep in and stifle her creativity. Yet another author I know switches between genres as he writes multiple novels.

If you find yourself flagging in your production even though the effort is there, or if you find it harder and harder to drive yourself to your writing desk each day, then consider the possibility that you're just a little bored. Shake things up. Bring in music, or take music away. Work on a laptop instead of a desktop, and move from room to room or even go to a public place. Try writing longhand or recording your prose into a tape player while you walk in the park or in your own back yard. Better yet, if you're a novelist take a stab at a short story; if you usually write in third person try changing it to first.

Stay flexible, stay sharp. Change is good for the writer's soul.

FUN WITH FEAR

In *Danse Macabre*, Stephen King wrote: "I recognize terror as the finest emotion and so I will try to terrorize the reader. But if I find that I cannot terrify, I will try to horrify, and if I find that I cannot horrify, I'll go for the gross-out."

Most of you reading this piece probably understand the "gross-out," though I'll tell you that different people have *very* different levels at which they'll be grossed out. I'm not going to give examples, though I easily could. And unless you're a horror buff you should be thankful that I don't. It could get really nasty.

What I want to talk about instead in this article is the difference between fear, horror, and terror? What do these terms mean? And how can the emotions that they label be important in writing? Well, here is how *I* define the terms, and why I think this trilogy of dark emotions is important, not just in writing straight horror but in all kinds of fiction.

Fear: Fear is a physical response to a threat. It is instantaneous, a reaction from the gut. It is built into your biology to enable you to cope with danger.

Terror: Terror is psychological. It is the expectancy of fear to come, the expectancy that at any given moment something will *jump out at you*, and that it'll be beyond your capacity to handle.

Horror: Horror is where fear and terror meet. It's when the physical and psychological come together and are united in the face of something...well...horrible. That is, something that stands, or shambles, or crawls, right there in front of your eyes and is: *coming for you*.

One night my wife and son and I were having dinner when from the back of the house came the sudden slam of a door. We were alone in the house. Or so we had thought. I remember looking up, seeing Josh and Mary staring at me, and how wide their eyes were. I remember how my heart was pounding. We were all experiencing intense *fear*.

This kind of immediate biological response involves a part of the brain called the "limbic system" and a connected set of nerves known as the "sympathetic nervous system." The latter is often called the "Fight or Flight" network, and every animal has some variation of it. It's there to keep us alive in the face of threats to our existence.

But for me, on that night of the slamming door, there was more than fear to the experience. I realized that I had to find the *maker* of that noise. It was in *my* house, after all. My family might be at risk.

I told Mary and Josh to go stand by the front door and *not* to wait around if I came running. And then I glanced down the hallway toward the back part of the house. The bedroom door was closed there, and I couldn't remember whether it had been closed before or not. Now I had to go down there and find out.

My fear began to give way to terror. Because now my imagination was running wild. There was no telling what waited for me, but my mind felt free to paint pictures of what *might* be waiting.

I started down the hallway very carefully, gaze focused on the closed door at the end, and just as I reached one hand for the knob another door slammed, from a direction I'd never expected. I came very close to needing fresh underwear and a heart transplant.

Fortunately, for me in that situation, there was no *horror*, no monster under the bed, no alien in the closet, no...clown laughing maniacally on a pile of pillows. Our heater was in the hall, hidden behind a half-door in the left side wall, and it wasn't working quite right. A little gas was building up before the heater ignited, pushing the door open a bit, and when the system did ignite the door would slam. That was the source of the sound, and for that reason I never got to any *horror*. I was very grateful. Because this wasn't a movie or a book, and real life horror is *not* fun.

There was another time when I *did* experience real life horror. I was seventeen, living at home on our farm in Arkansas, when one night we heard an absolute roar from the fields below the house. It sounded like I imagined a lion would sound, but this wasn't Africa and I was no great safari hunter.

Whatever made that noise, it drove our cattle wild, sending them stampeding across the field, bawling as if their tails were on fire. My older brother and I grabbed our guns and took off in the truck for the source of the commotion. Both of us were afraid, and I know I felt the beginnings of *terror* because I had no idea what that roar could be. As far as I knew, *nothing* in Arkansas could roar like that. But I'd read about cattle mutilations and could easily imagine something that *might* make that sound. Something...not of this world.

We reached the field where the cows were and they had quieted down a bit. I had to open the gate for us to drive through, and that was terrifying in itself because I kept thinking of what might come out of the darkness. My heart was beating so hard that it fluttered my shirt. But I got the job done and lived to get back in the truck.

There was a little hill awaiting us, and as we crested it and started down the other side the lights flashed out over the field and for a moment I saw—literally—hundreds of little glowing purple balls floating in midair in the darkness in front of us, floating a few feet off the ground. Paul David, my brother, slammed on the brakes and we slid to a stop. I looked at him. He looked at me. I could feel the hairs curling on my neck, and I've always had a lot of hair to curl. I could hear the cows moving about, right in the midst of those purple floaters. How could that be? How could that *be*? *That* moment was horror.

My brother was a braver man than I. He let off the brake, inched forward, and as the light from the headlights struck further into the field we saw suddenly that the floating purple orbs were eyes. But not alien eyes. It was the cows, their eyes wide open in terror as they reflected the headlights. I'd never seen them that scared before; nor have I since.

So what made the sound? We never found out. There were no tracks the next day, but we were missing a calf and we found its mother with her ears stripped to threads by the teeth or claws of...something. Before that night I often walked the farm in the darkness. After that night I seldom did again. Fear can go away, but terror and horror linger.

Emotional experiences cling like burrs to a person's mind. And fear and its offshoots are among the most powerful emotions. Creating such experiences and feelings in your readers will make sure they never quite forget your tales. But how do you go about it? How do you create emotions, especially fearful emotions, through the mere use of words?

I hope I've already given you *one* hint. You rely on your own experiences, not merely describing in rational words what you are afraid of, but using for fodder those moments when you yourself have been afraid. Ever been alone in an empty house as darkness closes in? Ever walked in deep woods and feared you were lost? Have you been close to having a car wreck, or maybe had one? Have you ever thought you were going to be robbed, or beaten up? Can you remember the way your heart worked in those moments? Can you remember how every sound and object had absolute clarity?

Can you recall the dryness in your mouth, the tightness of your bladder? Those are the things to use. It's not saying, "I'm afraid of snakes so I'll use that in my story." It's saying, "there was this one time when this snake scared the living you-know-what out of me and I'll use *that* in my story."

For a second hint, take the time to scare yourself, and notice the effects you get. I go for walks down the dirt roads around my place at midnight. Sometimes with the moon and sometimes not. There are trees on every side. I hear night birds. But there isn't a single streetlight. Once in a while you'll see a lonely house-lamp through the pines, that faint fog of a light that only serves to accentuate the greater darkness all around. Shadows follow me when the moon is up. I hear small animals crashing away through the brush, but they don't sound so small when you're standing alone on a rutted dirt road with the dark forest all around. I don't know if this will work for you, but it gets *my* heart rate up.

Another thing you can try is to arrange your writing environment to enhance the mood you're shooting for in a tale. Writing by candlelight sometimes works for me, especially if I pair it with eerie music like the theme song from *Halloween*. I also keep a few props around, Day of the Dead statuettes from Mexico, a headless horseman figurine from the movie *Sleepy Hollow*, and sketches and cover art depicting mad landscapes both physical and mental.

Use your own actual experiences of fear. Create new experiences. Write them down without holding anything back. This is the secret to generating the emotions of fear, terror, and horror in your readers.

Sow with darkness. Reap by the light of the moon.

WHY HORROR?

The two genres I love best are fantasy and horror. Fantasy was my first love, and you know what they say about your first. But though horror fiction came late to my life, when I was already into my early twenties, our relationship has been passionate and we're still seeing each other on a regular basis. Fantasy is beautiful and elegant; horror is dirty and a little trashy, not the kind of literature you bring home to momma.

So why do I read and write horror? Why does *anyone*? A writer should ask these questions of any genre they choose, and since I've had more success with horror fiction than with anything else I've written I've given the issue of why people like scary stuff a considerable amount of thought. As a psychologist, I've also done a little research into the subject.

One thing I've realized is that there's an important distinction between reading scary books and watching scary movies, even though I don't hear many critics discuss this difference. What I'm talking about is this: watching movies is often a social event while reading is solitary. Most of the time, people watch scary movies *together*. I don't think this completely changes the reasons that I've given below as to why people seek out horror fiction, but it enhances them. See what *you* think.

1). First and foremost, people like horror fiction, whether in print or movies, because it is *exciting*. When their bodies are physically stimulated, whether by something pleasant or something frightening, people are energized. Their muscles surge with blood. Their minds sharpen. They feel alive. As long as their excitement doesn't cross the line into true horror or terror, the feeling of being alive is a good one. This is why people ride roller coasters.

If there are other folks around, such as when people are watching a movie together, individuals can feed off each other's energies. This amps the excitement up even further, creating a more powerful effect. Music concerts do the same thing. Excitement is contagious.

Of course, some people find scary stuff *too* energizing, *too* intense, to the point where it evokes a sense of real terror. And they turn away. There are plenty of such people, and they tend not to be the fan base for horror fiction, but there are plenty more, such as myself, who enjoy a good scare.

2). A second reason why people like horror fiction is so that they can experience fearful events in a safe environment. They can have the delicious shiver without the mind-wrenching terror they would feel if such things happened to them for real.

Think about how nice it is to sleep all snug in your blankets when it's cold and raining outside your window. The presence of the freezing weather outside just adds to the pleasure you feel being safe *inside*. Reading horror fiction or watching a horror movie can produce much the same feeling, and if you watch the movie with friends the effect is enhanced. Friends are like those comforting blankets; they keep you feeling safe but let you have the thrill.

3). Horrific tales also let people test themselves against imagined threats. In a way, such stories allow folks to practice for something they might one day face, not monsters necessarily, but something just as dangerous. For children, play is a process of learning to be an adult, of practicing the things through games that they will—or might—one day have to do for real. In this sense, reading or watching horror is a type of play, of practice. What do you do if you are confronted with the possibility of death? What do you do if someone or something wants to kill you? Well, for one thing, you *don't* go in the basement.

I think this *testing* of themselves is more true for men, especially young men, than it is for women. Picture the stereotype of the young woman hiding her face from something terrible on the movie screen while the young man puts his arm around her to comfort her. There is some truth to this stereotype, although I've known women who deliberately pretended to be scared in movies to give their boyfriends the chance to express their protective instinct.

Whether it's biological or cultural, or probably both, men seem to have a greater urge than women to test themselves against outside threats. This effect is hugely powerful when men are together where they can show their disdain for the horrific. Together they can feel invincible, as if they can stand against anything. Perhaps in the distant past of the human race they had to. Perhaps in that sense, playing with fear may be coded into the male's genes.

Women, too, can face horrific experiences. In the real world they've had it pretty hard through the centuries, and this is reflected in the fact that women have traditionally been the choicest victims in horror fiction and film. Increasingly, women today are writing horror themselves. They aren't content to remain victims, and this, too, is a form of learning through play, even if it is sometimes very serious play.

4). There is something else about horror, though, for those such as myself, who might be called connoisseurs of the genre. That is, what is scary to most people isn't necessarily scary to us. There are actually few books that have truly scared me. *Ghost Story* by Peter Straub and *The Haunting of Hill House* by Shirley Jackson are two that did. Two movies that managed to creep me out were *The Exorcist* and *The Ring*.

Take a movie like *Alien*, however, which often makes the list of the top scary movies of all time. I loved *Alien*, but it *didn't* scare me. Instead, it had what I call the "coolness" factor, especially with that infamous chest-burster scene. *Alien* and its sequels were visually and emotionally exciting, but most of all they offered an imaginative adventure. Personally, this is the main reason why *I* read horror fiction and watch horror movies, to have my imagination stimulated. If you can get me to say, "cool," then I'll buy every book you write or watch ever film you produce.

At its heart, the enjoyment of horror fiction is irrational. But humans are not just rational beings. In fact, we're not *primarily* rational. We are emotional. And fear is one of the four major emotions that people experience—joy, sadness, anger, and fear.

Whenever you write, *whatever* you write, keep in mind the reasons why people might want to read the product of your hard work. Shaping your stories with an understanding of, and an appreciation for, why people like what they like can only help your chances of getting published. Giving them a good scare may not hurt either.

HORROR WRITERS: THE CRAZY TRUTH

I suppose all genres of literature are troubled by myths. You know, those pesky facts that everyone knows are true but which...aren't. Let's see: literary writers are pretentious wannabes, SF/fantasy writers are adolescents in adult bodies, poets are plain insane, and romance writers...well they just aren't getting enough! But some of the worst myths are told—and believed—about horror writers. Since I write horror, and I know a few dozen other horror writers, let me address some of the myths about my chosen field. Just ignore the nagging voice in your head that suggests I might be biased. Nothing could be further from the truth. I assure you.

Myth 1: People who write horror were physically or sexually abused as children by their parents or relatives. As I said, I know lots of horror writers. I don't personally know *one* who was so abused. In fact, most of them had happy childhoods, or at least childhoods that were no different from those of many others around them. My father died when I was thirteen and that was hard on me. But I always knew that I was loved by my parents and my upbringing was basically happy.

I do know that a very famous writer, Dean Koontz, who is generally known for his horror fiction even though much of what he writes isn't horror, has talked freely of the trauma of growing up with an alcoholic and sociopathic father. But even he wasn't sexually or physically abused. He was a victim of psychological abuse, and though that's certainly not something to minimize, there are many, many people who have had it far worse without being driven to write horror fiction. And most writers who *do* work in horror don't have even psychological abuse in their backgrounds. Their childhoods, strange as it may seem, were normal.

Myth 2: People who write horror are weird. Now, I'll admit, most of the horror writers I know have somewhat twisted senses of humor, and they may keep things around their workspaces that most people wouldn't tolerate, such as the skulls (fake for the *most* part) that I keep in my office at home. But I've always found that horror writers are the friendliest and most approachable people you can meet, especially at a writing conference. Every horror writer I know except one is married. Most have children who are well adjusted. Most also have other jobs and they do well in those jobs. They have friends. They're not any weirder than anyone else. (After all, we all know that it's the "quiet" ones you have to watch, and horror writers aren't usually quiet.)

Myth 3: Horror writers write their own fears out on paper. This is not *completely* a myth, really, but it's certainly not true in the simplest of senses. One time after I'd finished telling some family members about a story I was working on, my mother-in-law asked me how I could stand to write such things. She said she'd be scared to write about ghosts, or demons, or evil aliens, or monsters. She'd be scared they'd come after her. I told her, "well, I can write about them because I don't believe in them. If I believed in them I might be too scared to write about them myself." She was shocked; she didn't understand how I could write a scary story about something that I wasn't scared of myself.

I don't think that most people who work in horror actually believe in vampires and werewolves and ghosts and monsters even when they write about them. They are having fun with the concepts. Those things don't scare them. At worst, the vampires and monsters are metaphors for things like pain and death and disease that all of us fear.

But, let me clarify something. If I say I don't believe in monsters and ghosts, that doesn't mean I couldn't be scared by the thought of such things under certain circumstances. I'm probably as scared as anyone else in a "haunted house," because I can *imagine* the ghosts even if I don't, in my rational moments, believe in their ectoplasmic existence.

And, at least for me, when I'm writing a horror story, when I'm caught up in telling the tale, I *do* believe. Right now, I'll sit here and tell you that I put no faith in the concept of ghosts. But if I'm writing a ghost story and I'm alone, and it's storming outside, and I hear a strange noise that I've never heard in the house before, I *am* scared. Because I've worked myself into that state just through the exercise of imagination. I'm sure it's the same for many other writers of horror.

Now, there is one last "myth" about horror writers that *is* true, and I'll let you in on the secret. But keep it just between us. You know the saying that horror writers make better lovers? Believe me, *that* one is fact. I swear it on the *Necronomicon*.

THE HORROR LISTS

After many years of writing horror fiction and writing about it, I've developed some strong opinions about what is best and worst in the genre, and I've become—dare we say—haunted by the study of the genre's history. I've tried to read most of the works that shaped modern horror, and learn about the authors who crafted the early tales. This current piece is not really an essay on horror history but more a collection of lists to help those who want to know more about horror's past get started. Although these lists are a product of my own subjective understanding of the genre, they are not arbitrary. I believe that most literary historians would agree with me. See if you do.

Authors Who Shaped the History of Short Story Horror

It was the short story rather than the novel that created the field of horror fiction, and in my opinion the genre still works best at shorter lengths because it's easier for both writers and readers to maintain the emotional intensity on which horror fiction thrives. The following ten authors were short horror's most influential early practitioners, at least in the English language. Since most of these authors' works are in the public domain, great examples of their tales can be found free on the internet. I've included the web addresses for particularly telling examples.

1. Edgar Allan Poe: 1809-1849. Poe is a horror writer that even the literati respect, although his work is often labeled "crime" or "detective" fiction. Don't let those euphemisms fool you. Poe wrote horror. His fiction is full of grisly murders and dark emotions. He wrote often of madness.

Although an American, born in Boston, Poe lived for a few years in England and developed a great respect for the European tradition in fiction. Many of his stories are set in France and he became respected as an author there long before his worth was widely recognized in America. Poe has many famous stories, but one of my favorites is "The Fall of the House of Usher." You can find it free online at: http://www.pambytes.com/poe/stories/usher.html

2. Sheridan Le Fanu: 1814-1873. Le Fanu was an Irish writer who worked in many genres but who is best remembered for his mystery and gothic (horror) work. His vampire novella, "Carmilla," was published in 1872, some twenty-five years before Bram Stoker's *Dracula*, and is considered a major influence on Stoker's masterpiece. You can read "Carmilla" for free at:

http://www.english.upenn.edu/~nauerbac/crml.html

3. Ambrose Bierce: 1842-1914?. Unlike Poe or Le Fanu, Bierce is known more for his satire than his terror fiction, but his tales of the Civil War—in which he fought on the side of the Union—are master works of horror. Bierce was also American and is the source of one of the most famous literary mysteries of all time. He disappeared in Mexico in December of 1913 and no trace of him has ever been found. You can read "An Occurrence at Owl Creek Bridge," at:

http://www.pagebypagebooks.com/Ambrose_Bierce/
An_Occurrence_At_Owl_Creek_Bridge/

4. Guy de Maupassant: 1850-1893. Maupassant was French and is often considered one of the fathers of the modern short story. He, like Poe, did not have a strong grip on sanity during his later years. He was considered insane at his death, although a likely diagnosis today would be syphilitic dementia. Many of Maupassant's tales deal with phenomena that could either be explained by the supernatural or by the madness of the story's narrator. His most famous story is likely "The Horla," which you can read at:

http://www.eastoftheweb.com/short-stories/UBooks/Horl.shtml

5. Charlotte Perkins Gilman: 1860-1935. Gilman wrote very little horror fiction. Most of her work was nonfiction with a feminist slant. But she is important to the history of horror for her story, "The Yellow Wallpaper," which is a masterpiece of madness. The story is believed to be at least partially nonfiction and to reflect her own struggle with mental illness, particularly depression. You can read it at:

http://www.pagebypagebooks.com/Charlotte_Perkins_Gilman/
The_Yellow_Wallpaper/The_Yellow_Wallpaper_p1.html

6. M. R. James: 1862-1936. Montague Rhodes James is, in my opinion and that of many others, the premier British author of ghost stories. His tales have a certain quaintness, but that doesn't keep them from being downright scary. He wrote many stories but his best known collections are *Ghost Stories of an Antiquary* and *More Ghost Stories of an Antiquary*. One tale I particularly like is "A School Story." Read it at:

http://gaslight.mtroyal.ab.ca/schoolst.htm

7. W. W. Jacobs: 1863-1943. William Wymark Jacobs is another British author, and one who wrote mostly humorous stuff. However, several of his tales are definitely horror and were influential on many later writers. His most famous is "The Monkey's Paw," which you can find at:

http://gaslight.mtroyal.ab.ca/mnkyspaw.htm

8. Algernon Blackwood: 1869-1951. Blackwood is yet another British author. (What is it with the British and horror?) His tales are extremely atmospheric and remind me quite a bit of Poe, although I don't think his work is as good as Poe's. He definitely was an influence on many later writers, however, and there is quite a bit of critical material on him. Perhaps his most eerie work is "The Willows," which is a free download at:

http://www.gutenberg.org/etext/11438

9. Oliver Onions: 1873-1961. George Oliver Onions is another British ghost story writer, although no one ever uses the "George" when mentioning him. He has a number of collections of his own and has been frequently anthologized. Like many of the other British ghost "storyists," Onions' work can often be read as either supernatural events intruding into the real world or as the slowly developing madness of the main character. An excellent work that illustrates his themes is a novella called: "The Beckoning Fair One." It's found in one of Onions' collections called *Widdershins*, and you can download that book for free at:

http://www.gutenberg.org/etext/14168

10. H. P. Lovecraft: 1890-1937. Did you think I'd forget How-ard Phillips Lovecraft? Never. Lovecraft was an American author, a New Englander like Poe, who Lovecraft admired and emulated. Lovecraft is best known for creating the "Cthulhu Mythos." The basic concept is that there are beings on earth who predate humankind and who are either indifferent to humanity or inimical. These beings are originally from outside earth and have long been "asleep," although in the past some were worshipped as gods by primitive peoples. Some still have power today. One of my favorite Lovecraft tales is "The Statement of Randolph Carter." Read it for free at:

http://www.dagonbytes.com/thelibrary/lovecraft/
thestatementofrandolph.htm

Honorable Mention in Short Story: The two authors listed below are known for works other than horror, but each of them wrote one stand-out horror story that I want to mention.

11. Charles Dickens: 1812-1870: Dickens is often considered the greatest British author ever, and the vast majority of his work is far from horror fiction. The only "ghost story" to be commonly associated with Dickens' name is *A Christmas Carol*, which is not at all scary and which *I* don't consider horror. However, Dickens also wrote a story called "The Signalman," which *is* horror and which I enjoyed. You can find it at:

http://www.pagebypagebooks.com/
Charles_Dickens/The_Signal_Man/The_Signal_Man_p1.html

12. Lord Dunsany: 1878-1957. Lord Dunsany was of English-Irish descent. His actual name was Edward Plunkett, but few know him as that. Those who know *of* him think of him as a fantasy writer, and that is what most of his work can be categorized as. However, he authored one of the best horror stories ever written, in my opinion. It's called "Two Bottles of Relish" but, unfortunately, I can't find it free online. There are many anthologies that contain the story, however. Some are: *Great Short Tales of Mystery and Terror, Midnight Fright, Masterpieces of Horror, Stories for the Dead of Night*, and *Tales to Be Told in the Dark.*

Books that Shaped the History of Horror Fiction:

Up until the last three decades of the twentieth century, horror fiction was primarily found in short story form. There were relatively few novels that had a major influence, although those that did were big. A list of the most influential horror *novels* of the early days follows. Like the short stories discussed previously, most of these are also in the public domain and I've added links where they can be found for free online.

1. Horace Walpole: 1717-1797.*The Castle of Otranto*, 1764 is generally considered to be the first Gothic novel. It's still surprisingly readable and can be found online at:

http://emotionalliteracyeducation.com/classic_books_online/cotrt10. htm

2. Clara Reeve: 1729-1807. *The Old English Baron*, 1777 might be considered the world's first horror pastiche. The influence of Walpole's *The Castle of Otranto* is clear. The tale can certainly stand on its own, though. Download it at:

http://www.gutenberg.org/etext/5182

3. Ann Radcliffe: 1764-1823. *The Mysteries of Udolpho*, 1794 was certainly an early gothic novel but is largely remembered today because it was parodied by Jane Austin in her book, *Northanger Abbey*. "Udolpho" is a pretty standard work, but if you're interested it can be downloaded at:

http://www.gutenberg.org/etext/3268

4. Matthew Gregory Lewis: 1775-1818. *The Monk*, 1796, written before Lewis even turned twenty, was so successful that forever after the author became known as "Monk" Lewis. It can be viewed as the culmination of the first stage of the gothic novel's development, and for the time it was considered horrendously blasphemous and sexy. I think it still reads pretty well today. It's recently been released in a new print edition, but you can also download it for free at:

http://www.gutenberg.org/etext/601

5. Charles Brockden Brown: 1771-1810.*Wieland, or The Transformation*, 1798 was the first *American* gothic novel. Brown himself is one of the very first American novelists, and most of the eight novels he wrote were gothic in nature. He is often overlooked in the history of gothic literature but certainly deserves his place. This book is available in a print edition from *The Invisible College Press*. See their catalog at: http://www.invispress.com/

6. Mary Shelley: 1797-1851. *Frankenstein; or, The Modern Prometheus*, 1818 was an influence on the development of science fiction as well as horror. If anything in horror fiction's history can be considered a masterpiece it would be Frankenstein (and Dracula). If you haven't already read it, check it out online at:

http://home-1.worldonline.nl/~hamberg/

7. Charles Robert Maturin: 1782-1824. *Melmoth the Wanderer*, 1820 is an early "Deal with the Devil" novel. It was an influence on such disparate writers as Karl Edward Wagner in his stories of "Kane," and Anne Rice with Memnoch the Devil. It's a book that I personally find rather tough going, but many other writers have raved about it. You can find it free online at:

http://etext.library.adelaide.edu.au/m/maturin/charles/melmoth/

By the way, Maturin was Jane Wilde's uncle; Jane Wilde had a son named Oscar, who appears a little further down this list.

8. Nathaniel Hawthorne: 1804-1864. *The House of the Seven Gables*, 1851 is a relatively mild horror story but it does introduce the "house" as character, which was later exploited in many excellent haunted house tales. The book is easy to find in print but it's also online at:

http://www.online-literature.com/hawthorne/seven_gables/

9. Robert Louis Stevenson: 1850-1894: *The Strange Case of Dr. Jekyll and Mr. Hyde*, 1886 explores the inner monster, something very close to a werewolf, which may well live in us all. Almost a novella, this book is a quick but effective read. You can find it at:

http://www.bibliomania.com/0/0/46/86/frameset.html

10. Oscar Wilde: 1854-1900. *The Picture of Dorian Gray*, 1890 is a study of sanity and insanity that influenced many later novels of psychological horror. The author is known much more for his barbed humor than for his horror, but this is a masterpiece. You can find it at:

http://www.upword.com/wilde/dorgray.html

11. Bram Stoker: 1847-1912. *Dracula*, 1897 is considered the prototypical vampire tale, although it was certainly influenced by earlier works, such as "Carmilla" by Sheridan Le Fanu. *Dracula* is a great book, however, and well worth the read. You can easily find the novel in print, but it's also online at:

http://www.literature.org/authors/stoker-bram/dracula/

12. Henry James: 1843-1916. *The Turn of the Screw*, 1897 is sometimes considered the prototypical ghost story novel, although—in the British tradition—it can also be read as a tale of madness. I thought it was quite atmospheric and enjoyed it. It's widely available in print, but you can also read it online at:

http://www.online-literature.com/henry_james/turn_screw/

13. William Hope Hodgson: 1877-1918. *The House on the Borderland*, 1908 may be my favorite of all those listed here, although it's not the most influential on the field of horror. It really introduced surrealism to horror, which I enjoy. It doesn't have quite the tidy ending that some others here have, though. Download it for free at:

http://www.gutenberg.org/etext/10002

The Ten Most Influential Horror Writers of the Modern Period:

I'm going to somewhat arbitrarily define the modern period in horror as beginning in 1959 with the publication of *The Haunting of Hill House* by Shirley Jackson, although the ball didn't really get rolling until after 1974 when Stephen King's *Carrie* was published. The last *three* decades of the twentieth century produced a handful of "celebrity" horror writers whose names became bigger than any of their books. Other horror writers, because of movies made from their books, achieved a level of cultural influence far beyond the readers of their works. And, finally, there are some writers who have achieved a level of influence *within* the horror field that far exceeds their reputation in the broader world. I call these the "writers' writers."

Below is a list of the top ten most influential modern practitioners of horror. All of them are primarily known from their novels, and, with the exception of the "writers' writers," from the movies made from their works. (It's extremely hard for anyone to gain widespread popularity in writing today unless their material has been seen on TV or the silver screen.) I've included an example— one of my favorites—of each author's work, but these won't be in the public domain so you'll need to use the library or purchase them yourself. My comments are in parentheses.

The Celebrity writers. the Household Names

1. Stephen King: *Misery,* 1990. (Characterization is King's greatest strength.)
2. Anne Rice: *Interview with the Vampire*, 1976. (As much romance as horror.)
3. Dean Koontz: *Velocity*, 2005. (Koontz writes tightly plotted thrillers.)
4. Clive Barker: *The Books of Blood*, 1984-1985. (Barker's early stuff is true horror.)

The Movie Writers. The ones who are primarily known because of the Movies

5. Thomas Harris: *Red Dragon*, 1981. (The best writer in the serial killer genre.)
6. William Peter Blatty: *The Exorcist*, 1971. (Demonic possession for the modern age.)
7. Peter Benchley: *Jaws*, 1974. (Man as prey. A great subgenre.)
8. Robert Bloch: *Psycho*, 1959. (Horror of the mind.)

The Writers' Writers

9.Peter Straub: *Ghost Story*, 1979. (Literary quality horror.)
10. Joe R. Lansdale: *The Nightrunners*, 1987. (Raw, violent, in your face horror.)

The Books that Scared Me:

In my opinion, the following are the best horror novels of the modern period. Some might not be called "horror" in the strictest sense, but all are powerful books. The first two scared the daylights out of me. All the others had moments that were genuinely frightening, and many more moments where I turned the pages feverishly to find out what happened next and who would survive. None of these are in the public domain so you won't find them free online.

1. Peter Straub: *Ghost Story*, 1979.
2. Shirley Jackson: *The Haunting of Hill House*, 1959.
3. Thomas Harris: *The Silence of the Lambs*, 1988.
4. Dean Koontz: *Phantoms*, 1983.
5. Joe R. Lansdale: *The Nightrunners*, 1987.
6. Jack Finney: *The Body Snatchers*, 1955.
7. T. Chris Martindale: *Where the Chill Waits*, 1991.
8. William Peter Blatty: *The Exorcist*, 1971.
9. T. E. D. Klein: *The Ceremonies*, 1984.
10. John Skipp & Craig Spector: *The Scream*, 1988.
11. Robert R. McCammon: *They Thirst*, 1981.
12. Peter Benchley: *Jaws*, 1974.
13. Stephen King: *'Salem's Lot*, 1975.
14. James Herbert: *The Dark*, 1980.
15. Anne Rivers Siddons: *The House Next Door*, 1978.

The Best Horror Anthologies of the Modern Period:

I think the greatest works of horror are to be found among short stories. Below are my picks for the best anthologies of horror shorts of the modern period. These are divided between single author collections and multiple author collections. My comments are in parentheses.

Single Author Collections

1. Peter Straub: *Houses Without Doors*, 1990. (Not all of these are horror, but all are profound.)
2. Robert R. McCammon: *Blue World*, 1990. (McCammon is underrated. His work is superb.)
3. Dean Koontz: Strange Highways, 1995. (All the thrill of his novels at shorter lengths.)

4. Clive Barker: *The Books of Blood*, 1984-1985. (These stories changed the horror genre.)

5. Dennis Etchison: *The Dark Country*, 1982. (On the subtle side, but powerful.)

6. Stephen King: *Skeleton Crew*, 1985. (Better than most of King's novels.)

7. Karl Edward Wagner: *In a Lonely Place*, 1983. (Wagner could write horror with the best.)

8. Joe R. Lansdale: *By Bizarre Hands*, 1989. (Raw wounds and deep black humor.)

9. Poppy Brite: *Wormwood*, 1994. (Beautiful style melded with grotesque imagery.)

Multiple Author Collections

1. *Razored Saddles*, 1989. Edited by Joe R. Lansdale & Pat Lo-Brutto. (Horror westerns, including a couple of the most graphic horror tales ever penned.)

2. *Book of the Dead*, 1989. Edited by John Skipp & Craig Spector. (Set in the world of George Romero's zombies.)

3. *Dark Forces*, 1980. Edited by Kirby McCauley. (Just great stories from great writers.)

4. *Confederacy of the Dead*, 1993. Edited by Richard Gilliam, Martin H. Greenberg & Edward E. Kramer. (Another collection set in Romero's universe, but with the Civil War.)

5. *Hotter Blood*, 1991. Edited by Jeff Gelb & Michael Garrett. (Sex and horror.)

6. *Dark Voices IV*, 1992. Edited by David Sutton & Stephen Jones. (I may be biased on this one since it contains a story by me, but I think there's a lot of good stuff here.)

Nonfiction Books to Aid in Studying Horror Fiction and Horror Writers:

There are many good books out there that cover the issues of horror fiction and horror writers. Below is a list of some of the better ones, although I make no claim that they are the *best* ones. They are books that have helped me over the years in writing the articles I have, and books that I've just enjoyed perusing for their own merits. I believe that only one of these is in the public domain. I've included a link for it, and dates and publishers for the others.

1. Valdine Clemens: *The Return of the Repressed: Gothic Horror from the Castle of Otranto to Alien (SUNY Series in Psychoanalysis and Culture),* 1999, State University of New York.

2. E. Michael Jones: *Monsters from the Id: The Rise of Horror in Fiction and Film,* 2000, Spence Publishers.

3. Stephen Jones: *Clive Barker's A-Z Horror,* 1998, Harper Prism.

4. S. T. Joshi: *The Modern Weird Tale,* 2001, McFarland & Company.

5. Stephen King: *Danse Macabre,* 1997, Berkley.

6. H. P. Lovecraft: *Supernatural Horror in Literature.* (This is a pamphlet you *can* find online. It's a classic:
http://www.yankeeclassic.com/miskatonic/library/stacks/literatu re/lovecraft /essays/supernat/supern00.htm

7. Tony Magistrale & Michael A. Morrison (Eds.): *A Dark Night's Dreaming: Contemporary American Horror Fiction,* 1996, University of South Carolina Press.

8. Susan Jennifer Navarette: *The Shape of Fear: Horror and the Fin De Siecle Culture of Decadence,* 1998, University Press of Kentucky.

9. David Punter: *The Literature of Terror: A History of Gothic Fictions from 1765 to the Present Day: The Gothic Tradition,* 1996, Addison-Wesley.

10. Tim Underwood & Chuck Miller (eds.): *Feast of Fear: Conversations with Stephen King,* 1992, Carroll & Graf.

11. Stanley Wiater (ed.):*Dark Thoughts: On Writing: Advice and Commentary from Fifty Masters of Fear and Suspense,* 1997, Underwood Books.

12. Stanley Wiater: *Dark Dreamers: Conversations with the Masters of Horror,* 1990, Avon.

DREAM STORIES

I've always been cursed, or blessed, with nightmares. And they are often relatively coherent, with usable story lines. Several of my published stories originated as dreams; others are waiting to be turned into tales. Let me relate one to you.

In this dream, I'm hunting in the woods and it starts to rain. I find an old cabin, half fallen in, and go inside out of the weather. After a bit, lulled by the rain, I fall asleep. A voice awakens me, a woman's voice calling me to supper. I find myself lying on a couch and the house is warm with lights. I look around, confused, but then a woman opens the door to the room where I'm resting and tells me again to come on for supper. She is smiling and I realize she is my wife.

I follow her into a dining area where she's set a table with candles and food. She is young, maybe nineteen or twenty, with long blond hair. She is very beautiful. She smiles and kisses me on the cheek, and we sit down to eat. She is vivacious, happy, full of conversation, and soon my confusion is forgotten and I'm laughing and talking with her easily. She touches my shoulder or my arm as we talk, and I feel very comfortable. Then, suddenly, from the room above us, comes a loud, thump, thump, thump.

I jump, look up, then look at my wife. She's suddenly as pale as death and it seems as if she's physically aged several years. I see lines in her face that weren't there moments before. I start to get up, to go see about the sound, but she grabs my hand. Her eyes are bright. She tells me that it's nothing, that she'll go and make sure herself.

I settle uneasily back into my chair and she leaves the table. But she comes back a few moments later and sits down again. We resume our meal. Again we start to laugh and joke, and the sound is forgotten. Until it occurs again, louder: thump, thump, THUMP.

I jump up from the table and start for the stairs, but she rushes from her chair and grabs my arm. "No, no, no," she says. "It's nothing. Just ignore it. Please!" She is pleading. I can see it in her face. And again she seems to have aged a few years, more than the first time.

Reluctantly, I let her talk me into going back to the table. We sit and begin to eat again, but we are both subdued. Finally, we begin to smile a bit, though my wife's smile seems wan at first. But our mood lifts until we start to laugh again.

For a third time the sound comes tolling from upstairs, much louder now, rattling the ceiling above our heads, startling us. Thump, THUMP, THUMP! Once more I jump up and rush for the stairs. How can I ignore the sound any longer? My wife comes shouting after me, and halfway up the stairs she catches me, grabs my arm desperately. She begs, pleads again and again with me not to go upstairs, and now she seems much older, middle aged. Her blond hair even has gray strands in it, and her eyes are puffy and a little haggard. It is for her sake, for the naked terror in her eyes, that I allow myself to be led back to the table.

Again I sit. And I eat. But I'm waiting. There is no laughter in either of us now. And of course the sound comes again. THUMP, THUMP, THUMP! Loud as thunder now, loud enough to shake the house, loud enough to make my wife scream.

I leap up with an oath and run to the stairs. My wife grabs me but I shake her off. This time I will *not* be stopped. I rush up the steps, ignoring the cries behind me. My wife falls silent just as I reach the top of the stairs. There is a single door there, no landing or hallway, only a door. I try it and it's locked, but I put my shoulder to it. I burst it inward, throw it open.

A woman stands behind the door, an ancient and decaying crone. Her hair is dead white and sparse as winter straw on her head. Her eyes are like boiled eggs in a face of rotted and liverish flesh. I scream and stumble back. She speaks, in the voice of my beautiful, young wife.

"I told you," she says. "I begged you not to come up the stairs. But you just *had* to. And now you see what you've done! *See* what you've done!" I back further away as she steps out of the doorway onto the top of the stairs. She reaches out to me, says, "But I still love you." I turn and run, and run, down the stairs, out the door into the woods. Only once do I glance back, and the house is again the half ruin that I'd first seen when I came seeking shelter from the rain.

Only at that moment did I wake up, sweating and shaking, half expecting to see something ancient and smiling leaning over me. When I told my actual wife about the dream, she regretted that she hadn't been able to awaken me. I told her: "No, no. Don't *ever* wake me up when I'm having a nightmare."

She looked confused, as do most people when I tell them that I never want to be awakened from a bad dream. But where else can I have an experience that is both safe *and* more terrifying than any horror movie I've ever seen? And it's free! Plus, there are direct and indirect benefits to my writing. There are storylines and detail that I can use, and my memory provides me with emotions and images that help make my fiction more realistic. In dreams, I have been both detectives and victims. I've been children and adults. I've *been* the devil. And once I was a serial killer writing a novel on the wooden walls of my house in the blood of my victims.

If you want to use dreams to help your own writing, there are several things you can do. First, of course, you have to *remember* your dreams. Some folks believe that they seldom or never dream, but research shows that all humans dream every night. However, people are only likely to remember their dreams if they wake up after they're over, *and* if they then spend a few minutes *thinking* about those dreams. I suggest getting a journal to keep by your bedside, and then take time to actually write your dreams down after they occur.

But how can you write them down if you don't recall them? Well, to help you in the act of recall, here are a few hints. First, don't drink caffeinated products—colas, coffee, teas—for the last few hours before going to bed. Caffeine suppresses dreaming, as do most sleep aids. Second, know that, on average, typical sleep alternates with dream sleep throughout the night on a cycle of about 90 minutes, with 60 or so minutes of regular sleep and then 20-30 minutes of dream sleep. This means that your dreams should begin about an hour after you go to sleep.

People who remember their dreams best usually wake completely up at the end of the dream period. This means that if you set your alarm for about 1 hour and 15 minutes after you lay down to sleep, the alarm should go off and awaken you during a dream. Then you lay there and think about your experience. Of course, you might not want to do this on work nights, but try it sometime when you're on vacation, or if you plan to have a long nap on the weekend.

It may also help you remember dreams if you spend a few minutes *before* you got to sleep "ordering" yourself to recall your dreams. I've found that, with practice, I can set an internal alarm to wake myself up at certain times in the morning, and that I can also convince myself to improve my recall of dreams. And, whatever you do, don't get up immediately upon waking and go to the bathroom or to get a drink. In those few moments of doing something else your dream will be lost. Stay in bed, stay still, and *think*. What was I just experiencing?

There is another thing that I use to help my recall. If I can remember anything at all about my dreams, then I start to ask questions. "What time of day was it? Was the sun shining or was it raining? Was I inside or outside? Was there anyone else there that I knew?'

If you can improve your memory for the strange experiences that fill your nights, then you may tap into a rich new source of inspiration for your fiction. Give it a try. And, pleasant dreams! Or, if you prefer, unpleasant.

CRITICISM HURTS; OR, HOW I STOPPED THE BRUTALITY AND CAME TO LOVE WRITERS

Although I've discussed some examples of bad writing from currently publishing writers throughout this book, I haven't mention any authors' names with those examples. I thought I'd pursue that point here because it reflects on how I do my work these days.

When *you* read a book that you don't like, how comfortable do you feel in criticizing the writer's abilities in a public forum? I don't mean when you talk to your best friend about the book. I mean, what do you say about the author in your blog, or in your discussion groups (online or not), or in an Amazon review?

Once upon a time, I would publicly blast those I considered "bad" writers without a second thought. When I was growing up I read quite a few fantasy and SF novels by Lin Carter. I read them because there were a bunch of them available and because they were mostly pastiches of Edgar Rice Burroughs and Robert E. Howard, two authors I adored. But I never made any secret of the fact that I considered Carter a hack, even though Carter was alive at the time.

Many years ago I said in a number of public forums that most of the characters created by a famous writer, whose name I won't mention except to say that it was Stephen King, were predictable stereotypes. I felt not an iota of guilt concerning my words. After all, Stephen King was as rich as Croesus and as powerful in publishing as a...well, Emperor.

I don't feel so smug anymore. And I realize that at least some part of my criticism of King was based on jealousy. As a writer myself now, I know how much it hurts to get criticism on something you worked very hard on. I can also see, to my occasional chagrin, how comfortable most people are with dispensing such criticism. Writers, like actors and politicians, are public figures and the public can be rabid in expressing their like. Or their dislike. But writers and, strange as it may seem, even actors and politicians, are also people. They have feelings, and most of them are probably trying their best even if their best isn't very good.

I find these days that I tend either to avoid public criticism of living writers (dead writers are another story), or I leave out the names and focus on the writing problems themselves. For example, I hardly ever review a book on Amazon that I don't care for, even though I read plenty that aren't very good. If I mention a writing error in my *Illuminata* column I usually leave out the writer's identity.

Sometimes I've wondered if this is not cowardice. Shouldn't I speak the absolute truth and let the chips fall where they may? Well, after thinking about it, I don't consider myself a coward, and here's why.

If I'm writing a review that I'm paid for, I tell the honest truth as I see it, and I don't pull punches although I may seek for wording that is less than brutal. However, no one is forcing me to accept review assignments of material that I don't like. I find that I turn down assignments that would require me to really blast a writer's ineptitude. When it comes to Amazon reviews, which are unpaid, then I figure I can do whatever I damn well please. And in my own column I can choose to leave out an author's name if I want as long as I don't cheat my readers of the "lesson" to be learned in the column.

Finally, of course, I've learned as an adult that criticism is merely an opinion. Too often I have found myself loving a book that a friend of mine hated, or hating one that he or she loved. Criticism can be informed or uninformed, but it can hardly be "right" or "wrong" in the objective sense. Was Hemingway a better writer than Faulkner? They both won the Nobel Prize for literature but many people prefer one over the other. Is Stephen King better than Anne Rice? It depends on who you ask. They each have rabid fans.

And Steve (I call him Steve because he's a public figure and I feel like I know him), I'm sorry I criticized your characters once upon a time. I'm sure you worked hard on them. You're still as rich as Croesus, though.

AN ERROR IN DETAIL

As I mentioned in the last piece, I often find myself reluctant to criticize other writers publicly who I know are trying to make a living and who are, quite likely, doing the best they can. For that reason, even though I'm going to talk in this essay about a serious writing mistake that I've recently seen in print, I'm not going to name names.

I started reading a book not long ago by an SF/Fantasy author who has published many novels and short stories, and whose work I have admired in the past. This book I did not admire, and I went from reading, to scanning, to paging through, to tossing aside. The problem lay in the details, not in the details of grammar or punctuation, or even in the particulars of the prose, but in the details of the description on which the writer *chose* to focus.

For example, at one point the hero needs to burglarize a sorcerer's house to obtain an important item. The windows are barred, so he finagles a jack from a local watchman and climbs up the wall to where he can use the jack to force the bars out of the sill. So far, so good. But then we are treated to *three whole pages* of our hero struggling as he works on the bars. Every drop of sweat and quiver of muscle is lovingly described, which would be fine if our hero's life was at stake while he hung from a cliff a thousand feet in the air. Instead, we are literally left on the outside where it's boring looking in at what promises interest. The scene is simply wasted.

Later, after the hero gets inside the house with his companions, they awaken a guardian demon. *Cool*, I thought. Now we'll see our hero sweat for a good reason. I thought too soon. The buildup to the demon's actual appearance was full of extraneous detail that sucked the atmosphere from the scene, and when the evil being did finally appear it took less time to dispense with him than it had to get the bars out of the window.

Let me point out that the actual description of the break *in* was quite good. I could *feel* the hero tiring as he strained at the bars trying to force his way into the sorcerer's abode. I just didn't *care*. Nothing important hinged upon our hero's struggle at the window, and it had no real effect on his future actions. It was a waste of both the writer's and the reader's time.

Now, if the hero had been given only a few moments to get through the bars before a demon would be released, then we'd have tension. If the hero had come upon the barred window while trying to *escape* from the demon, we'd have tension. But just the fact that something is hard doesn't make it suspenseful. Changing a flat tire is hard, too, and requires a jack. But unless the difficulties of changing a tire somehow affect the plot, so what?

The break in scene, and others like it early in this book, felt very much like padding, as if the writer was trying to stretch a short story into a novel. In fact, I suspect that's exactly what he was doing, and that makes me a little angry. Maybe the guy needed the money, but it's still poor writing, and it may cost him a few bucks out of his pocket in the future. At least, he won't be earning any more money from me. *(Note: About two months after finishing this essay I was in the bookstore and noticed that this writer had two new books out with intriguing titles. I almost bought one, but flashed back to the last one I'd read and kept my wallet in my pocket.)*

Another book that I read recently, a thriller about angels and demons written by an author who regularly hits the bestseller lists (and no, not Dan Brown), had a wasted scene where the main character is going to inspect an ancient painting (it's still not Dan Brown). There was some mystery about the painting and I was geared up to find out what, and then the writer left us cooling our heels in an art gallery waiting area for nearly a full page while he described the jumbled arrangement of a bunch of cardboard boxes. I didn't toss that book aside because there weren't many such lapses, but even the one frustrated me and I don't feel the slightest urge to pick up more of this writer's books.

The real world is rich with, or perhaps cluttered with, immense detail. It would take me many pages just to describe what I see on my writing desk at this moment. Our brains are overloaded by all that immensity and tend to ignore everything but a few choice details. How much *more* the writer has to cut and prune away the excess detail so that readers can get to what they need to know. And while it's OK if my real-world eyes notice something unimportant, it's not OK for a fiction writer to.

Consider again what I see on my desk. Which of the opening paragraphs below suggests the better story? Which presents the details in a way that might tempt you to read a little further?

1. He sat at his black, Compaq EvoN1000c Pentium 4 laptop computer, which was "designed for Microsoft Windows XP" and which had "Intel Inside." To the left on his black metal desk was the single white sheet of a student curriculum report and a nearly full PC Accessories holder for 3 ½ floppies. To his right was a 1 liter (1.05 QT) bottle of Fiji "Natural Artesian Water" with a picture of greenery and a pretty pink bloom on one side. Also on his right was a 50 tablet bottle of Nature Made Super B-Complex vitamins, "with Vitamin C added," a 100 tablet bottle of Centrum Advanced Formula multivitamins, "from A to Zinc®," and a 150 tablet bottle of Original Rolaids antacid in peppermint flavor.

2. He sat at his laptop with a big bottle of Rolaids near to hand.

Choosing the correct details for a scene is far more about elimination than it is about addition. It's like panning for gold. You sift the material again and again until you're left with just the nuggets. Everything else gets tossed on the dross heap.

Show the readers only what they *have* to see. They'll thank you for it. And I'll be happy to name you in print.

ERNEST HEMINGWAY:
A WRITER'S LIFE AND DEATH

Author's Note: Fairly early in my writing career I began studying other writers, not just their works but their lives, in order to better understand this craft I'd involved myself in. Over the years I've written more than fifty short biographies of writers, but the majority of those were done as "work for hire" and I don't own the rights to them anymore. This essay and the next two on Jack London and Kenneth Bulmer are ones that I still have the rights to, and I thought I would print them here. It seems to me that we not-so-famous living scribblers might find some clues to success through studying the lives of our more famous dead brethren. My first choice is Ernest Hemingway, who is one of my favorite authors even though he never wrote SF, Fantasy, or Horror. But hey, even mainstream writers get it right on occasion.

Ernest Miller Hemingway was the son of a medical doctor, a man named Clarence Edmonds Hemingway who much enjoyed fishing and hunting. His mother was Grace Hall, a strong willed woman who had shown early musical talent and who always seemed to feel as if she had given up a promising singing career to become a wife and mother. Mama Hemingway was "high-strung" and had minimal domestic skills. Her six children (four girls and two boys) were placed in the care of a succession of nurses and nannies, hardly an optimal situation for the development of a mother/infant bond. Fortunately, Ernest was an independent and precocious child who learned early to walk and read.

Though Hemingway was born and grew up in Oak Park, Illinois, a Chicago suburb that was filled with more churches than saloons, he later rejected the lifestyle embodied by Oak Park. The single "place" that shaped him most was his family's summer vacation home on Walloon Lake in northern Michigan. Hemingway was only one-year-old when his parents bought land on the Lake and had a cottage built, and there he first learned about hunting and fishing and camping. Many of his earliest professional stories were set in the Michigan woods of his childhood. In fact, the character Nick Adams, who appears in these stories, is only a thinly veiled surrogate for Hemingway.

The young Ernest showed an early interest in and talent for writing. He wrote for his school newspaper and became an editor for it as a Senior. Some of his earliest writings were comedic pieces filled with a rather broad but satirical humor. He did, however, write dramatic fiction as well, often dealing with the Ojibway Indians of Michigan. His father occasionally treated members of the tribe and often took Ernest along.

Hemingway graduated high school during World War I and wanted to enlist. His father forbade it, and Ernest ended up working for a time as a journalist for the *Kansas City Star*. It turned out that Hemingway's eyesight was too bad to let him enter the army anyway, possibly because of injuries from boxing. But by mid-1918 he had joined the Red Cross and made it to Italy by that route.

Hemingway quickly got himself to the front where he could be involved in the fighting, and there is no doubt that he proved his personal courage in battle. He was wounded badly while carrying an injured soldier off the field, but still got the man to an aid station before passing out from blood loss. While in the hospital, Ernest met and fell in love with a nurse who was later to figure prominently in *A Farewell to Arms* (1929).

After Ernest's return to the United States, he continued to work at writing, but with little success. This strained his relationship with his parents, particularly his mother, who asked him to leave the family home and not return unless he was invited. Though the feud soon ended, it left a lasting mark on Ernest.

Soon, Ernest got married, to Hadley Richardson, and the couple moved to Paris, France. Ernest met many other writers in France and traveled extensively over Europe. He was selling newspaper features but struggling to get his stories published. Eventually, he managed to sell a couple of short story collections, but it was a 1926 novel, *The Sun Also Rises*, that established him as a major talent. The book was a bestseller and received critical acclaim in America and Europe. From there, Hemingway's fame rocketed upward.

It wasn't long, however, before Hemingway and Hadley got a divorce and Ernest married Pauline Pfeiffer. With his new wife, Hemingway returned to the States and settled in Key West, Florida. Then, he was punched squarely in the face by tragedy. On December 6, 1928, Ernest's father committed suicide by shooting himself in the head with a Smith & Wesson revolver. Though Ernest seemed to take the elder Hemingway's death in stride, it is notable that he also asked to be given the pistol with which his father had killed himself.

Over the next decade, Hemingway lived the prototypical life of the famous writer. He fished off Cuba, hunted in Arkansas and across the western United states, took in the bull fights in Spain, and went on safari in Africa. He wrote such books as A *Farewell to Arms*, *Death in the Afternoon* (1932), and *Green Hills of Africa* (1935). And always there was the drinking, the wine in Spain and the cold beer of his fishing trips, and in the evening after his writing was done the harder liquors.

The Spanish Civil War came and Hemingway went, to cover it rather than fight it. Hemingway seemed fascinated with the fierce excitement of battle, and he soon got further tastes of war by covering the Japanese invasion of China, and then World War II.

Between the Spanish Civil War and World War II, Hemingway got his second divorce. Another woman was involved and Ernest married *her* barely two weeks after his divorce was final. This marriage was to Martha Gellhorn, but their relationship lasted less than five years. Though the two were sexually compatible, Martha was far too intent on her own career for Hemingway's liking. He needed more support than she could give. In 1946, he married Mary Welsh with the hope of finding what he needed in a wife.

By the time of his fourth marriage, Hemingway had been living in Havana, Cuba for a number of years. There, after World War II ended, he picked up the pace again on his writing. He churned out *Across the River and Into the Trees* (1950), which many critics called a failure, then turned around and wrote his best work and one of the great classics of the English language—*The Old Man and the Sea* (1952). This book won him the Pulitzer and paved his road to the 1954 Nobel Prize in literature.

Though Hemingway had reached the pinnacle where his writing career was concerned, he was in poor health after years of heavy drinking and from suffering through one injury and illness after another, including gunshot wounds, broken bones, an air crash, and sicknesses of many kinds. He was diagnosed with diabetes, a mild case, and began increasingly to suffer bouts of depression in which he despaired of his ability to write. On July 2, 1961, Ernest Hemingway killed himself with a shotgun.

Hemingway's personality traits included that, 1) he showed frequent, severe depression in his later years and may even have attempted suicide by engaging in risky behavior, 2) he was clearly an alcoholic who had been warned frequently by doctors to stop drinking, 3) he showed occasional signs of paranoid thinking, 4) he insisted on being the center of attention, 5) rather than embellish his exploits, he seemed intent on living up to the wildest expectations people had of him, 6) he read voraciously, 7) he took frequent risks with his own life and seemed careless of danger, 8) he was accident prone, and 9) he had, at times, a strained relationship with his mother.

In looking at Hemingway's beliefs we find that, 1) he was an extreme individualist, 2) he placed strong emphasis on personal courage, 3) he seemed to accept a standard view of God and never completely rejected organized religion, 4) he was fascinated with death and the "honor" to be found in dying well, and 5) he believed deeply in love even though he was unable to maintain a long-term relationship with a single woman.

Finally, in examining Hemingway's writing we find that, 1) his gift for storytelling appeared during his teen years, 2) he was very disciplined in his approach to writing, 3) he glorified man in savage conflict with other men, or with such animals as the bull or the big game animals of Africa, 4) his stories and books were descriptive in a pure and austere way, and 5) he created a spare and lean prose that has made him one of the most, if not *the* most, imitated and influential American writers ever.

As a major element of Hemingway's life, we should particularly consider his enjoyment of what might be called "blood sports." This was illustrated clearly in his love of the "corrida," the bullfight. Hemingway was known as an "aficionado" of bullfighting, meaning that his knowledge and love of the sport was respected even by matadors themselves. Hemingway had many bulls dedicated to him during his time in Spain, and he wrote two nonfiction works on the subject, *Death in the Afternoon* and *The Dangerous Summer*, the latter of which was not published in complete form until 1985, years after Hemingway's suicide.

Bullfighting was not Hemingway's only blood sport, however. He enjoyed both watching and participating in boxing (see his short story "Fifty Grand"), and he was a dedicated fisherman. His best nonfiction book, *Green Hills of Africa*, was an unapologetic ode to big game hunting. Finally, Hemingway's fascination with the greatest of all "blood sports" led him to involve himself directly in three wars, World Wars I and II and the Spanish Civil War.

For such a successful person, there are a number of ways in which Hemingway showed immaturity. He married four times before finding a woman he could live with for more than a few years. And the children that he had from his marriages never seemed to figure prominently in his thoughts. His enjoyment of war was another example of immaturity, as was his habit of shooting lit cigarettes from the mouths of friends stupid enough to let him. Hemingway always had to out drink, out fish, and out *do* everyone. It was as if he poured all the maturity he could muster into his writing.

It seems to me that the most characteristic features of Hemingway's life were, 1) pride in his physical abilities and his writing, 2) a love of life, of food, drink, and adventure, 3) an ability to experience the world with passion and intensity, and 4) a radical individualism. These very characteristics may have made it impossible for him to tolerate the gradual loss of his health and talent. The thought of killing himself may, even, have comforted him. The fact that many would have loved to accomplish what Hemingway accomplished doesn't matter. Objective reality is nothing. In Hemingway's mind, he was losing a world that he had made his own, and a shotgun shell was his way to avoid final and inevitable defeat.

If you haven't read Hemingway, let me suggest some places to start. For novels, try *The Old Man and the Sea* before you read any of his others. Two of his best short stories, from the collection *The Short Stories*, are "The Snows of Kilimanjaro" and "The Short Happy Life of Francis Macomber." *Green Hills of Africa* is excellent nonfiction, but be aware that it does involve the hunting and killing of game animals. There is also a great little book called *Ernest Hemingway on Writing*, from Simon & Schuster, 1984, which is a collection of his comments about writing. These are mostly taken from his letters and put together by Larry Phillips, and there is great advice to be had in these pages.

Whatever you do, don't start with *The Torrents of Spring*. This is Hemingway attempting satire, at a very early stage in his career, and it reads more like juvenilia to me. In today's parlance, I thought it sucked.

JACK LONDON:
TWO-FISTED WRITER

Author's Note: Like Hemingway, Jack London is an icon in American literary history. He also is one of my favorite writers, and definitely not a "kid" writer as some claim. Of course, you know about Call of the Wild *and* White Fang, *but try* The Star Rover *or some of his short stories if you really want to see him rock. His "To Build a Fire" and "A Piece of Steak" are two of the best short stories ever written in English.*

Jack London was born in California in 1876 to Flora Wellman and W. H. Chaney, a writer and scientific astrologer. Chaney never married Jack's mother, however, and some eight months after the boy's birth Flora took John London as her husband and the father of her son. London was a quiet man, a talented farmer who was no match for Flora's ambitions and spendthrift ways. (She would almost certainly be considered "neurotic" today.) The family was often broke and moved frequently, living sometimes on farms and sometimes in the cities of Oakland and San Francisco.

Young Jack was an independent child, often spending his time alone. By the age of thirteen he'd saved enough money from working odd jobs to buy a small boat and had learned to sail it in the sheltered areas of the coast. He'd also discovered books and he read for long hours.

At seventeen, Jack took his first sea voyage, on a fast schooner bound for the far east. For the next several years, Jack alternated periods of steady labor as a "wage slave" with other periods of wild adventure, including a stint riding the rails as a hobo and a journey to the Klondike territory during the gold rush of 1896.

London's "adventures" provided fodder for the stories already bubbling in his brain, but it was the months of back breaking labor and thirty days spent in jail for vagrancy that made him a socialist. For the rest of his life, Jack London was to combine a powerful sense of personal individualism with an intellectual desire to see capitalism replaced with a system fairer to the working man.

Through hard work, an iron determination, a willingness to skate the edge of dangers both physical and intellectual, and a talent for words, Jack London powered himself into a position as one of the best known and most widely respected American writers of the turn of the century period. He wrote everything, from poems and stories, to scholarly articles on grammar, to informed tracts on socialism. His breakthrough to fame came in 1903 with the publication of *The Call of the Wild*, which was widely hailed as a triumph. *The Sea Wolf* in 1904 and *White Fang* in 1906 cemented London's position atop the publishing heap.

But while London's fortunes as a writer were increasing, the ship of his personal life had sprung its first leak. He left his wife of just three years (Bessie Maddern) and his two young daughters to marry Charmian Kittredge, who was often to prove more of a stress on his life than a balm. Charmian *was* better able than Bessie to share the adventures that Jack craved—she joined him in sailing, riding and hunting—but she was also immature and seldom tried to make Jack's writing life easier. As an example, for many years she resisted Jack's wish to hire a secretary, probably out of fear that another woman might steal her husband away.

Still, Jack London wrote well, turning out a thousand words a day despite whatever adventures, illnesses, or entertainments came his way. He wrote *Martin Eden* (1909), *Burning Daylight* (1910), *John Barleycorn* (1913), and *The Star Rover* (1914), all of which stand as important American novels, and he turned out short stories that changed the way readers and writers looked at the short form.

By 1914, however, London's health, spirit, and career were flagging. A series of emotional and economic catastrophes took their toll. After years of work and immense cost, London's dream home, called the "Wolf House," burned down just before he could move in. Arson was suspected. And, despite earning many thousands of dollars a year he was always in debt, partly because of the generous nature that saw him give money away like water, and partly because, like his mother, Jack was prone to making poor investments and having bad luck.

Even the debts might not have hurt London so badly if he had not begun to realize how people were taking advantage of him. The periodic bouts of melancholy that had occasionally plagued him over the years began to occur more frequently. He started to drink heavily, and for the first time since his youth began to drink alone and to show signs of drunkenness. His health deteriorated and he lost interest in those things that had once given him pleasure, including his writing. Finally, on November 21, a Tuesday night in 1916, Jack fell into a coma and despite heroic efforts to save him died late the next day.

For years it was believed by many that London died a suicide from an overdose of sister morphine. This myth seems to have gotten started, perhaps, from the fact that the initial doctor on the scene as London lay dying diagnosed the cause of London's coma as an overdose of morphine, two empty vials of which were reportedly found by the writer's bedside. When other doctors arrived, that diagnosis was changed—with agreement from the first doctor on the scene—so that on London's death certificate the cause of death is listed as "uremia," which is produced by the inability of the kidneys to remove toxins from the bloodstream. London had been suffering for some time from kidney problems.

Despite the death certificate, many later biographers accepted and promulgated the theory that London had died a suicide. In fact, London's "suicide" became "common knowledge," so much so that many reference texts simply assumed that the suicide was a fact. The resulting myth became widespread. There have been people who have tried for many years to correct the error, but until the late 1990s relatively few biographies consistently espoused the view that London died of uremia.

There are a number of important points about Jack London to consider, including aspects concerning his personality, his beliefs, and the recurrent themes found in his writing. Among his personality traits we find that, 1) he suffered from periodic bouts of moodiness that got worse during the later stages of his life, 2) he had a problem with alcohol, 3) he showed occasional paranoid thinking, 4) he often proved generous to a fault, 5) he was physically promiscuous, though capable of showing great emotional loyalty, 6) he would occasionally exaggerate or embellished his own exploits, 7) he had a strained and difficult relationship with his mother, 8) he was a voracious reader, and 9) he knew that he was, literally, a "bastard."

Among London's beliefs we find that, 1) he was politically a socialist, 2) he was personally an individualist with a strong sense of his own abilities, 3) he was an atheist, and 4) he accepted Darwin's theory of evolution and believed in taking a scientific approach to civilization.

Finally, in looking at London's approach to writing and the themes that he investigated, we find that, 1) his gift for words and storytelling revealed itself in his teenage years, 2) he was extremely disciplined in his approach to writing, both in doing the necessary research and in putting words on paper, 3) he often glorified the savage in conflict with other savages or with the violence of nature, 4) he explored the concept of reincarnation, 5) his stories were richly descriptive, and 6) he essentially created a new form of realistic and passionate fiction that changed the way later writers worked.

Much like Hemingway, who I considered in my last essay, Jack London was an aficionado of the "blood sports." He was a boxing fan, for example, and he wrote one of the best boxing stories ever put on paper, a tale called "A Piece of Steak," which appeared in *Best Short Stories of Jack London* (1945). Undoubtedly, London also witnessed dog fights in the Klondike, though there is little to suggest that he enjoyed such sport. In fact, London appears to have been rather soft-hearted where *animals* were concerned. Any soft-heartedness that London had didn't stop his race to cover the outbreak of war between Japan and Russia in 1904, however. His biggest complaint about that trip was the Japanese government's attempts to keep him away from the front and the killing.

Jack London was a master of diversity in writing. He wrote novels, incredible short stories, scholarly articles on grammar, and essays and books on socialism. He wrote quality literature that earned him a lasting reputation, and he churned out pot-boilers to make money. His novels explored such diverse fields as human evolution, savage man against savage nature, and thinly disguised autobiography, the last especially in his books *Martin Eden* and *John Barleycorn*. The former was a sailor, the latter a drunkard. London had been both.

Also like Hemingway, London often revealed an immature side to his personality. His most immature act was leaving his first wife after barely three years of marriage, effectively deserting two daughters who were both younger than three. Though he did offer monetary support to his children, he took little part in their lives until, not long before his death, he tried to make some amends.

Like Hemingway, London was also quick to dash off on an adventure without worrying much about those he left behind. A war might attract him here. The sudden urge to sail around the world might grab him there. He picked up and went. And despite the large amount of money he made from his writing, London still spent more than he made, often on spur of the moment purchases or ill-conceived speculations.

Again, like Hemingway, Jack London was an immensely proud man who lived life with passion and intensity. And he also possessed a radical individualism. He, too, at the time of his death, was experiencing increasingly poor health, partly because of drinking, and he seemed to have despaired of his ability to continue to write well. Even if he did not literally commit suicide, he certainly took little care to stave off his decline.

I suspect that in both London and Hemingway there existed a darkness and violence in the depths of their souls. Both were, in their way, death lovers. They wrote about it, thought about it, tempted it. I believe that death was no enemy to these men. It was a fate they had been writing their way toward throughout their entire lives.

KEN BULMER:
A DEATH IN THE FAMILY

Author's Note: The following is basically a eulogy written after the death of a writer who I greatly admired. I think it has something to say to the audience of this book.

Eventually, all writers start to lose their literary idols and influences. One of mine was Henry Kenneth Bulmer, a British writer who passed away at 12:30 AM on December 16, 2005 at the age of 84. Ken, as he preferred to be called, had been seriously disabled since a stroke in 1997, and yet, according to friends of mine who visited him, had maintained his dignity and sense of humor throughout the years. Ken's funeral was held in Tunbridge Wells, England on December 30, 2005. He is survived by his wife, Pamela, who he married in 1953, and by two daughters and a son.

Ken Bulmer was born in London in 1921 and became an early fan of science fiction. After a stint in the British Signal Corps during World War II, he returned home and began writing for and publishing SF fanzines. His first novel was a collaboration with another fan and was published in 1952 as *Space Treason*, but by 1954 he was writing independently and had turned pro. He wrote close to 170 novels and numerous short stories for British, American, and European markets. Many of his books were SF or fantasy, but many others weren't, and because he wrote under numerous pseudonyms and house names it's sometimes difficult to track down his work. Chances are you've read more than one of his books without knowing it.

Two of Bulmer's pseudonyms are of particular interest to fantasy fans, the one genre that I consider to be my favorite. He wrote three excellent sword & sorcery novels under the name Manning Norvil, each of which got better than the one before. These featured a character named Odan: The Half-God, and are *Dream Chariots*, *Whetted Bronze*, and *Crown of the Sword* God. Ken also wrote fifty-two books and a novella in the Dray Prescot Sword & Planet series, which were modeled on the Martian books of Edgar Rice Burroughs. Many of the Prescot books were written under the name Alan Burt Akers, although the later ones were credited to Prescot himself, who was the hero of the series. Only the novella and thirty-seven of the Prescot books were published in English, all by DAW Books. Despite the fact that they were written in English, the remaining books were printed only in Germany where there is a big Bulmer fan base.

Efforts are currently underway by fan groups to try and get the remaining Prescot books published in English, but money seems to be a sticking point in the process. Recently, Mushroom Books has started republishing the early works in the series in electronic format, and have been able to acquire the German-only ones as well. These are available in e-book right now, and can be found at Mushroom's website or at Amazon.

Several of Bulmer's house names might also be of interest to fantasy fans. He wrote two novels as Neil Langholm for a series about a Viking hero, #2 *The Dark Return*, and #4 *Trail of Blood*. He also wrote two books in the Gladiator series—long before the Russell Crowe movie—under the name Andrew Quiller.These were #2 *The Land of Mist*, and #5 *Sea of Swords*. He ghost wrote two novels for Barry Sadler in the Casca series, *Panzer Soldier* and *The Mongol*, and he wrote several books in the "Slaves of the Empire" series under the name Dael Forest. These were set in Roman times and seemed designed to capitalize on the Gor phenomenon, although they were extremely mild by Gorean standards. I'm still trying to figure out exactly which ones Ken did in this series.

Much of Ken's SF was written under the name Kenneth Bulmer, although he also wrote two decent fantasies under that name, *Kandar* and *The Diamond Contessa*. His SF would probably be defined mostly as space opera. *Some* of it certainly was, perhaps best exemplified by his "Ryder Hook" series under the pseudonym Tully Zetford, which were printed with the subhead "Star-Spanning Man of the Future." However, most of the SF works under Ken's own name contained generous doses of social commentary along with the adventure. Some were even social satires.

Bulmer's other pseudonyms included Frank Brandon, Rupert Clinton, Ernest Corley, Peter Green, Adam Hardy, Philip Kent, Bruno Krauss, Karl Maras, Chesman Scot, Nelson Sherwood, Richard Silver, H. Philip Stratford, and Ken Blake. Adam Hardy is probably the best known of these. Bulmer used it on fourteen books in the "Fox" series, about a kind of Horatio Hornblower character, and then wrote another six under that name in a series about the Falklands War. Many of the other pseudonyms were also used for series of war novels, but Ken Blake was a house name for some TV tie-in novels for the British series, *The Professionals*, a long-running crime show. Bulmer even wrote a western novel in the Jubal Cade series under the name Charles R. Pike. His was #11, *Brand of Vengeance*.

Bulmer served as president of the first amateur press association in Great Britain and remained active in SF/Fantasy fandom throughout much of his life. He was definitely a fan's writer and happily attended cons where he was a popular draw. In 1974 he was made a lifetime member of the British SF Association, a well deserved honor.

How good of a writer was Kenneth Bulmer? Well, I've come to realize over the years the truth of the saying, "one man's trash is another man's treasure." I have friends who consider Bulmer a hack. I can't agree. I tend to like his fantasy and historical work quite a bit more than his SF, but some of his fantasies are truly excellent. His Dray Prescot series was also an influence on my own Sword & Planet writing. (Although he had little effect on my horror and SF work.) And I'm certainly not the only one Bulmer has influenced. I personally know at least six writers from Europe and America who have written pastiches of the Prescot series.

I'll not make the claim here that Bulmer was a great writer in the sense of transcending his subject matter. I do know that I like him enough to systematically collect his work, and I think of him as a solid professional who consistently turned out interesting and imaginative stories. He even had a good dose of poetry in his soul, and he never forgot his roots among the fans.

For more about Bulmer, see his entry on Wikipedia, which lists most of his works. There's also a yahoo group dedicated to him. It's called Kregen, and I'm a member of it. Kregen was the name of the world where Bulmer's most famous character, Dray Prescot, had his adventures.

Ken, I miss you.

WHERE HAVE ALL
THE GOOD THEMES GONE?

At an SF convention a number of years ago I had a short, but rather cutting, disagreement with the fiction editor of a very large science fiction and science fact magazine. She was trying to be helpful with some suggestions about what editors look for in submissions.

Given the major magazine markets at that time, and now, I'm sure she really *was* helpful. The only problem was that I completely disagreed with her idea of what was good fiction and what was bad. In fact, I finally quit subscribing to her magazine because I found the fiction...well...boring.

Oh, the writing was technically flawless. It had nice musical phrasings and was accompanied by beautiful illustrations. But, unfortunately, nothing ever happened in the stories. They started out vaguely, and they ended even worse. I found them quite trivial, in the sense that they gave me no satisfaction from having read them. I didn't feel afraid, or sad, or happy, or filled with awe. They never even drove out the background noise of passing cars and the worries over the monthly bills. At least I would have liked them to do that.

Of course, I'm certain that the editor would disagree with me, and, who knows, maybe she's right. She is certainly better known that I am. But, as readers have said for many years, I know what I like. And the stuff in her magazine wasn't it. I also think that there are quite a few others out there like me, as indicated, perhaps, by the fact that subscriptions to her magazine plummeted to the point where they began to publish only online to save money and eventually went belly-up.

What my argument with this editor made me wonder was, where have all the good themes gone? She is still an editor, in a much smaller venue, and I believe she would routinely reject anything that smacked of space opera, or barbarian heroes. Even if it was good space opera she would reject it because, in a paraphrase of her words, "It's been done before." She seemed so caught up, as are many other editors and writers, in the pursuit of something new, unique, original, that she was forgetting about plot and story. I mean, why do people pick up fiction? They do so because they want to be entertained.

Now, I can see you asking where I'm coming from. And I have to tell you that I don't believe myself to be a blithering idiot who can't handle sentences of more than three words. But I work damn hard during the day. I'm a teacher, and reading makes up a great deal of my work, from essays, to textbooks, to scientific journal reports. I don't want to come home and struggle through some drifting, vapid, but "literary" short story. I want some action, some escape. What's wrong with that? I don't care if you have evil sorcerers, or FTL ships, or laser fights. I like that sort of stuff. I don't want to read *exactly* the same thing I've read before, but I'm asking, nay pleading, for writers and editors to realize that there is still a lot of ore in those old mines.

It seems that book publishers generally still realize this, though I'm not sure how long that will last. Personally, I find myself buying fewer and fewer new books and instead looking for older ones that I haven't read yet. But at least the publishers still print Star Trek® novels and books with elves and dragons in them. For magazines, though, it seems to me that some of the editors have forgotten that you have to give the customer what he or she wants. I don't think this is true of the small press so much as it is for the slicks, but the big magazines, including those for SF, Fantasy, and Horror, are seeing a steady fall-off in subscriptions and some of them are even moving away from fiction. Could it be they're not publishing the kind of fiction people like to read?

I'm not saying that writers should write pastiches. I hardly ever read pastiches. I'm not looking for hackwork that repeats some mindless formula. What I am saying is: don't ignore an idea, such as the generation starship, or the cyborg soldier, or a hundred others, just because it's been done before. And editors, I'm saying the same thing to you. The new is not inevitably better. Think of this. Reproduction is a pretty old topic. It's been done a few times in books and movies. But do you think people are tired of talking about sex? Do you think they're tired of *having* sex?

For SF, Fantasy, and Horror, too, there is still good wine to be found in old skins. The ideas that captivated my generation and others still hold power. Editors and publishers, if writers can find a way to dress up a great old idea in great new fashion, then give them a chance in the marketplace. If it's a choice between a lovingly written sword & planet novel that pays homage to Burroughs, and a literary quality short story set on Mars in which nothing happens but an argument between two characters, then I know which one I'm going to choose to read and which one I'm going to wipe my you-know-what on.

People still enjoy a well-told tale in the grand tradition. Let's give it to 'em.

WRITING WEATHER

In case you don't live where I live and aren't aware, southern Louisiana has a *warm* climate. It's mid-November as I write this, and in the 70s today. At night it drops into the 40s and 50s, occasionally into the 30s.

We had our first light frost where I live on the north shore of Lake Pontchartrain, across from New Orleans, on November 20, and tonight it's a little cool to be outside without a jacket. Throughout October and the first part of November, however, I could sit out on my deck most nights in a T-shirt and listen to the rattle of falling leaves on the tin roof. It's almost an imitation autumn.

But faux fall or not, even in a Louisiana October I found my energy levels for writing fiction start to surge. It has always been this way for me. I write better when it's starting to grow cold, and better yet in the dead of winter when the trees stand quiet and barren and waiting for spring.

Something in winter has always inspired me, and I believe it has to do with the edge of melancholia that is wetted in me by the first seasonal chill. I grow just a touch sad. Not depressed. I don't weep for lost summer or contemplate suicide. I'm merely a little more attuned to the darker emotions and darker thoughts that come creeping into my mind like the chill that creeps into our homes. And I find that in writing horror or fantasy those emotions are the engine that drives my imagination.

For me, I also find that rain—any rain but especially if it's cold—makes for good writing weather. If there's a little wind to spank the trees into motion that's even better. And if it's storming, I often turn off my computer and take a notepad and pen and venture onto the deck where the air can bite me. I like to huddle in a chair, close enough to the world so that I catch a faint mist from the raindrops as they explode against the corner of the roof. The writing comes easy then, or easier at least.

Do you have writing weather? I bet you do. Maybe it's in the spring when a young man's (or woman's) fancy turns to literature. Or maybe you write best in the wet, panting heat of midsummer, with a cold drink to blot the sweat on your forehead and a ceiling fan whispering lazily above you.

No more complaining about the weather. Let it help you instead. Find *your* weather and I bet you'll find your muse. One of them at least. I know I'm hoping for another frost tonight. Maybe the cold will bring me a tale, something wicked for whispering around a winter fire.

WHAT THE WRITER WANTS

Ever wonder what writers are really like? Ever wish you could find an easy way to break the ice with authors at parties so you can ask them to write up your brilliant idea for a movie? Or maybe you've considered becoming a writer yourself but are afraid you lack the qualifications? Don't worry. This little guide will tell you everything you need to know about writers and their desires.

1. Writers are eager to hear criticisms from readers about every element of their published work. They especially like it when such terms as "sucked" are used. After all, how can the writer get better without detailed feedback. Don't worry that you might hurt a writer's feelings. They are toughened to criticism, sort of like the marines of the artistic world.

2. A published book sells a lot of copies and makes the writer wads of cash so they will be happy to give *you* a copy for free. The mere fact that you'd like a copy of their work is reward enough. In fact, most writers have a large number of copies printed up at their own expense for just such a purpose.

3. You don't want to interrupt a writer at work, but, fortunately, most authors typically only work two or three hours a day. Here's some ways to tell whether they are working or not. A) If they aren't typing then they aren't working and can freely be interrupted. B) If they're reading then they aren't working and can be freely inter-rupted. C) Writing isn't a real job anyway so it's not like interrupt-ing them is going to upset them or anything.

4. In the introduction to this piece I mentioned that some people are afraid to approach writers about putting their personal ideas and stories into words. Balderdash! Writers never have enough ideas of their own and are desperate to hear more from perfect strangers. Of

course the writer will be happy to write that idea up and share the profits with said stranger. This benefits both parties.

5. Much like medical doctors and lawyers, writers are eager to give free advice and consultations on their area of expertise to total strangers. They are especially happy to fix grammar problems so that a work becomes instantly salable. When you work only two or three hours a day you have a lot of free time to fill.

6. Writers are superb party guests. They're good with words, after all, so they are always capable of engaging in witty repartee. If you really want to see them at their best, make sure to put them on the spot by asking them publicly to get up in front of your guests and tell a spur-of-the-moment story that is both poignant and funny.

7. In regards to #6 above, writers lead exciting lives, filled with frequent jettings to New York for champagne brunches with their agents, and with blockbuster, multi-city tours where they dine at only five star restaurants and sleep on silk sheets at only the finest hotels. These will be some of their most exciting stories. Make sure and ask them to drop in names of some of the famous people they've met, like Tom Cruise or Paris Hilton.

8. If you want to get your foot in the door as a writer, be sure and ask any writer you meet to read your manuscripts in progress. They'll be happy to do so, free of charge, and if they like it—which I'm sure they will—they'll be glad to recommend you to their agent, editor, or publisher. This will save you a lot of time and effort in getting your own writing career jumpstarted.

9. Writers are, of course, crazy. At least the good ones are. But this is why they are entertaining. Feel free to ask them such questions as: "What happened to you in *your* childhood?" Or: "I've always heard that writers are mostly gay. Is that true?" Part of the reason why writers are crazy is because they all drink heavily and/or do drugs. Ask them to tell you about their heroin binges with Stephen King.

10. Writers have a lot of groupies, and this goes for both male and female writers. They will be happy to share the largesse with you. You haven't lived until you've experienced a fivesome with a drugged-up, crazy writer who wants to role-play from their latest opus about the fourteen sexes of Planet Liango.

11. Writers believe everything they write. For example, if a writer has a ghost in their story then you can rest assured they believe in ghosts. Similarly, you can judge all writers' personal philosophies by studying their characters. Writers who create a racist character are certainly to be racist themselves. This is a guideline for finding common conversational points with the writer.

12. Writing comes easy for those who have the talent. One just sits down and words and sentences unspool from the central storage unit in the writer's magnificent brain. This makes writing actually the laziest job anyone could have. Writers have it made. Feel free to tell them this repeatedly. It's something they never get tired of hearing. Just watch their faces beam.

And now my fellow travelers, I must leave you for my muse has called and I sense an epic trilogy coming on. That could take me most of the rest of the day. Then it's off to chat with Brad and Angelina about my script for their upcoming movie.

Where's my nymphomaniac secretary with the coffee and the cocaine?

REST IN PEACE: SHORT STORY

Every once in a while you'll hear it. The short story is dead. Even the thought makes me mourn. I like short stories. I like to read them and I like to write them. They are a very different kind of art form from novels, and sometimes they are the *perfect* form.

No novel could express so well the ideas behind Tom Godwin's "The Cold Equations," Lester Del Rey's "Helen O'Loy," or Arthur C. Clarke's "The Nine Billion Names of God." No novel could maintain the absolute horror that suffuses the entire length of Joe Lansdale's "The Steel Valentine." John D. MacDonald's "Hangover" tells a story that could never be sustained at novel length, and yet it ends with—to me—the most horrific moment in all of literature. And there are reasons why "Flowers for Algernon" by Daniel Keyes and "Nightfall" by Isaac Asimov work better as stories than when expanded to novels.

We humans live our days as moments. Just as novels are made up of scenes, so too are our lives. Even if our lives are epic, we don't experience them that way. Usually a life is judged as epic only after the person is dead and being written about. The short story better reflects the reality of how we actually live. We lose it at the risk of losing ourselves.

Fortunately, I don't believe the short story form is quite dead, although I do think it's hurting. In the 1930s Robert E. Howard made a good living from writing short stories. James Sallis has talked of earning pretty good money from short stories in the 1970s, money that he could not get for those stories today. He writes novels almost exclusively now because there is no economic incentive to do otherwise. Heck, I made more money myself from short stories in the 1990s than I do now, which is part of the reason I'm writing a lot more nonfiction these days.

There *are* markets for stories today, of course, but the circulation for most magazines is down, money is tighter, and many magazines are cutting back on fiction, leaving a lot of competition for the remaining story slots. If you want to give your stories away for nothing you can find places on the net that might take them, although even there you'll find competition. But I don't believe any writer just starting out could make a living from short stories. I don't believe even an established writer could make a living unless, perhaps, they were picking up royalty checks on a lot of older stories and collections.

What does all this mean for those of you who still want to write short stories? Well, it means that you need to write them for other reasons than just to make money. And it means you need to be creative in finding outlets.

A lot of small online magazines run a mix of stories and poetry, and some of them are paying markets. I often find them by checking the links to other writers' blogs. Entering contests is another way to find possible markets, and newsletters like *The Illuminata,* local newspapers, and supplemental magazines sometimes use fiction.

Or join online writers' groups and work with other members to put together a contest or publish a group anthology. (I had a story in *The Parasitorium: Terrors Within,* which came out of a yahoo group on writing, and it received honorable mention in *Year's Best Fantasy and Horror* 2005 while the anthology itself was nominated for a Stoker.) Maybe some of you even have what it takes to start your *own* magazine. Do the things that connect you with other writers, and through those connections you'll find opportunities.

Finally, remember that if you love writing short fiction you need to support it wherever it appears. At the risk of sounding a little harsh, those of you who only read novels and never think about short stories (or poetry) should perhaps consider the following paraphrase of a rather famous quote.

First they came for the poets, but I wasn't a poet so I did nothing. Then they came for writers of short stories, but I never read or wrote stories and so I did nothing. Then they came for the novelists and the readers of novels, and I was one of those. But by that time there was no one left to do anything for me.

FIVE YEARS DOWN THE ROAD

Author's Note: The following is a retrospective that I wrote in October of 2006 for The Illuminata, *the online newsletter to which I contribute a writing column. It summarizes many of the major points that I've talked about over five years with that newsletter, and also reiterates some of the "tips" that I've given for writers in this collection. I thought it might be good piece to end part 2 of the book. I hope you find it useful.*

Five years for *The Illuminata* now. In that time Bret Funk, the editor/publisher, has missed putting out one issue. Dare we call it the "Katrina Issue?" I've been in a lot of magazines that didn't last that long or publish that regularly. Bret deserves kudos for his work ethic, and for his energy. But so do we who've scribed for this fine newsletter. I'm giving myself a figurative pat on the back even as I write this. And I wish *The Illuminata* happy birthday.

This makes the forty-fourth column that *I've* done for the newsletter. Maybe it's time for a retrospective, a look back at the main points I've made over the years. Here they are.

1. Ideas are everywhere for the plucking, in the fiction and non-fiction that you read, in the movies you watch and the people you meet. Childhood memories are one of the greatest sources, but don't forget your nightly dreams.

2. Ideas are only the beginning. You have to work your ideas, like kneading bread before you bake it. Put them through boot camp so that they can be all they can be. A good way to do this is to interrogate your ideas. Ask them questions. Demand answers. But don't necessarily accept the first answer you get. Dig deep.

3. Don't try to manufacture a style for yourself. Write and keep on writing, and your style and voice will develop organically.

4. Don't worry about money at first. Keep the focus on the words you're working. In the publishing world, the "writing" is the only thing you can control.

5. Develop your writing "tools." That is, educate yourself about vocabulary, grammar, and punctuation. You have to know the mechanics or you'll never write up to your potential. Just reading good writers will help you pick up the nuances of language and how it is used, but reference books are a necessity. If you need more, consider taking a refresher course at a local college.

6. Learn about other writers. See how they practice—or practiced—their craft. And don't ignore *any* genre of writing. Every writer and every genre has something to teach you.

7. The "telling" detail is the key to writing memorable prose. This is the detail that grabs and holds the reader's attention in any given scene. Mine your memories for such details. Think of events *you've* experienced. What details come immediately to mind? *Those* were the telling details for you.

8. Openings and endings are the most important parts of your work. Openings sell the piece you're submitting. Endings sell your next piece. Make 'em sing.

9. Readers like sympathetic characters.

10. Make contact with other writers. Let them help you flesh out ideas and give you emotional support. And return the favor. Writing really is a lonely business, but you don't have to be alone every second.

11. Rewrite everything. Multiple times.

12. Finish what you start, even if you can only get there by adding one good paragraph a day. Paragraphs add up to pages, and pages to stories and articles and books. Then submit what you've finished.

13. Learn how to properly format your submissions. There are plenty of books that can help, and you can usually find exactly the information you need in a magazine's "guidelines." These can be found inside the magazine itself, or, usually, online. Give the editors what they want in the way they want it.

14. You'll get rejections. Let them make you angry if you must, but *don't* let them make you stop.

15. Most importantly, *write*! Butt in chair; hands on the keyboard. Or however you have to do it. Just get it done.

PART THREE

I have wrought my simple plan
If I give one hour of joy
To the boy who's half a man,
Or the man who's half a boy.

—Arthur Conan Doyle

A WRITER ON THE RUN

Author's Note: After Hurricane Katrina beat the crap out of New Orleans in August of 2005, I became—for a while—a writer on the run. The following essay is the story of my first few months after the disaster.

New Orleans. Arkansas.
Arkansas. New Orleans.
Baton Rouge. Austin.
I'm a writer on the run. And though I know I'm not the only one, that doesn't help a lot.

When the approach of Hurricane Katrina drove us out of New Orleans, we went to that place where they have to take you in. We drove ten hours north to my mom's house in the little town of Charleston, Arkansas. Like a fool, I failed to bring my computer. I had disks with copies of my files, but halfway to mom's I remembered that there were things on my hard drive that I'd never saved on disk. I'd only emailed copies to my office computer, which was also trapped in New Orleans on the campus of Xavier University.

Why hadn't I brought my home computer? Maybe it was some hybrid of panic and complacency—panic at the thought of a category five hurricane rolling like a blitzkrieg toward us, complacency at the thought of half a dozen previous evacuations that had seen storms bypass us safely to the east. Then this latest storm hit, and the water came in, and I realized we weren't going back to New Orleans anytime soon.

Even without a computer I could have written. It doesn't take technology to create. I had paper and pens. But I didn't have the will. It takes commitment to write, and the only commitment I could give during those days was to the news. I wondered about my apartment and my things, and I watched in vain for pictures of my area. But mostly I wondered and worried about my friends, about whether they had gotten out or not. That worry intensified daily as I saw the city convulse in agony and insanity.

The local high school librarian was a relative of mine and we were able to use the internet there. I began to hear from a few friends, although there were plenty of others who had not yet checked in. And there was virtually no news about my university. I didn't know if I still had a job, or health care, or if I would get any pay for the fall semester. My fiancée, Lana, was in much the same boat, though not a boat as literal as those plying the streets of a slowly sinking New Orleans.

We could have stayed with my family for a month if need be. But my mom is nearly eighty-nine and she is fragile. She had just lost a daughter—my sister—a month earlier, and I didn't want to put more strain on her just when I should be doing things to ease her worries. Then we heard that they were going to let people back into the New Orleans area to get some things before closing the city off entirely. Besides my computer, I needed clothes and wanted to get a few books to read. Mostly I wanted to see if there was anything left of our home.

So back to New Orleans we went, scrounging for gas that was nearly impossible to find south of Eudora, Arkansas. To conserve fuel and ease the strain on our 1991 Thunderbird, we drove with the AC off and the windows down. We sweltered but we made it, even though we sat in bumper to bumper traffic for hours as we tried to get into Metairie along the one route allowed to us by the military.

I often complain about my bad luck, but I found out just how lucky I could be when we arrived at our apartment and found it intact. While many apartments around ours had roofs torn off, *we* even had electricity and a phone line. But we didn't have water or working toilets and we could not stay.

Even though I had my computer this time, leaving New Orleans again was harder than it had been before. We had no idea when we'd be allowed to return, and we had no true destination. After an aimless few hours on the road, we found—miracle of miracles—a seedy motel on the outskirts of Baton Rouge that had a single room for rent. We took it, and that night reached a decision.

Lana had been able to get in touch with her work and they wanted her to come to Austin, Texas. Any permanent relocation to Austin was impossible for me. I'd heard by then that my University *hoped* to reopen in the spring, and my son would also be trying to go to school in the city. I had to be with him. But we also needed money and Lana's boss had promised us a place to stay. Even though we were sick of the road and of living out of gym bags, seven hours in the car took us into Austin.

Lana's company put us up temporarily at an Extended Stay America, and for the first time in weeks I was able to set up my computer and get internet access. I hoped I might be able to make some badly needed money from writing, and within a day I was word-slinging again, but only on some nonfiction articles for which I had contracts and deadlines. I found that I couldn't write fiction. I tried. But while nonfiction can be produced with the mind alone, fiction requires something more. It takes heart. It takes emotion. And of those I was freshly burned out.

We spent just over two months in Austin, moving after a week into a one bedroom apartment with camp cots to sleep on and borrowed lawn furniture for a table and chairs. Lana worked across the street during the days and I alternated between staying home to write and going to the University of Texas at Austin where I'd been offered an office, a computer, and access to the libraries. (It's nice sometimes to have an academic affiliation.)

We found an eviction notice on our apartment door one day when we got home, but after some discussion with the manager of the complex we got that straightened out. Red Cross was generous enough to pay one month's rent for us, but the check was a little late in coming and the manager's assistant thought she was just doing her job by telling us to get out. I don't blame the Red Cross; they were swamped with pleas for help and I think they did a wonderful job as efficiently as they could. They even gave us a credit card worth 700 bucks, for the price of me standing in line for half a dozen hours, and that came in handy since we had no bedding, no cookware or dishes, and not a lot of clothes.

At the end of October I thought I'd been fired by Xavier University, along with about half the rest of the faculty. People who were being hired back were sent contracts via email. I didn't get one, although I didn't get a termination email either. I emailed the Vice President, in quite a state of panic as you might expect. Twenty-four hours later I got a note saying that my contract *had been* emailed but had apparently bounced; I got a new one. I've never quite gotten over that twenty-four hour period, though, when I thought my academic career was over and my future in doubt. I know that for quite a few of my friends that period of fear and doubt didn't end. They *were* fired.

Not long before Thanksgiving Lana's work moved back to the Greater New Orleans area and we came home too. My eighteen-year old son, Joshua, had been staying for a while at our apartment in

Metairie, a suburb of New Orleans. He'd previously been hanging with his mom in Mississippi but wanted to come home to be around his girlfriend. He found an eviction notice on that door too when he first came back, although he got that straightened out eventually. (We'd tried to contact the apartment office for weeks by phone but had gotten no answer.)

During the two months of our evacuation I completed almost thirty short biographical essays on writers, for a decent amount of cash, and wrote a grant that may just possibly have saved my job. After I got back to the New Orleans area I continued to turn out non-fiction, but even months later the fiction well remained dry. Part of it was just the grinding workload once we got back to school in the spring of 2006; we were badly understaffed and trying to teach with minimal facilities and support. But part of it was my still missing heart and lost emotions.

Will I get them back? I hope I will. I believe I will.

I guess we'll see.

Author's End Note: It's August 2007 as I write this addendum to "A Writer on the Run." It's been almost exactly two years since Katrina. Large parts of Greater New Orleans still lie devastated and Lana and I have actually moved thirty miles north to a small community called Abita Springs, Louisiana. I still work at Xavier, which is struggling to recover, but Lana and I both needed to escape the city. We have a place in the country now, and though I certainly don't enjoy the commute it's good to see trees and stars again. It reminds me of where I grew up.

I've made a partial return to writing fiction. Some nights my heart comes all the way up to the window on the wings of whip-poorwills. Sometimes it hides further back in the woods, and though I know it's there I can't quite catch it. But I'm putting food out for it; I'm building it a place to nest. I don't want it tamed all the way; I just want to pet it once in a while. I want it to come and sit with me again, like it used to, so it can tell stories to my fingers as they move on the keyboard in the dim light of the room where I sit to write.

READIN', WRITIN', AND ME

I hope everyone will forgive me for incorporating a little biographical material here toward the end of the book about how a country boy from deepest Arkansas grew up to be interested in writing. I like to hear these kinds of things about other writers, and I often wonder if there are similarities to be extracted from such remembrances.

I was born in 1958 and raised on a small family farm in the Arkansas River Valley, near the foothills of the Ozark Mountains. My father, J.V., was a farmer; my mother, Anna Bell, got up every weekday morning around 5:00 to go work at a chicken processing plant. I had three older brothers and an older sister, but all but Paul David were married and gone before I was old enough to remember much. Paul David was six years older than me. My other siblings were Jimmy, Dolores, and Raymond, at twenty, sixteen, and fourteen years older.

Our family raised cattle and always put in one cash crop, such as wheat, oats, maize, turnips, or black-eyed peas. We sold hay when we had extra. We also raised chickens and pigs for ourselves, and planted at least two vegetable gardens a year. I always felt that I worked pretty hard as a kid, although my brothers and at least one of my sisters-in-law would not agree. I remember my sister-in-law actually laughing out loud once when as a teenager I spoke of working hard. It hurt my feelings badly at the time and I suspect that's one reason why I really hate to be called lazy even today.

There was no kindergarten in Arkansas in those days and I don't know when I learned to read. I know I took to it like a bat takes to bugs. I remember having a few "Little Golden Books" before first grade, although I don't recall whether my parents read much to me. My father finished high school but I believe my mom stopped attending after the 8th grade. Both could read, certainly, but they both also worked extremely hard at providing food and a home for their five kids. There wasn't a lot of time for fun and games, and both my parents were also older. I was born on their twentieth wedding anniversary. My mom was almost forty-one, my dad a few years beyond.

Both my parents were also staunch Catholics, and this in a community made up primarily of Protestants. There was some prejudice there, although mostly just the occasional hostile word or look. I was slapped once by a girl on the bus for talking to her younger brother, who was my age. And once when I picked up some books for a girl who had dropped them I was told to: "Leave my books alone you dirty Catholic." Her older brother, a friend of Paul David's, promptly slapped the snot out of her and made her apologize. Years later she came to me privately and apologized again. I liked her for having that courage.

Starting at age six, I went to a Catholic grade school in Charleston, Arkansas for six years. I rode the bus since we lived miles out of town. Sacred Heart School had a tiny library that must have contained no more than 300 books. Most were stories about Catholic saints. I read them, but I only recall a few now. One was entitled *A Man on Fire*, about the life of Saint Paul. Another was about martyrs, and I'll never forget my horror at the brutal deaths so many early saints suffered, their bodies pierced by arrows, broken by stones, or crucified upside down.

The book that I enjoyed most, though, was about "The Littlest Guardian Angel," who had to fight a group of little devils on his first assignment. I wish I knew the actual title. I'd love to have that book. It would be interesting to read it again and see how it holds up. In my memory it's a wonderful adventure story.

Around third or fourth grade we were allowed to join a book club through our school, and we got paperbacks for 25 cents. I still have some of those books, including *Strange, Sudden and Unexpected*, *Is Something Up There*, *Dinosaurs*, and various books on football. (I wanted to be a pro football player in those days, or else be abducted by aliens.)

At this time we didn't have a lot to read at home other than the *Bible* and farming magazines. I read those, though, and I remember when my sister and her husband got a set of encyclopedias for their kids (Terry and John) and I would walk the half mile to their house to read them. I still recall one fantastic cover photograph of a brightly colored lizard against a red sand background. In my mind that background became an alien planet ripe for exploration, and the lizard a monster that I had to tackle to survive.

As I moved toward my teen years I became *addicted* to reading. I was happy when it rained so I could stay in the house all day with a book. I devoured mostly science fiction, fantasy, sports, and animal stories in those days. Edgar Rice Burroughs was my favorite, but not his Tarzan books. I read his Martian series and works such as *The Moon Maid* and *The Lost Continent.* Andre Norton was my second favorite. Books like *Breed to Come, Galactic Derelict*, and *Star Guard* ignited my imagination with images that burned even in my dreams. Other boon companions were the Black Stallion books of Walter Farley, and I loved the dog books by Jim Kjelgaard, especially one called *Desert Dog*, about a greyhound who has to learn to survive after being abandoned in the desert.

Other than the volumes I got from the book club, I picked up most of my reading material from the public library, where my sister, Dolores, worked. She knew what kind of books I liked and brought them home to me. Or sometimes when I went to town with my dad he would take me by the library and I'd check out as many books as they'd let me have at one time. Dolores had also *married* a reader. Roger read mostly westerns and through him I discovered Louis L'Amour. When I finished the books I'd gotten from the library I'd go borrow Roger's books. Eventually I read just about everything L'Amour published, and his stories impacted not only my later writing but the kind of life philosophy I developed.

It was around this time, however, that I got my sister in trouble with my mom. I read everything, regardless if it was age appropriate or not, and I'd borrowed a book from Dolores that had "sex" scenes in it. These were very mild by today's standards, but my mom, concerned by the book's cover, read a little of it. Needless to say, she wasn't happy, and though I got into trouble I'm pretty sure my sister suffered much worse. She didn't stop giving me books, though, so I bless her.

I soon began to get into difficulties for reading "too" much. I admit that I sometimes tried to avoid chores in order to read, and I'd frequently hide in the barn away from everyone else so I could read in peace. My mom was afraid I'd hurt my eyes, and I wear glasses so maybe she was right. Other than that, though, reading has always been and remains a staple of my life. I can't imagine what I'd have been like without books.

When I was thirteen my father died. He'd been born with a weak heart, although I didn't know it at that time, and he'd had a heart attack when I was seven. I'd been kept pretty much in the dark about that too, and never understood until later how he and my mom had lived for years with the possibility that he could die at any moment. On the morning of his death I'd gotten up early with him to work for a bit in the garden before I caught the bus to school. I told him that I loved him before I left, and I've always been glad of that.

At some point that morning he came in the house and sat down in a chair by the back door. He died there, with the door open.

It could easily have been me that found my dad when I came home from school that day, but my sister had hired a baby sitter for her two children while she went to work, and the sitter found him. She said later that she walked by the back door and saw him sitting there and said hello, but that when he didn't respond she went up to have a look and found him already cold. To this day I'm glad it wasn't me. I don't know how I would have handled seeing my father's corpse sitting bolt upright with his eyes open and glassy.

My mom took my dad's death very hard. She slept for a long time with one of his shirts under her pillow, and she drew a big black X on the bottom of the chair he died in and wouldn't let anyone move it. The hardest thing for me about the chair was that it sat right next to the bathroom I used at night and sometimes I was scared to walk past it. I loved my father, but I believed in ghosts in those days and didn't want to come around the corner and see him sitting dead in that place with the moonlight falling through the back window onto that chair.

My mom told me many times after my father died that she thought she would have died too if she hadn't needed to take care of me. I always felt a little weird about that, and I worried that she *would* die. I also worried that I couldn't live up to being the reason my mom survived, but this was a pressure I put on myself and was never something she tried to make me feel. Kids think about things in weird ways.

Anyway, mom and I kept the farm going during the weeks while Paul David came home from college on the weekends to handle things. My brother Raymond also came in frequently. We got through it, and by the time I was ready to go to college myself Paul David had returned to run the farm full time. I often think, however, about how incredibly hard my mother had to work during those years. She'd gotten permission from the chicken plant to come in an hour later than normal so she could get me up for school and fix me breakfast. But after putting in eight hours at the plant she'd come home to farm work, and then had to get me supper. It wasn't until I was a grown man with a son of my own that I realized how tough she had it. Frontier stock, I think you could call her.

Growing up in those days as a reader, I never considered being a writer myself. It didn't really occur to me that people like me wrote the books I was reading. I do remember penning a couple stories as a Junior higher, but it was strictly for entertainment value, not because I thought I'd some day be a writer and sell them. In High

School English we were *required* to write a couple of "fiction" items. I read my pieces and both were well received by my classmates. I remember getting criticism about the lack of realism from a classmate on one story, however. Even then criticism upset me, and I haven't changed much. It still hurts.

The critical student's story was also better received than mine and was highly praised by the teacher. It wasn't until a couple of years later that I discovered he'd plagiarized the story from an SF anthology. I found it out when he loaned me that collection, apparently forgetting that he'd thieved his tale from it. I never confronted him about it, but I never forgot either that the only person whose work had been judged better than mine had read a piece by a pro.

I first began thinking about becoming a writer when I started Arkansas Tech University in 1977. In my second year at Tech, while living with my brother Raymond and his wife Joyce, I wrote a western novel called *The Bear Paw Valley* on an electric typewriter that mom had bought me for school. It was essentially a Louis L'Amour pastiche. I was so unfamiliar with the process of writing that I just started typing at the top of page 1 and typed straight through to the end without even putting in chapter breaks. What an idiot, I was. But I still like "some" of the scenes from that book and, in fact, years later polished up one particular section and sold it as a short story called "Killing Trail."

Because I was flirting with the idea of writing I took an essay class with a man named Francis Gwaltney, the only writer of any kind of fame who'd ever come from my home town. That course remains the only writing class I've ever taken, and it didn't have anything to do with fiction. It *did* help me focus some energy and thought on writing, and eventually I took my western to Gwaltney, who read it and told me it was "unpublishable." He was right.

However, Gwaltney also told me I had talent and that he'd like to see something else from me, something more contemporary, more about the world I knew. And then he told me he'd send the result to his agent. I was ecstatic and immediately started another novel, mostly autobiographical, but before I'd completed more than a couple dozen pages and had a chance to show it to him, Gwaltney choked on a chicken bone and died while celebrating the publication of his latest work. I took that as a sign I was not meant to be a writer and gave it up.

In retrospect, abandoning writing because of Gwaltney's death was a childish reaction on my part. It may have been the right decision, however. I *wasn't* much more than a child, and though I had imagination I lacked both discipline and experience. I didn't write another word of fiction until some five years later while in graduate school at the University of Arkansas. I often worked very late at night while in grad school, and sometimes as a way to relax after finishing some research I'd type up a fictional scene, usually something with elements of fantasy or horror.

I was still doing a lot of reading, mostly short stories because grad school didn't leave much time for novels. Ray Bradbury was a favorite, and Arthur C. Clarke, and Robert E. Howard. Howard, dead since the 1930s, was either featured in or had a strong influence on two sword & sorcery anthology series I was reading at the time, *Flashing Swords*, edited by Lin Carter, and *Swords Against Darkness*, edited by Andrew Offutt. I'd also discovered horror fiction, especially H. P. Lovecraft. And horror anthologies were huge in the early 1980s. I had close to a dozen such anthologies edited by the late great Charles Grant.

I finally wrote a couple of stories that I thought were better than, or at least as good as, some of the stuff I was reading, and I bought a copy of *Novel and Short Story Writer's Market* and started submitting. The stories I had were "Death Turned Away," a horror piece, and "Shadow Dream," a fantasy. Both eventually sold, but at first I didn't have any luck. A couple of places were closed to subs and didn't even read my pieces. I got a couple of other form rejections.

By then I was well into writing a novel, a fantasy from a genre called sword & planet. It was entitled *Swords of Talera* and was influenced by Edgar Rice Burroughs' John Carter of Mars, and by the Dray Prescot books of Alan Burt Akers (aka Ken Bulmer). I was so excited by this book that I wrote on it in all my spare time, even by hand when I was home for Thanksgiving. That was absolutely the most fun I've ever had writing, and eventually that novel also sold, though I rewrote it several times first.

By the time I finished grad school in 1986 I had only submitted my two stories about four times and had no sales. But when I got to the Greater New Orleans area I continued to write while settling in as an Assistant Professor of Psychology at Xavier University of Louisiana. Then, in the fall of 1988, I decided to try seriously to write and publish. I constructed a mission statement for myself, allowing myself five years to get published and promising that I'd work on something writing related every day.

I subscribed to *Writer's Digest* and did indeed write almost every day, though often only half an hour or so. I began submitting more too, and started sending stuff to contests. In the spring of 1989 I got my first sale, a horror story called "Still Life With Skulls," to a magazine called *Twisted*. Within another week or so I had a second sale, a vampire story called "Messiah" to a magazine entitled *Dead of Night*. I was hooked then, and I date myself as a writer from that fall of 1988.

Over the next decade I sold a lot of short stories and poetry, but I knew if I wanted to get any name recognition I needed to write novels. I revised *Swords of Talera* and began submitting it, but sword & planet fiction had fallen out of favor with publishers in the mid 1980s and there were no takers. A small magazine finally ran it as a serial in 1998 where it won their Reader's Choice award for that year. That was enough for me to write a sequel, *Wings Over Talera*, which was serialized in 2000 by the same magazine group and was also named Reader's Choice winner.

Horror had taken a hit and fallen into a slump in the early 1990s as well, but I had long wanted to write a novel in that genre so in 1995 I started one. I called it *Cold in the Light* and it took me almost four years to complete because at the time I was also serving as chairperson of the Psychology Department at Xavier, and I was the doting father of a wonderful little boy named Joshua.

I'd first met Mary Rocker in 1986, right after arriving in the New Orleans area. We started dating but had only been seeing each other about four months when she announced that she was going to adopt a baby who was soon to be born. When Josh arrived in June of 1987 I immediately fell in love with him. Mary and I were married a year later and I completed the adoption process so that Josh became my legal son. He'd been my "real" son from the first moment I held him.

After *Cold in the Light* was finally finished I started a serious search for an agent. The first one that said he would accept me as a client turned out to be a fraud, and I was lucky to discover it before any contracts were signed. The second agent to accept me seemed like a good fit, until after only a couple of months she developed a serious health crisis and retired from the business. I was so discouraged that I quit writing and submitting for six months. I told myself it was permanent, but I couldn't stay away and I know now I'll never quit.In 2002 *Cold in the Light* finally sold, without an agent and to a small press publisher.

In the years since 2002, I've had a few writing successes and a few disappointments. *Swords of Talera* was eventually published as a paperback in 2007 by a small press publisher, and the same publisher also brought out the two sequels, *Wings Over Talera* and *Witch of Talera*, the latter of which I wrote in 2003. I'm proud of that trilogy and happy to see the books in print, although I wish they would have sold more. At least *Cold in the Light* and the Taleran novels have been praised by nearly everyone who has read them, and it has been such a wonderful feeling to get letters and emails from fans who enjoyed my work. Still, I wish *more* people had read them.

One thing I like to know about other writers is their influences. Mine are legion. Edgar Rice Burroughs is probably number one, both on the content of what I like to write and, to a lesser extent, on my style. Robert E. Howard is second, especially for content. Dean Koontz is an influence on my thriller work, both in content and style, but he has had very little influence on my short horror fiction or my fantasy. Stylistically, I see elements of many other writers in my fiction, Ray Bradbury, Louis L'Amour, John D. MacDonald, and Ernest Hemingway. Ken Bulmer was an influence on my fantasy. Of course, everything I've ever read has ended up somewhere in the mix.

I like to think of myself as a flexible writer, of being able to write in a lot of *different* genres and styles. I've written SF, horror, sword & sorcery, sword & planet, westerns, children's stories, mainstream, and experimental tales. I've had quite a bit of poetry published, and a lot of nonfiction essays. The latter have been mostly on writing or about writers, but I've also published a fair amount of scientific stuff.

In 2003 Mary and I separated and eventually divorced, although both of us remain close with Josh. Josh has also accepted Lana Jackman, the woman who has been a balm for my soul these last few years and who become my wife in October of 2007. In those same years (2004 – 2007) I've been writing more nonfiction and less fiction, even though fiction is what I love most. There are a couple of reasons, 1) nonfiction pays a lot better, and 2) some interesting nonfiction projects have virtually fallen into my lap. Despite that, I look forward to having more time one of these years to focus again on fiction. I want the feeling back that I had in those long ago days when I was scribbling madly on *Swords of Talera*. I wasn't thinking about publishing then. I wasn't thinking about money or name recognition or even whether anyone else would like what I'd written. I was just wondering, what comes next?

DEATH BY PROSE

Author's Note: Below is a slightly different perspective on my history as a writer from that offered in the previous essay. I'm still trying to figure out which one is closest to the truth. I think this one's a little funnier. It's never been published, however. I wonder why.

I've killed a few agents and editors and magazines in my time, some professional writers and publishers. I didn't start out to, but I've killed and gotten away with it. And not even a Sherlock Holmes could pin the crimes on me.

The reason I've gotten away with it is because of the murder weapon I've chosen for my modus operandi. No "Clue" type weapons for me. No knives or guns or knotted ropes. No candlesticks or wrenches. Not even a lethal-but-hard-to-detect poison whose recipe I extracted from my copy of *Deadly Doses: a writer's guide to poisons*. No, my weapon of choice has been...prose.

I began my spree when I was only nineteen. Like most serial criminals I started with someone I knew, someone close to home. I was in college at the time, with an interest in writing. Having completed a gun-slamming western that was a poor pastiche of a bad Louis L'Amour novel, and having fully envisioned the approval and riches that would soon be heaped upon me, I went to see my English professor, who was a relatively well known and respected novelist with about a dozen notches on his typewriter for books he'd written. He was also the only novelist I'd ever known who came from my populous hometown of Charleston, Arkansas, which boasted almost 1500 residents.

Anyway, I took my shoot-em-up to this professor and he read it, and came back and told me—rightly—that it was unpublishable and that I should put it aside for ten years and then look back at it to see how embarrassing it was. However, he also told me that I showed great promise and that he'd like to see me write something more contemporary. If I did, he said he would send it to his agent for consideration.

His words hooked me. I'd shown..."promise!" A real live published author had declared so. At home that Friday evening I started a new novel, set in my hometown and in the modern day (1978 that is). The words just flew onto the paper from my typewriter, and by Monday I had nearly twenty fresh pages written.

I was aching to show my professor what I'd accomplished. Only, he didn't show up for classes that day. Or any day thereafter. Unbeknownst to me, the insidious toxins of my prose had already been at work, and over that weekend the man, the writer, the person who had seen promise in my work, choked on a chicken bone and died. I'd claimed my first victim. There *would* be more.

Again, like many serial offenders, I lay low after that first crime. For almost ten years I didn't produce another drop of fiction. But in 1988 I started "writing" again, and soon had constructed a nasty little piece of stalking-horse-prose called "Haunting Place."

Three of the first few magazines that I sent "Haunting Place" to accepted it. The very first two to accept it even paid me. But you're probably asking yourself, if the first one bought it why did the others need to see it? The reason is that none of those magazines, after accepting my tale, lived to put out another issue. This, of course, kept my story free to be sent to some other poor and unsuspecting magazine struggling to survive.

Lately, the pace of my crimes has accelerated, as is true of most serial killers. Two small vampire magazines winked out like Christmas lights just after publishing stories of mine. A fantasy novel I wrote was serialized in a Texas magazine. That magazine vanished within two months of publishing the last installment. A series of barbarian stories sold to a magazine group in Florida and they published several of them before dying of the accumulating toxins. They had even asked me for more in the series, unaware that the disease they'd taken to their bosom had already metastasized. The list goes on.

Finally, I even began to recruit other writers as accessories before the fact in my crimes. For example, a friend from my writing group had acquired an agent and knew I was struggling to find one. He recommended me to his New York connection, who promptly solicited my completed manuscript for a horror/thriller about monsters running rampant through the dark and misty woods of Arkansas.

So, I sent my opus off and waited to hear. And waited. After two months I followed up with an email. No response. And suddenly my friend stopped hearing from this agent as well. So did another local writer who I knew used the same agent. Emails and attempts to reach the man by phone were met with in-space-no-one-can-hear-you-scream silence, and the agent's webpage was no longer being updated.

I cracked. Now that others were involved I felt it impossible to hide my crimes and confessed to my friend, telling him that his agent was most likely dead at my hand, or, rather, at my prose. He didn't believe me. How could he, I suppose. I'd established myself by day as a mild mannered professor, a law abiding citizen with a wife and child and a house in the suburbs. Only at night when I turned on my computer and sat at the keyboard did the beast rise.

I never heard from my friend's agent but my friend finally did after several months. Had the man been deathly ill? That was my bet, although the fellow didn't say why he'd been out of touch. I think I know how he must have survived, though. He told my friend after reappearing that he'd: "decided to get out of representing fiction." It would have been that which saved him from my toxic prose.

As for the present essay—a story of the horror of trying to get published and finding instead that one is an inveterate murderer—should it be accepted? Should it, by any chance, be published? I just have one question: Do you feel lucky?

Well, do you?

INTERVIEWS

30 May 2007: Interview by Shauna Roberts. (Reprinted with permission.) Shauna makes her living as a freelancer for medical and scientific journals and magazines, and is also a fiction writer, working primarily in the genres of SF, fantasy and romance. Her blog can be found at: http://shaunaroberts.blogspot.com/

Interview with speculative fiction author
CHARLES ALLEN GRAMLICH

Shauna: Congratulations, Charles, on having two new sword-and-planet novels, *Swords of Talera* and *Wings over Talera*, published this spring by Borgo Press, and thank you for visiting my blog.

CAG: Thanks, Shauna. And thanks for inviting me today.

Shauna: The Talera Cycle fantasy trilogy is being published by a small press, as was your 2002 horror novel *Cold in the Light*. What do you see as the major advantages and disadvantages of working with a small press?

CAG: Well, the major disadvantage is money. Small presses don't have much of it, so authors can't expect any significant gob of cash up front. But, on the positive side, many small presses provide better royalty rates than the mainstream publishers, and if your book sells you can do OK. Small presses also typically don't have much in their budgets for promoting writers either. An author really has to push their own work, but I think that's become more common at the mainstream presses as well. Unless you're a huge name.

An advantage of the small press is that the author can often have more input into covers and back cover copy than typical of mainstream publishers. And with many small press publishers the relationship between author and publisher becomes quite personal.

I've very much appreciated the personal attention I've gotten from Borgo Press, and from The Invisible College Press before that.

Shauna: In *Swords of Talera*, as in many fantasies, an ordinary person suddenly finds him- or herself in extraordinary circumstances in which the normal rules of life do not apply, and the person must become heroic to survive. Hundreds of thousands of us in southeastern Louisiana experienced just such an adventure after Hurricane Katrina. What heroic qualities did you discover in yourself after the hurricane? Did you rewrite any sections of *Swords of Talera* to reflect your new first-hand knowledge?

CAG: *Swords of Talera* was first written long before Katrina. But it was revised for paperback publication after Katrina. You're absolutely right that many of us here along the Gulf Coast experienced the kind of dislocation after the hurricane that Ruenn Maclang did in *Swords of Talera*. Although I didn't create any new scenes for the book solely based on my experiences during and after Katrina, I think that living through the tragedy of the storm added new depth to many of the revised scenes. I ended up spending two months in Austin, in a two-room apartment with lawn chairs for furniture, so I began to understand the dislocation that Ruenn suffers in the book. That certainly came through in the revisions.

I was amazed at the heroics shown by so many all along the Gulf Coast after Katrina, and the heroics of those who came from all over the country and from Canada and other countries to pitch in. I don't know if I discovered any heroism in myself, but I saw and met many heroes in action and that certainly bled through onto the pages of the book.

Shauna: You appear briefly in *Swords of Talera* as yourself. Was it difficult to create a character who was stripped down from flesh and blood and soul rather than built up from a skeleton? How did you go about turning yourself into a character?

CAG: There is a long tradition in Sword & Planet fiction, beginning with Edgar Rice Burroughs, of framing these stories with a connection to a real person who is being "told" the story or who has been given a "manuscript" or "tapes" that reveal the tale. I think it's a fun tradition and wanted to honor it myself. I appear strictly in the introduction, however, and show up less and less throughout the introductions in the sequels. I have no plans to have myself transported to

Talera, which is what the writer Lin Carter once did in one of his own Sword & Planet series.

As for it being hard, it was actually very easy, one of the easiest things I did in the book. There wasn't really much "making it up" involved. I've been called a "character" anyway, usually with some pejorative adjective for a modifier.

Shauna: *Swords of Talera* is an old-fashioned read, modeled after the books of Edgar Rice Burroughs and originally appearing in a magazine in serialized form. What do the Talera Cycle and Burroughs' books offer readers that is missing in modern fiction?

CAG: Writers like Burroughs and Robert E. Howard knew that "story" is of paramount importance. Certainly you want great characters and interesting plots, but most people read for the story. Sometimes I think that many modern writers have forgotten that. They've become too self-conscious, or have been too heavily influenced by the slash-and-burn techniques of TV, and they've forgotten how much fun a "well-told tale" can be. Burroughs and Howard often had plenty going on under the skins of their stories, but they never forgot that a piece has to work as a "story" first.

One big publisher rejected *Swords of Talera* because they said it was too old-fashioned, but I took that rejection as a compliment because that was exactly what I hoped to achieve with this book. There's still a lot of flesh on the bones of those old tales. To reject them because they're not "the latest thing" is to follow a fad that will disappear itself before long.

Shauna: The theme of freedom is an important one in *Swords of Talera*. Slaves constantly look for a means of escape, and complete strangers risk their lives to free slaves. Why did you choose this theme to be so prominent? Will later members of the trilogy have different themes?

CAG: Slavery has a long and complicated history in human affairs. Outside of murder, it's arguably the worst thing one human can do to another. Slavery has touched almost every human society, past and present, and the legacy of slavery is still affecting our country's history today. Growing up in the South, and teaching for the last 20 years at a predominantly African American university, has taught me a lot about the horrors that existed with slavery, and it is a topic that I'm interested in even though I find it difficult to understand how anyone could ever practice it.

As Ruenn Maclang says in the book, however, "chains are not always made of metal." Actual slavery appears more prominently in *Swords of Talera* than in either of the sequels, but the whole trilogy is about freedom and about how we must be vigilant against those who would take it away from us, whether it be from outside our society, or from within.

Shauna: The relationship between the protagonist, Ruenn, and the alien Jask is fascinating. What in the character of these two enemies allows them to forge a friendship and trust each other?

CAG: Jask and Ruenn may literally be from different worlds, but they have two things in common that made it inevitable that they'd come to like and respect each other. First, they each have a strong sense of personal honor, a sense that one pays one's debts. Second, they both understood what it was like to be isolated and alone among their fellows. Jask really wrote himself as a character and I enjoyed watching his growth very much. If I continue with the Taleran series he will certainly show up again.

Shauna: How does being a psychologist influence how you create characters?

CAG: Long before I was a psychologist I was reading Burroughs' John Carter of Mars series and the stories of a hundred other writers of adventure fantasy, like Robert E. Howard, Andre Norton, Poul Anderson, and Kenneth Bulmer. The characters in the Talera books owe much more to the great writers who came before me than they do to my formal training in psychology. While I consciously work psychological elements into the characters and plots of my horror fiction, as with *Cold in the Light*, I made no attempt to do so in the Talera trilogy. We're all a product of our experiences and training, of course, so there may be psychological elements to the stories that I don't even recognize myself. If so, they're largely accidents.

Shauna: Thank you again for allowing me to interview you.

CAG: My pleasure. Great questions. They really made me think.

* * * * * * *

July 2007: Interview by Richard Tucker at Xavier University of Louisiana. (Reprinted with permission.) This appeared in This Month at Xavier, *Volume 38, No. 7.*

Psychology Professor Has Tales to Tell

We'd be lying if we said that Edgar Rice Burroughs (of Tarzan fame) is alive and teaching at Xavier, but there are those who would say that's not too far off the mark.

Enter Dr. Charles Allen Gramlich, by all appearances an unassuming professor of experimental psychology and, unbeknownst to most, a prodigious crafter of yarns and spinner of tales. He is the author of several novels and numerous short stories, most of which fall into the genres of science fiction, fantasy, or horror.

Three of his novels have already been published: the horror/action-themed *Cold in the Light* (2002) – whose sci-fi elements have drawn comparisons with the early work of N.Y. Times bestselling author Dean Koontz (Strangers) – and his fantasy, adventure-themed *Swords of Talera* (2007) and *Wings Over Talera* (2007) – which some critics have likened to the works of the legendary Burroughs [think John Carter: Warlord of Mars].

This summer he is anticipating publication of his latest novel, *Witch of Talera*, the third and perhaps final chapter in what he calls the Talera Cycle – his fantasy adventure series in which a 19th-century Earthman is mysteriously transported into a world dominated by ancient warriors and deadly beasts.

Although the Talera trilogy is just now being released in book form, it dates back to his college days; in fact, Gramlich wrote the first installment during late night breaks from his graduate research. But his interest in the genre and his love of writing goes back much further than that.

"I grew up reading adventure stories like Tarzan and John Carter and they really struck a chord with me," said Gramlich. They were also ready companions for a young boy growing up on a farm near the foothills of the Ozark Mountains six miles away from his nearest neighbor.

"When I first started 'telling' stories to myself as a pre-teen, without writing them down, I set almost all of them in a fantasy landscape that was essentially an expanded version of the farm where I was growing up," he said, explaining that the seven ponds in the area became the seven seas of his fantasy world. "Even today some of my fantasy stories take place in a variation on that original world building."

"I love telling a good story; that's what I am looking to do whenever I write," he said. Initially Gramlich wrote for his own amusement, but after sharing some of his stories with his college friends, he began to realize he had some talent in that area. Much to his chagrin, however, he had launched his writing career in what mainstream publishers dubbed "the waning years of the popularity of the adventure/fantasy genre" – thus the huge gap from creation to fruition.

However, he eventually caught the eye of the now-defunct Startling Science Stories magazine, which published the trilogy as a four-part series in 1999. He also earned the magazine's Reader's Choice Award for that year.

Oddly enough, the novel he wrote in between volumes of the Talera series – *Cold in the Light*, a horror novel about earth-evolved humanoids run amok in rural Arkansas [think along the lines of *Predator*] – was published in book form first. It was also much harder to write.

"Cold has a lot more sub-plots than the Talera series," said Gramlich. "I had a basic concept and an ending, but unlike the trilogy I didn't plot out the story before I started writing because I didn't want to know all the answers up front. I wanted to even surprise myself."

Today all four novels are available through amazon.com and other on-line retailers, and Gramlich is hopeful that they might soon find their way to retail stores. And while book sales have not reached the point where he is ready to give up his day job, he admits the additional income has provided more than few extra luxuries.

"Let's just say I make enough money that I'm not wasting my time doing this," he laughed.

For Gramlich, who has taught at Xavier since 1986, fiction novels represent just one facet of his writing repertoire. Over the years he has published more than 70 short fiction stories, 60 poems and 100 nonfiction and academic writings.

Oddly enough, his fictional writing has been shelved this summer while he completes some more "educational" projects for the publisher of his Talera trilogy (Borgo Press), most notably a student guide for writing effective term papers.

Of course for some students, writing term papers is an adventure in itself.

KIDS INSANE

BY JOSH GRAMLICH

Note: The following story is by my son, Joshua, who was seventeen when he wrote it for a school English project. You're probably wondering if I helped him. Well, other than correcting some punctuation and a few grammatical issues, I helped not at all. I couldn't have written a story this good when I was his age. I think it deserves a wider audience. I hope you enjoy.

The wheels turned fast on the bike as Bryce pedaled down the street. He had never ridden so fast. He had just left his house and wasn't planning on going back. He and his mother had just been in the worst argument they'd ever had and he couldn't take being in the house any more. He was on his way to Adam's place. Adam was his best friend. They had been close for over ten years, but Bryce wondered if tonight would test that friendship.

* * * * * * *

They started the night on their bikes as they sped down Houma Boulevard. They were heading toward the service road. With adrenaline running high, they both pulled off under a bridge. The night was gloomy and the sky dark. Even the streetlights seemed shadowed.

"Are you ready," asked Adam, his short blond hair spiked with sweat from their ride.

Bryce brushed back his own hair, which was dark and tangled. "I don't really have a choice," he replied.

With that said, they hit the road. They soon turned right down Danny Parkway and began counting blocks. "Four blocks," George had told them.

"Where is he?" Bryce asked his friend as they stopped at the corner.

But Adam was turning away down a small alley. By the time Bryce caught up, Adam was already hiding his bike.

"OK. Where is he?" Bryce asked again as he parked next to his friend.

Before he could get an answer, a soft whistle floated through the air. The whistle startled Bryce before he realized that it had to be George, who was nineteen and two years older than either of the other boys.

"Come on," Adam told Bryce.

They turned and walked back up the alley together to find George waiting at the exit onto the street. He wore the leather jacket that he always wore, no matter the heat, and his lip ring caught the dim light. There were no cars passing by, although there rarely were at this hour. The three friends greeted each other by a special hand shake. Each of their right hands had K.I., for Kids Insane, tattooed between the thumb and forefinger. It was their group sign and they were the only three members. They did everything together.

As they walked farther up the block, George's eyes shone bright with the reflected glisten of a black diamond. Approaching that street-jewel, he pulled out a straight metal tool. Adam and Bryce watch the road for any movement. Behind them, they heard a car door open. Spinning around quickly, the two found George hopping into the front seat of the 2004 Subaru STI. He had already begun ripping things apart under the steering wheel. By the time Adam and Bryce climbed aboard, the forty thousand dollar machine was spitting out an evil growl through the performance exhaust. In a matter of seconds they were speeding down the street to the music of the turbocharger.

* * * * * * *

The stereo thumped from loud music as the room fogged up. The fluorescent lights gave everything an unfamiliar glow. Empty boxes and bottles lay scattered and stacked everywhere. Sprawled on the floor lay Adam and Bryce, their hearts still beating hard from what had just happened.

Bryce marveled at the lazy turning of the ceiling fan over his head. Then he sat up to watch George counting their money out on the bed. The sight of that wad of cash sent electricity through Bryce's body. They'd stolen a few things in their day, but nothing that had paid as good as tonight's boost. Their world had changed and the music thumped alone. No one wanted to ruin the moment with speech. They were invincible.

* * * * * * *

Rays of violent sunlight pierced through Bryce's eyelids. He sat up to find that George was gone and a soft breeze accompanied a bright sun through the window. Adam still lay next to him on the carpet. Bryce's stomach stung as if he hadn't eaten in a week. Realizing that it was only ten o'clock, he figured he would just go home. As he got up to leave, his head throbbed in pain. He stumbled wearily to the front door.

Nothing that had happened last night felt real. Why had he gone along with stealing the car? On his walk home all he felt was guilt, no more happiness. He also feared that he would somehow get caught. He had covered this route many times, for he lived just down the street from George. The road had never felt like this, however. He remembered every last thing that had ever happened in these two blocks. His whole life had been lived here. He was saddened by the memories of riding his bike and playing baseball with all the neighborhood kids. He remembered how innocent he used to be.

Opening the door to his house felt odd since he'd planned never to come back. Last night had changed that. He felt bad for telling his mom he hated her. She had brought him up better than that. It was moments like these that he appreciated her, but he never got a chance to tell her these things. Walking into her room, he found an empty bed. And there was nobody in the bathroom or the living room, either. Feeling let down, he plopped onto the couch and closed his eyes.

* * * * * * *

When his eyes opened again, he found himself in a dark world. He was still on a couch, just not his own. He was at some sort of house party, but he wasn't sure where because he couldn't even see straight. The voices were murderous to his ears, the images frightening to his eyes. Blue lighting changed the shade of everything, and strobes appeared to slow the world down. The voices he heard came from two black figures with twisted faces floating above elongated necks. In fear, he put his head into his hands.

The music vibrated his insides to the point where he could barely sit up. A sharp pain arose in his back. The pain circled around and around, getting heavier each time it passed his heart. It became so unbearable that he had to look up to see if something was there. When he did, he saw the hand of a girl gently rubbing his back. She had ash-blond hair, streaked with bronze, and blue eyes that promised much.

"What's going on?" Bryce asked.

"Are you okay?" the girl responded with her caressing voice.

He didn't know how to answer. He couldn't say how he really felt, but it seemed like he would die if he shut his eyes again. He opened his mouth to say something, but before a single word could get out a clash of smashing glass silenced everything but the music. In seconds there was a big crowd gathered right in front of him.

With a surge of returning reality, he stood up to see what was happening. He caught a glimpse of Adam throwing his fists around. Then he saw George. His two friends scuffled with three football players who were twice their size. Bryce immediately jumped up and pushed his way through the crowd. But before he could get close enough to help his friends he heard the back door slam open. Everyone jerked their heads around to see two guys dressed in black beaters and covered in tattoos. One of them held a wooden bat, the other a crowbar.

In an instant, the newcomers had taken charge of the fight. Their weapons swung, struck, came away bloody. The three jocks were laid out in seconds. Bryce froze as Adam and George both looked toward him. Both had an evil look of power in their eyes.

George turned and walked out front. Bryce followed.

"What just happened?" Bryce sternly asked George.

"Adam needed help, so I helped. Where were you?" he added sarcastically.

Bryce just shook his head. A gentle tear rolled down his face for the first time in three years, for the first time since his father had died in a wreck.

"Aw, is the poor baby gonna cry?" George mocked.

Bryce turned without a word and walked away. He had nowhere to go. He hardly knew where he was. He just had to leave. He couldn't take this anymore. What had started as fun, as a pact between friends, had turned darker, deadlier.

Sometime later, he found himself soaked in sweat and standing in front of a black iron fence. The fence ran for about three miles around the park. Bryce hopped over it, just as he had so many times before when his group went out there after hours. He walked around the whole park until he found the picnic area where he used to come on weekends with his mom and dad. He walked up to the tree where they had always sat and collapsed against it. There he stayed for hours. He would never have left if his cell phone hadn't rung. It was Adam. Bryce didn't want to talk to his old friend but he had little choice. He agreed to meet him at George's.

* * * * * *

When he arrived at George's, he saw that the party had moved here. There must have been fifty people hanging around. Someone mentioned the cops running everyone off from the other place, and Bryce's veins exploded out of his arms in anger as he remembered what he'd seen at *that* party.

George and the two tattooed thugs whose violence had won the fight a few hours ago stood on the porch like they owned the world. All three were smirking. All three looked like they'd enjoy *another* fight. Bryce frowned and tried walking past, but he felt a strong arm grab him.

"What's your problem?" one of the men barked at him.

"You are! All of ya'll are! This is just so stupid. Where's Adam?" he demanded.

"He should be in my room," George informed him. "You do know that nobody can mess with us now, right? K.I. is expanding. Adam's down with it. Why can't you be?"

Without a response, Bryce jerked away and stormed through into the hallway where George's room was. There were people lined up all down the hall. Pushing his way past, Bryce finally reached George's door. He could see the fluorescent glow seeping from under it. With memories flushing through his head, Bryce opened the door, knowing that his oldest and best friendship was on the line. But it wasn't Adam who he saw on the other side.

"Hey, your name is Bryce, right?" a voice inquired.

"Yeah. You ummm... You're Lauren's friend, right? Melissa?"

"Yeah, you remembered. So why did you leave earlier? The party was just getting started."

"Because," he said, "I've never seen Adam act like this. This isn't who I am. This isn't who Adam is. I'm just sick of this. I'm done. I only came so I could tell him how I felt. Do you know where he is?"

"Jeez, you got some attitude! I think he's in the big bedroom." She turned away.

Two years ago, Bryce had stood outside Adam's house as a giant white truck parked across the street. From it came what seemed to be hundreds of boxes. These boxes were to be put into the house just across the way from Adam. The most important luggage to come off the truck, however, was Lauren. She was beautiful, with shoulder length hair of ash-blond. She had a nice golden tan to match the highlights in her hair. Bryce fearlessly walked across the road that day and talked to her. Ever since, they had been together. They didn't see each other every day, and they'd had their ups and downs, but for the most part they were a happy couple. She let him do pretty much anything he wanted, which made him happy.

Walking down the hallway, Bryce thought of Lauren. He suddenly felt so overwhelmed with everything that he went in the bathroom. He normally hated talking on his cell phone; he didn't even know why he had one. Regardless, this was one of those things he had to talk to Lauren about. He pulled out his Samsung and shot the numbers on the key pad. He patiently waited for her to answer her cell. He'd learned long ago not to bother calling her house because nobody ever answered there. His patience soon turned to disappointment as he received no answer.

With a sigh, he gave up, then decided to go talk to Adam and just get it over with. He walked into the master bedroom without knocking and found Adam talking on his own phone.

"Hey, let me call you back later," he said importantly into the phone. He punched the end button, then stared hard at Bryce. "So, what's up?" he asked

Bryce could hardly look at him. "You're what's up. Why are you acting like this?"

"This is what we always wanted," Adam insisted. "We have power now."

"No, it's not what *we* always wanted. Maybe it's what George always wanted. What me and you wanted was to start up K.I., the best paint crew in the N.O. We don't even tag anymore. You never used to be like this. So why are you acting this way? Cuz I don't like it. It's just not you."

"Well I hate to break it to you, but we're in it for real now. We've crossed the line. Two of those jocks died. The other is just hanging on. You should have done more than just stand there and watch. It was one of the most incredible feelings in the world. The power! Our old life is over. We live a new life of crime, violence and hot girls now."

"It may have made you feel good, but it makes me sick. I know the old Adam would have felt the same way, too, but you know what? I'm done. I quit this. All I want to do now is go and find Lauren. She's the only person I have left in my life."

"Oh really, is that what you think? You think she loves you? She's been living it up behind your back for a year now. Every day that you're not together. Where have you been? Why do you think she's been so nice to you lately?" Adam's words were bitter, and almost gleeful.

Sudden tears started to cluster hotly in Bryce's eyes. He wanted to jump on top of Adam and beat him until there was nothing left. He could picture it in his head. His veins pulsed harder and harder. Bryce had once loved Adam as a brother. Now he hated him as an enemy.

Not being able to stand the sight of a friend who was no longer a friend, he simply turned and walked out. He headed toward the front door but was stopped by the girl who had rubbed his back so lovingly at the earlier party, the girl with the bronze streaked ash-blond hair. She didn't stop him physically, but by what she was doing. He saw his love being given away on the couch in front of the whole world. Instead of making a scene, he once again simply lowered his head and went.

He walked straight out of the front door and onto the street. He dug in his pocket for anything, just to see if there was anything left in his lonely life. There was one last thing, one small, metallic object. And he knew exactly what to do with it. He strode down the block, the same block that he had grown up on and had once loved. Now it was a block that he no longer knew. He went to his house and inserted the object from his pocket into the lock. He went to turn it and it didn't turn.

"What!" he muttered to himself. Why wouldn't it work?

He tried again and again and again, until he faced the reality that it would never work. The one place he'd thought he would always have was a place where he was no longer allowed. He looked through the window to see if could locate his mother. The only thing he saw was emptiness. Everything was gone, no couch, no table, no T.V. It was all gone. He now had nothing. He took his nothing and stumbled to the street. He sat on the curb and buried his head against his knees and cried, not just a few tears but a shower of weeping.

He had messed up. He never should have become friends with George. He should have treated Lauren with more respect. He should never have told his mother the things he had. Was that why she had gone? Now, he was himself empty, with absolutely nothing left except for one thought.

He took off his t-shirt and stalked down the street. There was a sleek little blue sports car that he knew of. Wrapping his hand with his shirt, he swung his fist harder than he ever had before. Smashing the window in, he reached inside and unlocked the door. He didn't care if he got caught.

He looked for anything, but all he found was nothing. He was looking for money, but wound up with a 350z. He didn't want it, but he needed it. He reached under the steering wheel just as George had. He could see the front door of the closest house opening. A man stepped outside on his phone and looked Bryce straight in the eyes. He threw his phone down and charged toward him. Bryce scrambled through the wires and grabbed two, ripped them in half and sparked them. As he slammed on the gas, the car roared to life and Bryce was gone.

Once again he had stolen a car. Once again he felt so guilty.

* * * * * * *

He drove for twenty minutes before pulling into the parking lot of a shopping center. He was hoping the stores would be open. However, they were all closed. Exhausted and out of ideas, he laid his head on the steering wheel and cried. He cried and cried and cried. He had nothing left. Why was he still alive?

He thought about K.I. and realized how big of a crock that was. Friends are worthless. He thought about Lauren and how big of a lie that was. Girlfriends are worthless. He thought about his mother and how big of a pain she was. He thought about how much he still loved her, but she apparently didn't love him. His plan was to go into the gun store and steal any gun he could find. He was going to drive up to the cemetery and say goodbye to the only person who still loved him.

He would have pulled the trigger on his father's grave, but then it hit him, just like the bullet would have. He remembered all the times his dad had told him that he loved him and just wanted the best for him. His dad was his hero. He and Adam always used to do stuff with his father. Every since his dad had been gone, though, there was no one to look up to but George.

That was over with now. Bryce wanted to make his father proud of him. He put his hand up to his mouth and bit as hard as he could. In a mouthful of blood, he removed everything that reminded him of this stupid city. As he spit a chunk of his hand out of the window, he put the car into gear. He headed towards the interstate. What lay ahead of him he was not sure, but he was about to find out.

FIENDS BY TORCHLIGHT INTRODUCTION

Author's Note: In 2006, I was honored by Wayne Allen Sallee, the noted horror author, when he asked me to write the introduction for a collection of his stories. That collection appeared under the title fiends by torchlight *from Annihilation Press. I actually wrote two different versions of that introduction. Below is the one that* didn't *appear in the book.*

1985. Chicago. A reign of terror begins. It goes virtually unrecognized at first. But within a year the word spreads; people start to wake up to the name Wayne Allen Sallee.

Sallee is a writer, of course, not a serial murderer. I'm pretty sure our lives are safe with him—as long as he doesn't get writer's block. Whether our minds are safe *from* him is another question.

I met Wayne at a New Orleans SF Con. It was late last century, years after his 1985 debut in *Grue #1* with a raw wound of a story called "Rapid Transit." That tale was selected a year later by Karl Edward Wagner for *The Year's Best Horror Stories XIV*, and Wagner, known for an ability to recognize new talent, was dead on again. "Rapid Transit" has been reprinted seven times in three languages, and Sallee has grown into the promise of that story.

Since "Rapid Transit's" birth, Wayne has appeared eleven times in *Year's Best Horror*, has received twenty-nine honorable mentions in *Year's Best Fantasy and SF*, and has been named five times as a finalist for the Bram Stoker award, the most prestigious award given for horror. In critiques that I've written about Wayne, I argue that he's among the top five horror writers alive today who work primarily in the short form, along with such masters as Dennis Etchison and Ramsey Campbell.

Sallee's work reminds me of Campbell's, in fact. His stories are intensely introspective and psychological. His characters dwell in isolation, sometimes through their own fault, sometimes through the fault of others who cannot handle their differences. And make no mistake, Sallee's characters *are* different. They come from a land few writers have visited, because Wayne Allen Sallee has lived a life few writers have lived.

Wayne grew up with cerebral palsy, and though that's not the *reason* he writes, the experience has ferociously shaped—some say "warped"—his characters and the lives they inhabit. To make matters worse, in 1989 Wayne was hit by a car and the injuries were severe. Doctors stole bone from his right hip to repair his left arm. The repairs weren't perfect. Wayne once used his left hand to write because the palsy mainly affected his right side. Now he types with two fingers and sitting in any one position creates intense discomfort. It is a "discomfort" that Sallee transmutes and passes on to his readers.

Wayne's stories are graphic; he's linked occasionally to the Splatterpunks. But that label doesn't fit him well because the violent imagery and energy of his work is absolutely realistic, not stylized. Wayne's writing really is *about* "discomfort," about internalized physical and emotional pain. Unlike softcore horror, which ends with the monster defeated, the end of the world denied, Wayne leaves us looking at the hardcore darkness within.

The collection you're holding is a logical progression in an extraordinary career. It's a message coming in from a shadow dream. Give it a listen.

—Charles Gramlich
New Orleans, 2006

ABOUT MY NOVELS

COLD IN THE LIGHT

Back Cover Blurb:

Where the beings known as the "Whoun" came from, only a few know.

What they're going to do next is anyone's guess.

But in the Ozark Mountains of Arkansas, where a decades old conspiracy has started to unravel, a cop and a doctor are about to find out. Against an enemy from their nightmares, the two will have to fight, to save the life of an unborn child who isn't human, a child that will change their world forever.

In the brooding forest, they'll learn what it means to fear the dark.

And the light.

Reviewer comments:

"Charles Gramlich has created very interesting characters that would scare the bejebbers out of anybody." —Conan Tigard, *The Reading Nook*

"From the first scene it pulls you into its vortex of action, intrigue, conspiracy, and gore." —David Lanoue, Author of *Haiku Guy*

"I wasn't even planning on reading this when I started it. I was just glancing at the first page and the book hooked me; a great start and it held me all of the way through. It had lot of really great action scenes and a good strong story." —Lance Storm, Professional Wrestler

"...a spine tingling horror/adventure yarn. Gramlich's rich yet lean prose makes for a very fast paced thriller that packs a magnum punch, like an out of control motorcycle heading down a dark country road. This is definitely one book you will be reading with the lights on. *Cold in the Light* reads like the better tales of modern thriller authors such as Dean Koontz or John Saul." —J. D. Charles, Staff Reporter for the *Logan Banner*

"*Cold in the Light* has it all: conspiracies, hidden agendas, alien intelligence, and a frightening monster—and that's the first twenty pages!" —Bret Funk, Author of *Path of Glory*

"If you're a fan of horror, but like a twist of dark, demented humor thrown into your nightmarish reading, such as that of King or Barker, then you will probably enjoy the debut novel of Charles Gramlich." —Ethan Nahte, *Live 'n' Loud*

"Charles Gramlich meshes a hard-hitting action story with the modern world of evolutionary possibility." —Matthew Herridge

"Full of action, horror, and conspiracy thriller-type suspense, this is a book that succeeds on many different levels. Gramlich is one of those rare writers with the enviable ability to understand and sympathize with a wide assortment of characters (including some non-human ones)." —Book Lover

"The protagonists are believable, the antagonists are frightening, the plot twists are perfectly timed, and the story is top notch and definitely original. I am still not sure what genre this belongs to and that in itself is congratulatory!" —Chris Gruber

"I found his descriptions vivid and bone chilling..." —Ryad

"Charles's writing leaves a shiver on the spine that doesn't go away with the rising of the sun." —Richard Bamberg, Writer

SWORDS OF TALERA

Back Cover Blurb:

SWORDS OF BLOOD AND GLORY

Talera is a world of alien warriors and dangerous beasts, a world of swift and deadly swords raised against incredible odds. For Ruenn Maclang, an Earthman mysteriously transported to Talera, this strange and violent planet is a potentially lethal puzzle. To stay alive, Ruenn must quickly learn the discipline of the sword and the bitter stench of battle. And he must uncover the secrets of Talera, a world very far from natural.

But living isn't the only thing Ruenn has to do. His brother is lost somewhere on Talera, and the woman he loves is slave to the brutal Klar. If he hopes to save them both, Ruenn Maclang will have to risk his honor and his life. He will have to become Warlord of a world, and a greater swordsman than he ever dreamed possible.

Reviewer comments:

"I found this book to be a real page-turner..." —Scifimatter Brad

"*Swords Of Talera* harkens back to the days of my youth when I discovered John Carter of Mars, Carson Napier of Venus, and Tarzan of the Apes. All of course by Edgar Rice Burroughs. In this new novel, Mr. Gramlich's character is transported to another world of exotic people and exotic creatures, forced to battle his way across it in search of his brother. If you ever liked these interplanetary romances, this is the book for you." —Randy Johnson

"I took a chance on this because I'd seen the author posting on a SF forum I haunt and he had promised something along the lines of the old Edgar Rice Burroughs' John Carter of Mars, a series I had loved as a kid. Actually I think in truth he's selling himself short here because this book has more fresh ideas and solid action per page than just about everything else I've read all year put together." —W. Nelson

WINGS OVER TALERA

Back Cover Blurb:

SWORDS OF SORCERY AND FATE

Talera is a world of warriors and heroes, not all of whom are human. It is a world where sailing ships ply the skies as well as the waters, and where beasts are as likely to hunt men as be hunted by them. On Talera, beauty and steel are equally dangerous weapons, and sorcery is the deadliest talent of all.

For Ruenn Maclang, an Earthman who has won a place on this mysterious planet, his sword is a constant companion, and battle a daily promise that is seldom broken. But what will Ruenn do when the battle is against the woman he loves, and against the brother he has lost? And what will he do when he's faced with a deadly choice: kill his brother...or die?

Reviewer comments:

"Ruenn Maclang returns in book two of the Talera Cycle. He's still looking for his brother and boy does he find him. Mr. Gramlich continues to explore his world, introducing us to more peoples, more beasts, and more battles. This time it's for his love's country and life. The tale moves along briskly, making one wish the book were longer. I'm ready for the third volume. —Randy Johnson

BIBLIOGRAPHY

This Bibliography is divided into two sections. Section 1 contains books that can be used as "tools" to help you write better. These are books you'll use every day and which you'll need to buy and keep handy on your desk. Some of them you probably already have (or at least their equivalents). Section 2 contains books that deal with the issues of words, language, and writing in a more general way. Many of these are fun to read as well as being helpful with the subtleties of our English tongue. And don't forget that there is a lot of writing help on the net, as well, ranging from dictionary and encyclopedia sites to blogs and essays by writers at all levels of expertise.(Note: some of the books listed below may also exist in newer editions than are given here.)

Section 1: Tool Books.

1. Your best tool is a general purpose dictionary. Two good ones are:

Ehrlich, E., Flexner, S. B., Carruth, G., & Hawkins, J. M. (eds.). (1982). *Oxford American Dictionary* (reissue ed.). New York: Avon.
Guralnik, D. B. (Ed. in Chief). (1986). *Webster's New World Dictionary of the American Language* (2nd ed.). New York: Prentice-Hall.

2. Another good tool is a thesaurus in dictionary form, such as:

Laird, C. (Ed.). (2003). *Webster's New World Thesaurus* (Reissue ed.). New York: Pocket.
Morehead, P. D. (Ed.). (2001). *New American Roget's College Thesaurus in Dictionary Form.* New York: Signet.

3. You will certainly want a guide to help with punctuation and grammar. There are many such books, but a good one is:

Shertzer, M. (1996). *The Elements of Grammar* (Subsequent ed.). New York: Longman.

4. For those problem words and phrases, try the following:

Shaw, H. (1987). *Dictionary of Problem Words and Expressions* (Rev. ed.). New York: McGraw-Hill.
Strunk, W., Jr., & White, E. B. (1979). *The Elements of Style* (3rd ed.). New York: Macmillan Publishing Co., Inc. *(Note: There is a 4th edition of this but the 3rd is more commonly cited.)*

Section 2: General books dealing with writing related issues.

Appelbaum, Judith. (1988). *How to Get Happily Published*, (3rd ed.). New York: Harper & Row, Publishers, Inc.
Asimov, Isaac. (1981). *Asimov on Science Fiction*. New York: Doubleday & Company.
Block, Lawrence. (1981). *Telling Lies for Fun & Profit*. New York: William Morrow.
Bradbury, Ray. (1992). *Zen in the Art of Writing*. New York: Bantam Books.
Burroway, Janet. (1992). *Writing Fiction: A Guide to Narrative Craft*, (3rd ed.). New York: HarperCollins Publishers.
Cameron, Julie. (1992). *The Artist's Way*. New York: Jeremy P. Tarcher/Putnam.
Cameron, Julie. (1998). *The Right to Write*. New York: Jeremy P. Tarcher/Putnam.
Card, Orson, Scott. (1988). *Characters & Viewpoint.* Cincinnati, Ohio: Writer's Digest Books.
Card, Orson, Scott. (1990). *How to Write Science Fiction & Fantasy.* Cincinnati, Ohio: Writer's Digest Books.
Claiborne, R. (1983). *Our Marvelous Native Tongue.* New York: Times Books.
Fowler, H. W. (1965). *A Dictionary of Modern English Usage* (2nd ed.). New York: Oxford University Press.
Gardner, John. (1983). *On Becoming a Novelist.* New York: Harper & Row.
Goldbert, Natalie. (1990). *Wild Mind: Living the Writer's Life.* New York: Bantam.

Goldberg, Natalie. (2006). *Writing Down the Bones* (expanded ed.). Boston, MA: Shambhala.

Gordon, K. E. (1983). *The Well-Tempered Sentence*. New York: Ticknor & Fields.

Gordon, K. E. (1984). *The Transitive Vampire*. New York: Times Books.

Grambs, David. (1993). *The Describer's Dictionary*. New York: W. W. Norton & Company.

Johnson, E. D. (1982). *The Handbook of Good English*. New York: Facts on File Publications.

King, Stephen. (1981). *Danse Macabre*. New York: Everest House.

King, Stephen. (2000). *On Writing*. New York: Pocket.

Lamott, Anne. (1995). *Bird by Bird: Some Instructions on Writing and Life*. New York: Anchor Books.

Maass, Donald. (2002). *Writing the Breakout Novel*. Cincinnati, Ohio: Writer's Digest Books.

Maass, Donald. (2004). *Writing the Breakout Novel Workbook*. Cincinnati, Ohio: Writer's Digest Books.

McCrum, R., Cran, W., & MacNeil, R. (1986). *The Story of English*. New York: Elisabeth Sifton Books—Viking.

Morrell, David. (2002). *Lessons from a Lifetime of Writing*. Cincinnati, Ohio: Writer's Digest Books.

Newman, E. (1974). *Strictly Speaking*. New York: Warner Books.

Newman, E. (1975). *A Civil Tongue*. New York: The Bobbs-Merril Company, Inc.

Plotnik, A. (1986). *The Elements of Editing* (Reissue ed.). New York: MacMillan Publishing Company.

Safire, W. (1990). *Fumblerules*. New York: Bantam Doubleday Dell Publishing Group, Inc.

Soukhanov, A. H. (Executive Ed.). (1986). *Word Mysteries & Histories*. Boston, MA: Houghton Mifflin.

Train, J. (1980). *Remarkable Words with Astonishing Origins*. New York: Clarkson N. Potter, Inc.

Welty, Eudora. (1984). *One Writer's Beginnings*. New York: Warner Books.

Wilhelm, Kate. (2005). *Storyteller*. Northhampton, MA: Small Beer Press.

Yudkin, Marcia. (1988). *Freelance Writing for Magazines and Newspapers*. New York: Harper & Row.

Zinsser, W. (2006). *On Writing Well* (30th anv. ed.). New York: HarperCollins Publishers.

Zinsser, W. (1988). *Writing to Learn*. New York: Harper & Row.

www.ingramcontent.com/pod-product-compliance
Lightning Source LLC
Chambersburg PA
CBHW021223090426
42740CB00006B/355